Early American Pottery and China

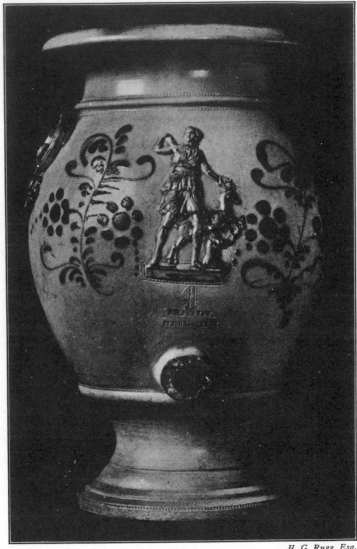

PLATE 1

Stoneware from St. Johnsbury, Vermont

Early American Pottery and China

by
John Spargo
Author of *The Potters and Potteries of Bennington*, etc.

Charles E. Tuttle Company
Rutland, Vermont

Representatives
Continental Europe: BOXERBOOKS, INC., *Zurich*
British Isles: PRENTICE-HALL INTERNATIONAL, INC., *London*
Australasia: PAUL FLESCH & CO., PTY. LTD., *Melbourne*
Canada: HURTIG PUBLISHERS, *Edmonton*

Published by the Charles E. Tuttle Company, Inc.
of Rutland, Vermont & Tokyo, Japan
with editorial offices at
Suido 1-chome, 2-6, Bunkyo-ku, Tokyo, Japan

Copyright in Japan, 1974 by Charles E. Tuttle Co., Inc.

Library of Congress Catalog Card No. 74-78148

International Standard Book No. 0-8048-1135-0

First edition, 1926 by the Century Co., New York
First Tuttle edition, 1974

PRINTED IN JAPAN

TABLE OF CONTENTS

v

Table of Contents

LIST OF ILLUSTRATIONS

vii

List of Illustrations

List of Illustrations

ix

List of Illustrations

FOREWORD TO THE NEW EDITION

IT IS WITH DELIGHT that I welcome this new printing
of my late father's book *Early American Pottery and
China*, for I like to boast a little that I had a part in its
making.

The book is really a companion work to his treatise
The Potters and Potteries of Bennington, published in the
same year. It grew out of my father's desire to track
down the sources of the many pieces of pottery and
china that were then, as even more so they are today,
erroneously attributed to Bennington. Once started, the
work was expanded to include a great many other
American wares.

During the late teens and early twenties, it was my
task to drive my father thousands of miles over New
England and New York State country roads and byways
in quest of Bennington ware—the best of it now to be

Foreword to the New Edition

seen at the Bennington Museum, which he founded—
and whatever other treasures might turn up. Not only
did we comb back-road antique shops, barns, and farm-
houses. There also were trips to the sites of defunct
potteries, where frequently we dug for shards. Occasionally, we'd seek out an old-time potter, who usually
was a philosopher, and spend an enthralling hour or so
as he recounted his wanderings. My part ended with the
driving, however, and then the real work began.

The research that went into the production of this
book is almost unbelievable. The months of letter
writing, the trips to museums and libraries, the searching
of endless records and cross-references would stagger any
but a dedicated scholar. And that my Dad surely was.

As his foreword points out, the book, a pioneer work
in its field, was never intended to be a checklist of American potteries. Rather, it is a handbook for the collector,
as valuable today as it was in 1926. I am sure that the
reader will find it entertaining as well.

GEORGE H. SPARGO

Nestledown
Old Bennington, Vermont

FOREWORD

This book is written by a hobbyist for his fellow-hobbyists, gentle folk and kindly as a rule, though people who do not know the charm of hobby-riding may think them as cracked as some of their "pots" too often are. The purpose of the book is as modest as the hobby. It is simply to assist the amateur in order that he may pass safely and with confidence through a field notoriously full of pitfalls.

The book is not in any sense a history of American pottery and china, though it is largely given to historical record. The reader is warned not to seek in its pages a detailed account of all the numerous potteries which flourished in many parts of this country during the seventeenth and eighteenth centuries and the first three quarters of the nineteenth century. Such a history, assuming that the materials

Foreword

for it existed, would be a voluminous affair, no matter how compressed and confined to the baldest recital of essential facts. Even a mere catalogue of all the potteries which existed in the United States up to the Centennial of 1876, with particulars of their location, ownership, date of operation, character of wares made, and similar data, would be a formidable undertaking.

More important than the bulk of such a catalogue, however, is the fact that when made it would only partially serve the purpose for which this handbook has been written. However valuable such a record might be, it would not meet the needs of the amateur collector whose hobby is early American pottery and china. Such a collector wants to know what to collect, and why; to be aided in identifying and classifying specimens, and to be intelligently informed concerning their history, their contribution to the development of ceramic art in this country, their makers, and so on.

In a great many cases, perhaps a majority, potteries known to have existed in this country prior to the Centennial year have no claim to the attention and interest of the collector. Serviceable the wares produced in such potteries might be, and generally

Foreword

were, but lacking all distinction, the products of one pottery being remarkably like, and practically indistinguishable from, the products of scores of others.

Of course, there are many factors which enter into collecting. A piece of pottery or china may be of interest primarily for ceramic reasons. It may possess some inherent quality, some merit of shape, design, glaze, color, or body composition, that compels the interest of the ceramist as such. He will be moved to find out all that can be known of its history. Such a piece is a sort of document to be transcribed and interpreted. On the other hand, a red earthenware jar, identical in every particular with other red earthenware jars found in scores of places, may be beautiful. It may possess some quality of shape, color, glaze, or body composition which will make it most attractive. Quite regardless, therefore, of any attribution to a particular pottery, or even to a particular locality, such a piece will possess interest and value. That its interest is esthetic, rather than ceramic, does not do away with the fact that some collector will prize it.

On the other hand, we may find collectors greatly stirred by a coarse and ugly earthenware or stoneware pot or jar, simply because it is known to have

Foreword

been produced by a certain potter, or to have some other historical interest. Such a piece of pottery may be insignificant and even contemptible as pottery, yet it may be regarded by enthusiastic collectors as "a beautiful specimen." The commonplaceness of the object itself is not regarded; what counts is the historical interest.

For reasons which are almost as varied as the wares themselves, special interest has been centered on the products of certain potteries. Sometimes the interest is to be explained by some quality in the wares themselves—beauty in some cases, quaintness in others. Sometimes the interest arises from the fact that some noteworthy individual was connected with the making of the ware. Often, indeed, there is no obvious explanation of the interest, or, rather, of why the interest is not equally extended to other wares of a like kind. There is no obviously good reason why the collector who takes keen delight in a hound-handled pitcher, which he believed to have been made at Bennington, should be ready to discard it when he learns that it was made at Jersey City or Baltimore. All through the Middle West, for example, one encounters many good specimens of pottery, mistakenly regarded as Bennington ware,

Foreword

and highly valued on that account, which in fact were made in Ohio. Convince the owners that they were made in Ohio, and, instead of giving the specimens a new interest, in nine cases out of every ten you rob them of the interest they had.

Such collectors make the mistake of too narrowly specializing, and miss thereby a great deal of the finest pleasure to be derived from a more liberal pursuit of their hobby. Fortunately it is no part of my present task to attempt to reform anybody.

"Reforming schemes are none of mine." This is a guide to the game, not an attempt to reform it. Yet I may be permitted to express the hope that the amateur collector who reads these pages will find his interest broadened beyond any narrow specialization, so that he will welcome the addition of a new fact to his knowledge of American pottery with even greater zest than he welcomes the addition of a new specimen to his collection.

I hope that the effort to explain in non-technical language many of those technical matters which the collector must know in order to understand his hobby has not been unsuccessful. Had the book been intended as a manual for specialists and experts, some of the pages devoted to this task would

Foreword

not have been written at all, while others would have been written quite differently. In order to get a maximum of satisfaction from any collection of pottery and china, even the most modest, one must understand the principal technical processes involved, and the terminology applied to them.

My thanks are due to the friends and fellow-hobbyists who have generously aided me with information and advice or with photographs of specimens to be used as illustrations. Mrs. Florence V. Paull-Berger, curator of the Wadsworth Atheneum, Hartford, Connecticut; Mrs. Rhea Mansfield Knittle, of Ashland, Ohio; Miss Jane Wolfe, of the Pennsylvania Museum, Philadelphia; Mr. Homer Eaton Keyes, Editor of "Antiques"; Mrs. William Whitman, Jr., of Simsbury, Connecticut; Mr. George S. McKearin, of Hoosick Falls, New York; Mr. J. B. Kerfoot, of Freehold, New Jersey; and Mr. Stephen Van Rensselaer, of Peterborough, New Hampshire, have all been most helpful and gracious. They are all good hobby-riders, and my best thanks are tendered to them for their courtesy and friendship.

While attempting nothing like a check-list of American potteries, I have added several carefully

Foreword

arranged chronological lists of potters in the hope
that they will be of great assistance to collectors.
For the same reason I have arranged a selection of
marks.

JOHN SPARGO.

Nestledown,
Old Bennington, Vermont,
July, 1926.

Early American Pottery and China

Early American Pottery and China

CHAPTER I

SOME ELEMENTARY PRINCIPLES

I<small>F</small> you are an advanced collector, or a professional expert—the curator of a museum with an important collection of ceramics, for example—you may as well skip this chapter. It is not intended for people like you, who have studied deeply and long since known all that is written here, and much more. It is intended for humbler folk of more limited knowledge; for small dealers who cannot specialize on pottery and china, but yet need to be able to buy and sell with intelligence and discrimination, and for amateur collectors whose enjoyment of a delightful hobby is restricted because they have never

[3]

comprehended certain basic processes, or understood the rather complicated terminology of the subject.

By way of a start, let us consider the widespread confusion in the use of the terms "pottery," "china," "earthenware," and "porcelain." It is truly astonishing that so many people who have spent the time, labor, and money necessary to the assembling of creditable and interesting collections, and so many dealers of antiques, have never taken the trouble to learn the meaning of these terms, but use them without discrimination or understanding. "I have an interesting piece of old pottery," writes one amiable collector, and then proceeds to describe a porcelain vase. A lady enthusiast writes a pretentious volume wholly devoted to the old-fashioned printed earthenware, and entitles the book "Old Blue China." A rather successful dealer in antiques writes and offers a "china platter," which is obviously not china at all, but earthenware. The catalogue of an auction mart lists as an "early earthenware pitcher" a fine example of early nineteenth-century American porcelain. These illustrations of the prevalent confusion might easily be extended to fill many pages.

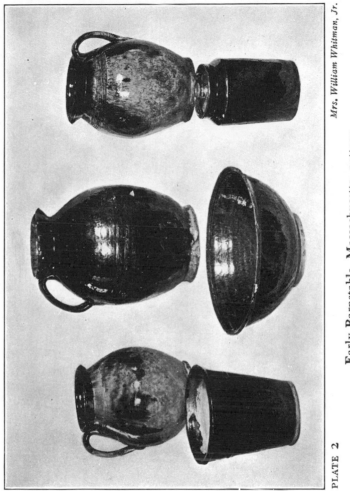

PLATE 2

Early Barnstable, Massachusetts, pottery

Some Elementary Principles

As the basis of an intelligent system of classification we must begin by sharply differentiating between pottery and china. It is true that the distinction which is now pretty generally followed by English and American authorities is not universally accepted. French writers, in general, do not accept it, but use the word *potterie* to embrace every product of the potter's art ranging from the coarsest earthenware to the finest porcelain and including all the intermediate forms. It is not probable that the amateur hobbyist to whom this discussion is addressed will be bothered by this divergence of the practice of French writers on the subject from that generally accepted throughout the English-speaking world. If we are to avoid confusion, we shall do well to follow the English practice rather than the French. That practice is to limit the application of the word "pottery" to those wares which are entirely opaque and without any degree of translucence.

The definition is very simple, and so is the practical test. All that is necessary is to submit the specimen one desires to classify to the test for translucence by holding it up to a strong light. If it is entirely opaque, it is pottery, not china. Its primary

[5]

classification is determined. No matter whether it is coarse or fine, hard or soft, glazed or unglazed, ornamented or plain, if it is opaque and entirely void of translucence, it is pottery and not china. There is one apparent exception to this rule which must be noted. We shall have occasion to refer to it more fully when we come to the consideration of china. For the moment, it will be sufficient to observe that a translucent material may appear to be opaque when it is in a dense and heavy mass. A thin fragment broken from that mass, however, would be translucent. On the other hand, a similar fragment of pottery would be opaque.

This division of ceramics, which we shall call "pottery" as distinguished from "china," embraces a wide range of wares. It includes the stoneware jugs and jars; the ornamental terra-cotta wares; the great variety of earthen wares ranging from common flower-pots of red clay to the greatly prized platters with their quaint printed designs, and from the coarse slip-decorated dish made in Pennsylvania a century and a half ago to the most elaborate and colorful of Staffordshire figures. Earthenware is a synonymous term applied to all ceramic wares which are opaque.

Some Elementary Principles

All wares produced by the potter's art which are not pottery are china. That is only another way of saying that wares which are not absolutely opaque, but possess the quality of being translucent in any degree, are to be classified as china and not as pottery. Here, again, it does not affect the classification whether the ware is coarse or fine, hard or soft, glazed or unglazed, plain or ornamented. If it is in any degree translucent, it is china.

We have already noted the fact that a translucent material may in certain circumstances appear to be opaque; that the translucent quality, while actually present, may not be apparent. This can be easily understood. Take, for example, a bottle made of dark glass, such as an ordinary flask of dark amber or green glass. If the bottle be held up to the light, it will be seen to be transparent. If, however, at the time the bottle was made, some of the same material, from the same container, was pressed into a cube nine inches in diameter, let us say, that cube would not be transparent. It would not be penetrable by ordinary light-rays. Yet, if the cube were to be smashed it would be found that the fragments of it possessed the same quality as the bottle.

[7]

In like manner, from the selfsame batch of prepared material, a potter might make a plate, for example, and some heavy object such as a column several inches in diameter. The plate would be translucent, but the column would not be. And yet, *because the translucent quality was resident in the material, any fragment broken from the column, approximately equal in thickness to the plate, would also be approximately equal to it in translucence.*

Having made clear the essentials of this basic primary category, we may as well clear up a widespread misunderstanding with regard to its nomenclature. China and porcelain are not, as many people think, different wares. *The two words are only different names for the same thing.* "I have a beautiful lot of old china, but somehow I have never happened to get hold of a piece of old porcelain," said a dear old lady as she displayed her treasures. She did not know that china is a synonym for porcelain. Neither did the dealer who advertised that he had "a splendid assortment of both china and porcelain" for sale. There are many collectors and dealers who are no better informed.

It will remove confusion if we consider the subject historically a bit. Porcelain was originally made in China. Prior to its introduction into England from that country the English potters made only earthen wares; that is to say, wares that were opaque. In popular usage the porcelain brought from China was called "China ware"; that is, ware of Chinese manufacture. When the British potters began to imitate the Chinese product, "China ware" became a recognized trade description for that type of ware. It will be readily understood why and how the term "China ware" came to be much more widely used in England than the word "porcelain," a word derived from the Italian *porcellana*, a cowry-shell, by way of its French adaptation *porcelaine*. The original Italian is said to have been applied to the cowry-shell as a name because of some fancied resemblance of the shell to a pig's back, *porcella* meaning a small pig. The ceramic term "porcelain" is supposed to have been suggested by a fancied resemblance of the quality of the ware to the polished surface of the cowry-shell.

So we are again confronted by the peculiarities of our own language. "China" as a name for porcelain is virtually confined to the English-speaking peoples. All that matters is that we thoroughly understand that the two names refer to the same thing. It does not matter which of the names we use, or if we use both names interchangeably, so long as we understand that they both equally designate any product of the potter's art which is translucent.

PASTE

The statement is often made that all china, or porcelain, whichever term is preferred, is divided into two major groups or classes; namely, "hard paste" and "soft paste." This classification is also of English origin and is more generally accepted throughout the English-speaking world than elsewhere. By many writers, particularly those of continental Europe, the terms "natural porcelain" and "artificial porcelain" are preferred. These terms and those used by the English refer, practically, to the same distinction. The French also indicate it by terms analogous to the English, *pâte dure* and *pâte tendre*.

It can hardly be said that any of these terminologies is wholly satisfactory. They are all too arbitrary to be wholly applicable, and any attempt to apply them to individual specimens soon brings one up against difficulties not to be easily surmounted. Words like "hard" and "soft" are relative in their meaning, not absolute. Iron is *soft* by comparison with steel but *hard* by comparison with lead, for example. So in practice it is not possible for any human being to make of these terms a standard that will prove infallible in its uniform application to individual specimens.

By "paste" is meant, of course, the mixture of clay and other materials of which the body of the ware, as distinguished from its glaze or other covering, is composed. The word "body" is often used instead of "paste." Some writers prefer this, and in their discussions we find reference to hard and soft *bodies*, instead of to hard and soft *pastes*. The original Chinese porcelain which European potters sought to imitate was not only translucent but extremely hard. This hardness manifested itself by the metallic ring of the ware when sharply struck, but it was also apparent from the vitreous appearance of the edges when fractured. Moreover it was practically impossible to tell from the fractured surface where the body ended and the glaze began. Here we have several characteristics of what is variously designated the "hard paste porcelain," "true porcelain," and "natural porcelain."

Early American Pottery and China

In trying to imitate this Chinese ware, as early as the sixteenth century, the potters of England and continental Europe reached some interesting results. Not being aware of the fact that the secret of the Chinese ware was not a chemical formula but the quality inherent in a certain kind of clay called kaolin, and possibly laboring under something of an obsession attributing to the "mysterious Oriental" a chemical knowledge he did not in fact possess, these imitators made their experiments along chemical lines. By the latter part of the sixteenth century Florentine potters were making a translucent ware called porcelain. It differed from the Chinese product in important respects. It was less vitreous than the Chinese ware, and the glaze was softer than the body, differing from it in substance and therefore subject to crazing and chipping as the result of unequal expansion and contraction.

The Florentine process was not long continued, and was in fact entirely forgotten. Then, in 1671, an English potter, the famous John Dwight of Fulham, discovered and patented a process for making what he called "porcelaine," and "the mystery of transparent earthenware." This was not porcelain at all, but what that learned authority,

PLATE 3
Chert factory, Mount Jasper, New Hampshire

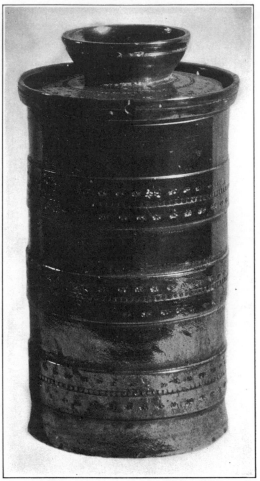

PLATE 3   *Mrs. William Whitman, Jr.*
Churn made at Boscawen, New Hampshire

Some Elementary Principles

Professor Church, has called "a porcellaneous stoneware." In 1695, almost a quarter of a century after Dwight's process was patented in England, a Frenchman, M. Chicanneau, at St. Cloud, France, by his own independent researches hit upon a process that was quite similar, at least in its essential features, to that of Dwight; and we now know that Dwight's process, independently arrived at by experiments, was quite similar in its essential features to that used in Florence in the previous century.

One thing is common to the three processes, and, indeed, to all experiments made along the same general line. They all attained their measure of translucence through the admixture of glass with clay. They differed in the relative proportion of glass to clay that they used. In some cases the amount of glass used so far exceeded the volume of clay that the product can hardly be classified as anything but glass. The matter is not so simple as that, however; while the *material* used was that of the glass-maker, the *methods* used in its manufacture were those of the potter. The Florentines made a mixture consisting of 24 parts of sand, 16 parts of a glass (composed of rock-crystal 10 and soda 8), and 12 parts of a white earth. Then they took 12 parts of this mixture and added 3 parts of white clay, and this constituted the body of the ware. It was fired and then glazed with a lead glaze, or enameled with a tin enamel. It differed quite radically, in all essentials save only its translucence, from the Chinese ware of which it was an imitation. The same thing is true of the later English and French wares of this type. That is why they and all similar products are called "artificial" porcelain.

In Germany, in 1710, a young chemist—or perhaps alchemist more accurately describes him— introduced a true porcelain that was at once recognized as being like the Chinese, not only in its superficial appearance but also in the nature of its body and glaze. The name of this young German was John Frederic Böttger. He was then twenty-four years old, and was a protégé of August II, elector of Saxony, who had an experimental pottery at Dresden. It has been asserted that Böttger had received information of the Chinese secret brought from China by some traveler, but, so far as the present writer knows, there is no credible evidence of that. In any case, original discoverer or copyist, the fact is that he was the first European to make a true hard-paste porcelain. By one of those happy

Some Elementary Principles

and fortunate coincidences which loom so largely in the romance of history, at about this time a wealthy German iron-founder, named John Schnorr, riding in the country near Schneeberg, Saxony, one day observed that his horse was finding it difficult to raise its feet. On making an examination he found that the clay was very white, extremely plastic, and adhesive. He appears to have conceived the idea of using it to make hair-powder, then so much in demand. He proceeded to carry this idea into effect. Böttger came across some of this hair-powder and, apparently suspecting that it was a powdered clay, experimented with it. Thus was discovered the supply of kaolin which was to make his discovery of the Chinese secret commercially useful and to revolutionize the industry.

True porcelain, as distinguished from artificial, is composed of kaolin and feldspar, the latter being also known as *petuntze*. This feldspar is probably best described as partially formed clay, or clay in the making. Unlike the true clay, kaolin, it is fusible. At great heat, instead of being vitrified, as other plastic substances are, it melts and becomes a white milky glass. Permeated and mixed with the kaolin it produces the translucence which characterizes porcelain. The body so constituted is called *hard* paste in contradistinction to the body of the porcelain which is called *soft* paste, not because the body actually is harder, although that is generally true, but especially because of the fact that it is fired at a much greater temperature, standing a degree of heat that would either crumble or fuse the other. Its greater power of resisting the action of fire is indicated much more than its actual greater hardness in the sense of resistance to penetration or pressure.

Long as this section on pastes already is, there yet remains to be considered another important branch of the subject, one which has occasioned much confusion. It is not easy to state it clearly in a paragraph, and it is too important to be hastily passed over. As already noted, the English potters at first made the artificial porcelain, using glass. Early Bow and Chelsea porcelain wares were of this type. Those famous potteries used a mixture of sand, pipe-clay, and glass for their bodies, and covered these with a glaze of flint-glass rich in lead. The use of glassy mixtures of this type was fairly general in English potteries during a great part of the second half of the eighteenth century. We must

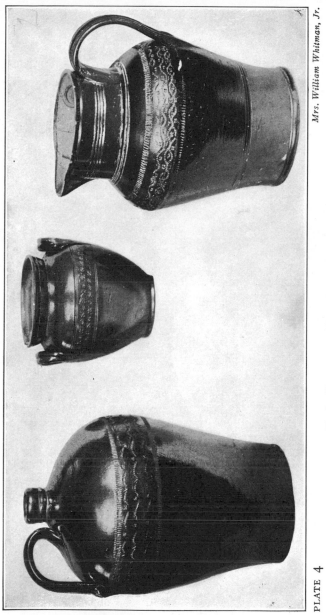

PLATE 4

Early Boscawen, New Hampshire, pottery

Some Elementary Principles

bear in mind that in spite of the invention of so-called porcelain by Dwight in 1671, it was not until some eighty years after that event that the manufacture of porcelain on any really important scale was developed. Notwithstanding the fact that Böttger's discovery of 1710 had given rise to a considerable German industry along greatly superior lines, and that from 1713 onward the German potteries at Meissen and elsewhere, as well as other factories in Austria and Russia, had been turning out a true porcelain, fairly comparable to the Chinese, the English potteries at first devoted themselves to the artificial type having glass and sand as its most important components. They seem, however, to have encountered great difficulty in making ware of this type, particularly in firing it in the kilns. Quite naturally, they sought to overcome this difficulty, and as early as 1749 we find Thomas Frye, of the Bow pottery, taking out a patent for a process in which bone-ash was used with a smaller amount of glass. From that time onward the use of calcined bones steadily increased, and the proportion of glass was correspondingly lessened. With the manufacture of porcelain, the older artificial type may be said to have begun to decline almost as soon as it was fairly started. Yet it was not until 1800 that Josiah Spode entirely abandoned the use of glass and made porcelain of a paste or body composed of china-clay, calcined bone, and feldspar.

We may fairly look back upon the period 1750-1800 as one of transition, during which the artificial soft-paste porcelain composed largely of glass was, by an evolutionary process so gradual and subtle as to be almost imperceptible, supplanted by a new type distinctively and characteristically English. To this day this porcelain, composed of kaolin, calcined bone, and feldspar, just as in Josiah Spode's day, with proportions of the ingredients varying somewhat in different factories, remains the standard English type. The degree of softness of the paste depends on the amount of bone-ash that is used.

While some writers insist on calling this type "natural" or "true" porcelain, there is really no justification for doing so, and much confusion has resulted therefrom. It is in fact an artificial type quite as certainly as the other soft-paste variety composed largely of glass. It would be much better, in the judgment of the present writer at least, if the terms "natural" and "true" could be limited in their application to the hard-paste porcelain composed of kaolin and feldspar. On the other hand it would seem to be desirable to provide for the English type which derives its character from bone-ash a separate classification, as a subdivision of "artificial" porcelain. That would greatly simplify matters and materially lessen the obstacles to be overcome by the amateur collector.

Bearing in mind the fact that this book is expressly designed to meet the needs of the amateur, presumably unfamiliar with the great body of literature on the subject, it may be well to warn the reader against an all too easy misinterpretation of the preceding summary of English porcelain. It must not be inferred from the brief account given of the evolution of artificial soft-paste porcelain in England that no natural hard-paste porcelain is or has been made in that country. In fact, such porcelain has been made there from the middle of the eighteenth century to the present time, and in certain important branches of its manufacture—notably Parian and biscuit porcelain—the English potters have attained high rank. As early as 1755 Richard Chaffers, one of the pioneer potters of

Liverpool, put a thousand golden guineas in his holsters and set out on horseback for Cornwall "to find and purchase kaolin and feldspar soaprock for the purpose of making true porcelain equal to that of the Chinese." That he made something which he regarded as true porcelain is certain. He presented the first piece to his friend and business rival, Josiah Wedgwood. Such specimens of this ware as have survived cannot be regarded as true porcelain, however, in the judgment of the most competent authorities.

William Cookworthy, a chemist, of Plymouth, and pioneer of the Plymouth and Bristol potteries, was the first English potter to make genuine hard-paste porcelain. He obtained a patent for his process in 1768. He had been studying the subject for at least twenty-three years and perhaps longer. We know this from a letter on the subject written by him in 1745. It is of some interest to recall that at that early date he was interested in experimenting with what was described as "an earth, the product of the Cherakee Nation in America, called by the natives *Unaker*." This "Unaker" was simply kaolin of fair quality found in Virginia. In 1765 or 1766 kaolin from South Carolina was used by Wedgwood

Some Elementary Principles

and others. When Cookworthy found a plentiful supply of both feldspar and kaolin in Cornwall near the town of Helston, the quality of the kaolin being superior to the American, hard-paste porcelain became a commercial possibility in England.

The patent Cookworthy received was for "a kind of porcelain newly invented, composed of moorstone or growan, and growan clay, the stone giving the ware transparence and the clay imparting whiteness and infusibility." Cookworthy's claim to the honor of being the first sucessfully to make hard-paste porcelain in England is beyond question. From that time to the present hard-paste porcelain has been made in England, but to a less extent than the soft-paste, and with less success—always excepting the specialized branches, like Parian and biscuit, in which the English potters have excelled.

CHAPTER II

PRINCIPLES OF CLASSIFICATION

THE application of the principles and defini-
tions set forth in the preceding chapter will have
suggested to the amateur collector the division of
his collection into two major classes. The first,
pottery or earthenware, includes all the opaque
wares; the second, china or porcelain, includes all
the wares that are, in any degree, translucent.
We need a more detailed classification than this,
however. It is necessary to subdivide the major
group according to varieties. A complete guide to
such a classification that would meet every test and
requirement is not possible in such a work as this.
It would require a volume by itself. It is possible,
however, to offer the guidance of a helpful outline,
and a collector cannot acquire much more from
books alone. He must depend upon observation of
actual specimens and familiarity with them.

Principles of Classification

The translucent wares generically classed as china are subdivided according to the character of their paste composition. We do not need to discuss further the significance of the various terms, hard and soft, natural and artificial, used to describe the different types. Some writers divide porcelain or china into two categories, called natural and artificial. Other writers, while adhering to the same division, prefer to call the categories hard paste and soft paste. The difference is one of terminology only, and is not important. The inadequacy of this division as the basis of classification has long been recognized, and some modern authorities have advocated a third category. The present writer agrees with this suggestion. While the English bone porcelain is properly described as artificial, as explained in the preceding chapter, it differs so radically from the other artificial soft-paste porcelain that it can fairly be said to be almost as different from it as either of the two is different from the hard-paste type. For this reason, and the additional reason of the large place in modern ceramics taken by the English type, it would seem to be desirable to subdivide the soft-paste porcelain. This gives us three divisions as follows:

[23]

(1) Natural—hard paste—kaolinic.

(2) Artificial—soft paste—alkaline (glass).

(3) Artificial—soft paste—calcareous (bone).

The distinctive features of these three types cannot be satisfactorily explained by means of the printed page alone. No matter how careful, painstaking, and precise an author may be, mere verbal descriptions must necessarily fall short of the ideal of a perfect instructor. The amateur collector should bear this in mind, and contrive somehow to examine and compare some well authenticated specimens of each type. Merely looking at them will not suffice. He should handle them, so as to be able to know how different they are to the sense of touch. Variations of texture, of density, of glaze produce subtle differences not to be defined or described, or learned otherwise than from this close practical observation. Not as a substitute for books, therefore, but rather as an auxiliary to them, an interpreter, actual specimens are necessary. The amateur who desires to understand his porcelains will do well to begin with a good specimen of Chinese porcelain as a norm or standard. It need not be very old as Chinese porcelain is rated. When he has examined this with great thoroughness, so that he feels he has formed a perfect mental picture of it, he should proceed to the next stage. This consists in examining two or three good pieces of European hard-paste porcelain, noting carefully the points of conformity with the norm. If access can be had to a museum collection, it will probably be possible to obtain permission to examine authenticated specimens.

The beginner will find it much more helpful, at this stage, to confine himself to two or three pieces than to attempt to study a larger number. Attention should be centered upon indications of inherent quality and all other things disregarded. To attempt to study the variations of design, decoration, and other superficial things, is to invite mental confusion. To compare the weight and texture of pieces, and to strive to acquire that subtle power of sensing these qualities which will enable one to be fairly certain in making classifications, should be the aim.

The next stage is to get hold of representative specimens of each of the two types of artificial, or soft-paste, porcelain. This is not at all a difficult matter. If one or two good examples of the old type of artificial soft-paste porcelain—the alkaline, or glass, type—can be had and compared with one or two of the English artificial soft-paste type, containing much bone ash, it will be apparent at once that these types differ quite radically from true—hard-paste—porcelain and from each other. So marked are these differences that little difficulty should be experienced in forming a reliable mental picture of each type, a good working understanding of the essential characteristics. The writer does not believe that much more aid to this part of the classification of china can be given by means of the written word alone. All pretensions to do much more he regards as approaches to charlatanry.

Even the most experienced connoisseur will sometimes encounter a specimen which he cannot classify with certainty, except that because of its translucence he is certain that it is porcelain and not earthenware. He will be quite unable, without destroying the piece, to determine positively whether it should be classified as hard paste—natural—or soft paste—artificial—or whether it should be described as alkaline or calcareous. By breaking the piece he could tell perhaps, though even then he might not be absolutely certain. How foolish it must be, then, to pretend that the knowledge can be gained from books!

In magazine articles and a certain class of "popular" handbooks, it is sometimes said that the collector can easily tell whether a specimen is hard porcelain or soft porcelain by the use of a knife or file. The theory is that a knife or file will cut into soft porcelain, whereas hard porcelain will resist all attempts to cut into it, even with a file. The reader of these pages is warned most earnestly not to apply this test to any specimen for which he cares. As a test it is worthless, and it may mar, or even destroy, a good piece. It is true that a file will cut into the body of a piece of soft-paste porcelain; it is also true that a good sharp file will cut into the hardest porcelain. The writer has demonstrated this many times. Many a good specimen has been irremediably spoiled by ill advised attempts to use this test. There is another objection to it; namely, the fact that it is predicated upon a division that is too arbitrary and too simple. In the case of American porcelain in particular, and also of English porcelain, though perhaps in less degree, there is no such simple rigid division in fact. As Barber long since pointed out, the degrees of difference are so slight and so numerous that it is not possible to decide where hard paste ends and soft paste begins. Starting at one end with hard paste we find specimens ranging from the very hardest to those which we are disposed to classify as soft. Any extensive collection of soft-paste porcelains is almost certain to contain some which closely approximate hard paste in all external and readily ascertainable features. Even if the file test were reliable when applied to the extremes, it is fairly obvious that it could not be usefully employed in those cases where there is such a marked convergence to the center.

Equally worthless and untrustworthy is the so-called foot test. By this is meant that hard-paste porcelain can be readily distinguished from the soft-paste variety by the simple expedient of examining that portion of the piece upon which it rested while being fired in the glazing-kiln. It is held that if this part is unglazed and rough, the specimen under consideration is to be classified as hard paste. It has been pointed out by Barber and others that it is common enough to find soft-paste porcelains which possess this feature. In some cases the fact is the result of accident; in others of the deliberate removal of the glaze from the foot before firing, to prevent adhesion to the bottom of the sagger. The foot test is of no value.

There are some tests that are indubitably reliable of themselves, which are of little or no practical value to the collector. By subjecting to a great heat the pieces one desires to classify, it would be possible to determine with great accuracy which pieces were hard paste and which soft paste. Obviously, however, in the hands of the amateur this involves the risk, and the probability, of the destruction of valuable specimens. As a laboratory method applicable to the testing of samples on a commercial scale, it has its uses and merits, but as a working method for the collector it is as impracticable as anything that can be imagined. Much the same can be said of the chemical test. By pulverizing the bodies, or parts of the bodies, of a number of specimens into powder, and using acids, the presence of phosphate of lime, which, in the form of bone-ash, enters largely into the composition of the English type of soft-paste porcelain, could be readily demonstrated. This method would be good enough for application to samples on a large scale, but it is obviously not one for the everyday service

[29]

of the collector. He is hardly likely to subject a valuable specimen to that testing process.

There are some useful rough-and-ready tests of real service and merit, however. Perhaps the best of these is the fracture test, as Barber observes. If the piece under examination has been accidentally broken or chipped, examination of the break will show, in a majority of cases, whether the specimen should be classified as hard paste or soft. This test is frequently available, on account of the fact that so many specimens come to the collector in a damaged state, permitting its application. It will be well for the amateur collector to gather together a number of such pieces and submit the fractured edges to close scrutiny and comparison.

In some cases it will be found that the fractured edges are smooth and glassy, betokening the vitreous character of the ware. This vitreosity is more or less uniform throughout the entire thickness of the ware; there is no sharp distinction separating the inner body from the outer glaze, but instead it is hard to tell where the glaze ends and the inner body begins, even with the aid of a strong glass. Pieces having these characteristics can be confidently classified as hard paste. In the case of soft paste the fractured edges will be found to be rather rough in the middle. Instead of the glassy surface of the broken edge there will be a granulated or flaky surface inside, only the two sides showing a thin glass-like margin of the thickness of the glaze. If the broken edge of such a piece be touched with the tip of the tongue, the absorbent quality of the body will manifest itself at once. Where these conditions exist classification as soft paste may be confidently made. If one cares to touch with the tip of the tongue a sheet of glass and then a soft brick, he can thus obtain a very good idea of the different sensations produced by "tasting" the two types of porcelain body.

As a rule, then, for pieces thoroughly representative of the two extremes, the fracture test is a useful one—when there are fractures to which it can be applied. It is only rarely that the collector will be willing to break a specimen for the sake of obtaining a chance to apply the test. That, of course, is a serious limitation. Another limitation is that, even where there are fractures to which it may be applied, it is not always a sure guide to determining the classification of paste that belongs to neither extreme type but somewhere between them.

Another test, useful to the collector, but extremely limited in the range of its applicability, is that of color. It is the easiest to use, but it requires intelligent discrimination and good vision. Allowance must be made for accidental discolorations, for example, and also for peculiarities in the clays used. As a general rule, the tendency is for hard paste to show a bluish tint, and for soft paste to show a mellow ivory tint. If on holding a specimen up to the light it is seen that the white has a cold bluish quality, it is strong reason for calling it hard paste, for that is the characteristic of vitreous wares. If, on the other hand, the white has a warm, mellow, ivory quality, that is strong reason for calling it soft paste, for that is the characteristic result of the use of bone-ash and of relatively low-temperature firing.

The expert relies upon this color test to some extent, but not as a specific test. He forms his opinion, more or less subconsciously or intuitively, from the sum of impressions derived from touch, color, weight, and general appearance. The writer does not hesitate to say that no human being can with certainty classify every piece of porcelain submitted to him. Whoever pretends to such knowl-

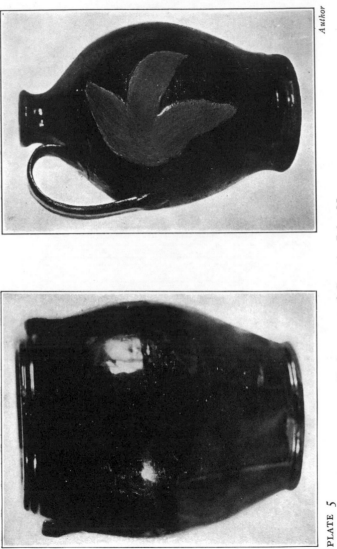

Author

Early wares of Captain John Norton

PLATE 5

edge can be set down as a charlatan. In general, however, it is possible for an experienced connoisseur to tell whether a piece is hard or soft paste. A special sense seems to be developed which enables one to judge, in the dark even, by the touch and the weight of the piece alone, with surprising accuracy. The writer has frequently demonstrated this.

Of course, there is no mystery in this at all. It is a special faculty, developed by much experience and practice, and gained in no other way. Not infrequently when the writer has been asked to determine the proper classification of some specimen of china or earthenware, and has done so, he has been asked, and sometimes challenged, to explain the grounds upon which his decision is based. "Please tell me how you can tell. Show me the trick. Let me into the secret," wrote a correspondent, a physician of eminence noted as a diagnostician. Strange as it may seem, he did not realize that his question was as irrational as it would have been to ask him to say exactly how he detected symptoms and read their meaning, and to teach the "trick" in a letter to a casual correspondent. Even if he could explain his methods, it would take him a very long time, and then if the questioner really wanted to learn the trick he would have to devote years of patient study, careful observation, and special training of ears, eyes, or fingers. Easy short cuts to expert knowledge do not exist in ceramics any more than in medicine, music, or any other branch of knowledge.

Now we must turn to the classification of pottery, the various types of earthenware. Even at the cost of some repetition which may prove irritating to some, for the sake of the novice let us recall the fact that all the opaque wares are classed as pottery and that earthenware is a synonym for the latter term. To call an earthenware platter "china," for instance, is as foolish as it would be to call a pewter platter "silver" or "glass."

Roughly speaking, pottery wares are all divided into two major classes, and the basis of the classification is the same as in the case of porcelain; namely, hard paste and soft paste. Given ordinary intelligence—and one is bound to assume that every collector possesses that!—it is not at all a difficult matter to carry over into the pottery division of ceramics the process of classification already learned in the division of porcelain.

Principles of Classification

Take the matter of hardness, for example; as in the other great divisions of ceramics, this term is not used primarily to indicate relative hardness as that term is generally understood in contradistinction to softness; that is to say, superior resistance to penetration, or pressure, which is the ordinary connotation of the term, is not the quality that is primarily indicated by the word in its application to pottery. What is meant more than anything else is the quality of resisting the action of fire in a superior degree, a quality resulting from the materials employed, their admixture and compression, and the high temperature used in firing them. With such allowances as almost suggest themselves, the fracture test described in the discussion of porcelain classification can be applied to the classification of pottery also. If one takes fragments of an ordinary stoneware jug or jar, and examines the fractured edges and compares them with the fractures of various other earthen wares, he will see at once what is meant. Composed of plastic clay which has been mixed with sand to prevent cracking, the chief characteristics of stoneware are its compact texture and its hardness—the latter term being now used to connote both its great resistance

[35]

to penetration and pressure and its capacity to with-stand extreme heat. This hardness is partly due to the nature of the materials used and their special preparation, and partly to the degree of vitrification produced by the intense heat at which the ware is fired in the kiln.

Where fractured a piece of stoneware will appear hard, uniform, and vitreous. The tongue test shows it to be non-absorbent. It is analogous to hard-paste porcelain in these respects. If, next, we take a fragment of ordinary *majolica*, let us say, and examine its fracture, we shall find its body to be rough and uneven, perhaps flaky or granular. Applying the tip of the tongue to it we shall find that the body is decidedly absorbent. Similarly a piece of *Delft* ware would show the same general characteristics as the majolica, while, on the other hand, a piece of *basalt* or a piece of *jasper* would show the same characteristics as the stoneware.

As in the case of porcelain, classification of earthenware acording to the paste composition can only be approximate and general. It is not possible to achieve absolute and unvarying exactness. Just as the translucent wares do not conform to absolute standards, but represent almost every possible gra-

[36]

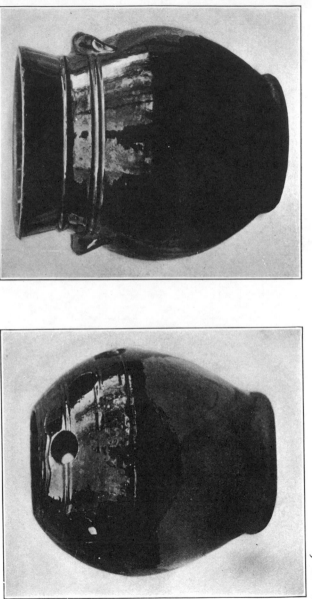

PLATE 6

Huntington, Long Island, pottery

dation, so do the opaque wares. In general, however, it is possible to tell by touch and weight—and in the *biscuit*, or unglazed state, by appearance—to which of the two great divisions the piece belongs, whether it is hard paste or soft paste.

Having thoroughly assimilated these principles the amateur collector is now in a position to take a further important step toward the classification of a collection including a fairly wide range of wares. Let us take a number of the wares which most interest collectors, and see how, in the light of the principles thus far explained, we can assign them to their proper categories. By doing this we shall see how readily all wares, both pottery and china, fall into one or the other of the two great divisions. and thus we shall understand the importance of classification according to paste composition.

Under the head of hard-paste wares we shall place first of all, of course, all varieties of china, the translucent wares, which we have definitely decided are not to be classified as soft paste. This brings into our category an immense range of varieties and types of ware. It is futile to attempt to list these, and so we must be content with this general statement at this stage, leaving until later the necessary amplification and interpretation. All *Parian* belongs to this division. There can be no exception to this rule, for Parian is a true hard-paste porcelain. Virtually all the *biscuit china* comes under this head. While there are some exceptions to this rule, which we shall note as occasion arises, for our present purpose the generalization will serve. Soft-paste porcelain is almost invariably glazed. It would not be serviceable without glazing because of its porosity and absorbent character. As applied to china the term "biscuit" denotes entire absence of glaze of any kind. Chaffers, the distinguished English ceramist, has aptly likened biscuit china to a new clay tobacco-pipe without the least gloss on it. It is pure white unglazed porcelain. The fact that it is biscuit china is strong presumptive evidence that it is hard paste.

All types of *stoneware* are classified under this head. This includes not only the ordinary coarse stoneware crocks and jars, and other common domestic utensils, but the many beautiful products which are not ordinarily thought of as stoneware at all, but known only by special names. The fine *basalt* ware produced by Wedgwood and other noted English potters is really a highly developed

form of stoneware. All basalt pottery is embraced
in the category of hard paste. The same thing is
true of *jasper* ware, which Wedgwood introduced
and developed to such a high degree of perfection.
It may be doubted whether the art of the potter
has ever been more finely expressed in modern times
than in this beautiful ware. Under this same head
we must include all the finely ornamented *salt-
glazed ware* produced in England toward the end
of the eighteenth century, and now so much sought
after by collectors. Under this head, also, are
classed the molded ornamental stoneware pitchers
and vases produced by Doulton and other famous
English pottery firms. All the laminated wares,
from the *agate* of Whieldon to the *scroddle* of Bennington, are hard-paste wares. So, too, are the
dense earthen wares containing a large percentage
of flint, known as *stone china* and *ironstone china*.

It will be seen that what at first appeared as a
simple matter of definition assumes impressive proportions when we set ourselves to the task of classifying china and pottery. Although we have done
little more than scratch the surface, the amateur
will find in the foregoing summary of hard-paste
wares a good many guide-posts. It is difficult to

see how an intelligent understanding of ceramics could be arrived at in any other way. The second division, the soft-paste wares, is not less important than the other.

To begin with the translucent wares, china, it is hardly necessary to say that the great majority of specimens of English china which the average collector is likely to be interested in belong to this category. All specimens clearly identifiable as bone-paste porcelain belong to this division, of course. By way of generalization not much more can be usefully said concerning porcelain with reference to this classification, for reasons already discussed at some length. From time to time, in dealing with special examples, it will be possible to add to this generalization. Under this head must be included all *majolica*, no matter where made. *Delft* also is invariably to be classified as soft paste. This applies not only to the old Delft made in Holland, but to all the wares of the same general type, having a tin-enameled surface, which all bear the name derived from the Dutch town, even though made in English potteries. *Queen's-ware* belongs to this same class, and so do virtually all types and forms of *luster-ware*, all the transfer printed *Staf-*

Principles of Classification

fordshire tableware so commonly miscalled "old china," and all the earthen wares designated in the trade as "common white" and "common yellow." The printed wares of Liverpool, Sunderland, and Leeds, so much desired by the modern collector, are all soft paste. To the same category must be assigned all the numerous types of mottled glazed ware produced in so many American potteries and designated *Rockingham*. This applies to the Rockingham ware of Bennington, exemplified in hound-handled pitchers, toby mugs and bottles, cow creamers, and the like, and it equally applies to the immense range of wares of the same general type ranging from worthless nondescript rubbish to really fine examples of American pottery made in New Jersey, Pennsylvania, Ohio, and elsewhere. All the so-called *flint-enamel wares*, of which those produced at Bennington under Christopher Fenton are best known to collectors, are to be classified under this heading as are virtually all the slip-decorated wares, of which the *tulip ware* of Pennsylvania is the best example.

We have not exhausted the subject, and the summaries given under both heads are far from complete, but they are representative enough, and

[41]

comprehensive enough, to enable the collector to proceed with confidence to the classification of his wares. It is not enough, however, to know how to classify one's collection according to the composition of the bodies of the several specimens. The collector should know something about glazes and enamels in order to pursue his hobby intelligently. It is not necessary, of course, for him to possess precise and detailed knowledge of the composition and use of glazes and enamels. It is no more necessary for him to know the formulæ of the glazes and enamels used than it is to know the formulæ used in the composition of the paste. But just as it is imperative that he should know the difference between hard and soft pastes and how to distinguish them in order to be able to classify specimens intelligently, so he should know enough about glazes and enamels to be able further to develop that classification.

This is not a technical manual on the manufacture of pottery and porcelain, and it is no part of our purpose or aim to enter into any extensive account of the composition and use of glazes and enamels. All that we shall attempt is such an exposition of elementary principles and facts as will

PLATE 7

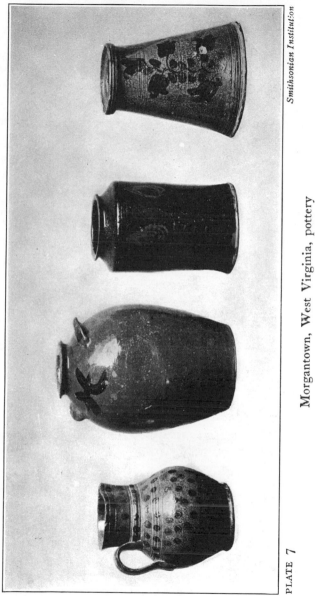

Morgantown, West Virginia, pottery

Principles of Classification

enable the collector to classify his specimens still more precisely by giving due and proper attention to the glaze or other covering used. This knowledge is of the greatest possible importance in the pottery division of ceramics. When first fired, and before being glazed or enameled, all products of the art of the potter, whether opaque (pottery) or translucent (porcelain), are in what is called the "biscuit" state. Once we have grasped the distinction between hard- and soft-paste bodies, it will be easy to understand the importance of glazing. Soft paste far antedates hard paste. The latter requires firing at a high temperature, and therefore presupposes a considerable development of the art.

At some remote period, far beyond any written records of the race, men discovered a means of making their vessels of clay more useful by overcoming their porosity and absorbent character through the use of a thin coating of glass, which is what glaze is, as the word itself implies. The softer the paste the more absorbent the vessel, and, consequently, the greater the need of glaze. Stoneware, being extremely hard and non-porous, can be used without glaze and is usually only lightly glazed. We may roughly describe glaze as a specially prepared glass that is finely ground, mixed in water, then spread over the ware and re-fused by firing.

We can divide all glazes into two great classes; namely, the alkaline and the plumbiferous. The first class includes salt glaze, as well as the glaze that is formed in the manner already described, by mixing ground silicious materials with water and fusing them on the body of the ware. The second class includes glaze produced by sprinkling some sort of lead sulphide on the ware and fusing it by heat, also the mixing of oxide of lead with other ingredients in water, covering the ware with this, and then fusing it by the application of heat. Salt glaze is usually found on stoneware. The composition of the body of this ware, and the high temperature at which it is fired, make it peculiarly adaptable to salt glazing. The simplest form is attained by throwing salt directly into the oven or kiln in which the ware is. This is done when a high temperature has been attained. At this temperature the salt is volatilized, and the vapor rising from the ware, acting upon the vapor of the sodium chloride, produces, in combination with the chlorine of the salt, hydrochloric acid. The soda acts upon the silicate of the ware and forms a silicate of soda, covering

[44]

the body of the ware with what is really a coating of soda-glass.

How pulverized lead sulphides, dusted upon the ware and fused by heat, form a protective coating to the body, making it more impervious, is too obvious to require description. The novice will not find it easy to distinguish between the alkaline and the plumbiferous glazes. Sometimes, indeed, the expert cannot do so with absolute certainty by any method short of an actual chemical test. As a rule, however, the two can be distinguished. In the case of lead glazes, whether applied in powdered or liquid form, there is a smoothness which is not found in the case of the salt glaze. The latter, especially when produced by throwing salt into the oven or kiln, is apt to be characterized by fine granulations which cover the ware with little pits, giving it something of the appearance of the skin of an orange. Examination of a few pieces of old stoneware will make clear what is here meant.

We are now ready to go a step further and again to classify glazes according to another standard. All glazes are divided into two subdivisions; namely, the transparent and the opaque. Suppose we have a piece of ware in the biscuit state which we desire to cover with a coating of transparent, colorless lead glaze. We have a ground mixture of the materials of which ordinary glass is made, and to this we add oxide of lead. We mix these in water and cover the ware with the liquid mixture, generally by dipping. We next place the ware in a kiln or oven, and at the proper temperature fusion of the materials takes place and the ware is covered with a transparent colorless glaze. If we desired to color the glaze without losing its transparency, we should add the proper metallic oxides in the right proportions. Vegetable coloring would not do and is never used.

Suppose, however, we wanted to hide the body of the ware completely. It might be that we desired to give to a dark and unattractive body the external appearance of being light. We need only to add oxide of tin to our glaze to make it opaque. We could also get the opaque result by adding other substances, such as ochers, clays, and so on. In reality we ought not to call the result a glaze at all. Glass and glaze are synonymous, and when you get away from transparency and attain its opposite, complete opacity, it is a misuse of language to call it glass. So the best authorities insist that, instead

Principles of Classification

of dividing glazes into transparent and opaque, we ought to confine the term "glaze" to the transparent types, whether colored or not, and describe the opaque type as "enamel," which is really what it is. It does not much matter what we call it, however, so long as we understand clearly what is meant. The coloring of the opaque type is attained precisely in the same manner as the coloring of the transparent.

NOTE A: There has been greater controversy over this ware than any other. Many experts have contended that none of the ware bearing the name was made at Lowestoft; that at most it was decorated there, being made in China. The accepted standard for all Lowestoft is the Oriental type; that is, a hard-paste body. There is a good deal of ware, classified as Lowestoft, which has a soft-paste body, however, quite akin to Bow. Most British experts call this by some such name as "pseudo-Lowestoft."

Soft-Paste Types

1. All "bone china"
2. All "artificial" porcelain
3. Delft in all forms
4. Majolica
5. Queen's-ware
6. All the lustered wares
7. Transfer printed earthenware of all kinds
8. Bow
9. Leeds
10. Liverpool
11. Sunderland
12. Common white earthenware
13. Common yellow earthenware
14. Sgraffito ware
15. All slip-decorated earthenware
16. Rockingham (see Note B below), also called "tortoise-shell" and "mottled"
17. Flint-enamel ware
18. All "marbled" or "veined" wares

NOTE B: The reference here is to the ware covered with brown glaze, either mottled and somewhat resembling tortoise-shell or plain, to which the name "Rockingham" is generally applied. It should be added to the foregoing, perhaps, that the fine, costly, and elaborately decorated ware called Rockingham, and much referred to in English works on ceramics, is also of the soft-paste type.

[48]

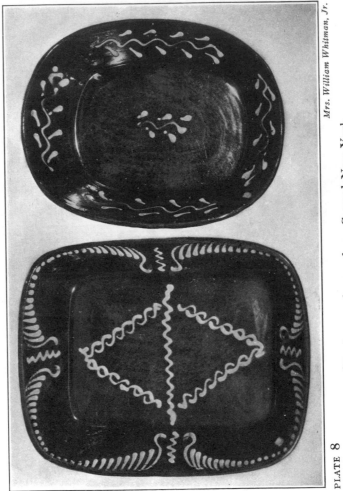

Slip-decorated ware from Central New York

PLATE 8

CHAPTER III

AMERICAN POTTERIES BEFORE THE REVOLUTION

LIKE the word "antiques," the term "early American" applied to pottery and china is elastic in definition and conveys only a vague and uncertain meaning. That goods made within the memory of men and women still living, who can well remember the making, should be classed as "antiques" is simply amusing, of course. Yet the shops are crammed with such things, and many a woman whose attire, cosmetics, and demeanor bespeak a desperate, but altogether admirable, determination not to be classed as old, and who would be offended if described as belonging to an antique age, will cheerfully apply that designation to chairs, lamps, coverlets, bric-à-brac, and so forth, less aged than herself. What a comedy this tragic business of living is!

In the case of our native potteries, however, there is some justification for the use of the term "early

[49]

American" in a rather loose sense, so as even to embrace some potteries in which men still living were employed. It is fairly obvious that 1860, for example, which from the point of view of the Bostonian is quite "late," is from the point of view of Seattle so "early" as to be almost prehistoric. These are extreme cases, of course, but they serve to emphasize a fact that must be constantly borne in mind; namely, that the course of the development of our country and the manner of its growth compel us to use such terms as "early" and "late" in a rather empirical sense. When we remember that the first kiln of ware made in East Liverpool, Ohio, one of the most important pottery centers of the world, was fired in 1840, whereas in Pennsylvania the industry goes back to a full century before that date, it is easy to understand that "late Pennsylvania" and "early Ohio" may refer to the same period.

Of course, the earliest of all American pottery goes back to prehistoric times, to the mound-builders and the cliff-dwellers, but in the present work we shall not concern ourselves with this. Neither shall we make any attempt to deal with the pottery of the later aborigines with its wide range from the crude earthen vessels of the Indians of the eastern part of the country to the really admirable creations of the Pueblo and other Western Indians. These prehistoric and aboriginal examples of the potter's art are excluded from our present consideration, not because they are lacking in ceramic interest—for in fact they are of great interest from that point of view—but for quite other reasons.

The interest which attaches to all examples of prehistoric pottery, and to the greater part of those of a later period, made by the aboriginal tribes before the incursion of the white man and his civilization, is primarily archæological and ethnographical. They are documents really, among the most important documents from which what we know of those earlier peoples and races has been learned. And just as this prehistoric and aboriginal pottery is primarily important for the light it sheds upon the great problems of archæology and ethnology, contributing materially to the construction of such pictures as we have of the manner of living of peoples of a remote past, so, for an intelligent understanding of the pottery, considerable knowledge of archæology and ethnology is necessary. Even a cursory examination of the literature devoted to prehistoric and aboriginal American pottery will show why the subject requires specialization, and why by common consent it lies outside the limits of the hobby to which this volume is devoted. Acknowledging himself greatly interested in much of this pottery, purely as pottery, the writer confesses that his knowledge of archæology and ethnology is too elementary and too limited to warrant his forming any opinion or judgment concerning its classification, much less offering advice and guidance to others.

Brief as the story of our nation is when compared with that of the European nations, much of its essential early history is obscure. We do not know, for example, where or when the first pottery was made by the pioneer settlers of European stock. We know that the first settlers in Virginia soon established small potteries in which simple domestic utensils of coarse earthenware were made. By 1650 there were several such potteries in the settlements of Virginia, but so far as the writer has been able to discover there are no records extant which show definitely where they were or by whom they were conducted.

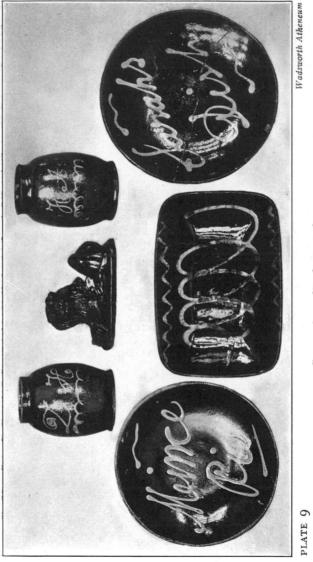

Connecticut slip-decorated ware

PLATE 9

American Potteries Before the Revolution

It is a remarkable fact that, notwithstanding the great importance to the people of the manufacture of articles of such fundamental utility as cooking-utensils and drinking-vessels, the keepers of the early records of our towns rarely considered the establishment of a pottery a matter worth recording. In dozens of instances the writer has made, or caused to be made, careful examination of the early records of towns in which potteries are known to have existed at an early date, only to find that no mention of the potteries was made by the recorders. The establishment of a grist-mill is generally noted in the official records, and so is the establishment of a sawmill. Even the establishment of a distillery is usually noted. The delver after facts can, as a general rule, ascertain when and by whom these enterprises were started, but in the case of potteries that is usually not possible; in most cases the only references to these disclosed by examination of the local records are in the descriptive clauses of deeds of title. There is nothing unusual in the fact that the records of Virginia do not inform us when, where, or by whom the earliest potteries were established.

We should naturally expect to find that among

the early Dutch settlers in New York were some who possessed a practical knowledge of potting. Who the first potter was or where his pottery was located we do not know. In the list of burghers of the "City of Amsterdam, New Netherland," April 18, 1657, occurs the name of Dirck Claesen, "Pot-Baker." In the list of freemen of the city of New York, 1697-98, we find the names of John Dewilde, "Pottmaker," Dirck Benson, "Pott Baker," and John Euwatse, "Pottmaker." Whether Dirck Claesen of New Amsterdam was the first of the Dutch settlers to practise the potter's craft the writer of these pages has been unable to determine with any degree of certainty. We may safely assume that he made earthenware stew-pans, milk-pans, beer-jugs, platters, and other simple utensils. We do not know where his pottery was. Barber in his "Pottery and Porcelain of the United States" credits to Professor Isaac Broome, the noted sculptor and modeler, the discovery of the remains of an old kiln a mile or two below South Amboy, New Jersey, and suggests that the first pottery of the Dutch settlers was located there. So far as the present writer knows, there are no records bearing on this point, nor are there any specimens of pottery bearing the mark of Dirck Claesen or any of his contemporaries, or credibly attributed to any potter of the period. We can only note the names of these early potters and the dates of their occurrence in the records.

At least as early as 1684 there was a pottery at or near Burlington, New Jersey. If only some authenticated specimen of the ware that was made there could be unearthed, the addition to our knowledge of American ceramic history would probably prove to be of great interest and the utmost importance. The information we have concerning it is exceedingly scanty and fragmentary. Such as it is, however, it would seem to warrant the belief that at this pottery was made the first white ware ever made in the colonies. There are no known examples extant, but in all probability the output of this pottery was a white stoneware, of fine texture, salt-glazed, resembling the admirable white salt-glazed ware produced in England by John Dwight, the Elers, and others, and now so eagerly sought after by collectors.

Dr. Daniel Coxe, of London, one of the principal proprietors of West New Jersey and sometime its governor, was the proprietor and founder of this pottery, in many ways the most interesting of all the potteries of the colonial period. He appears never to have visited America himself, but to have acted through his agent, John Tatham, and his son, Daniel Coxe, Jr. In the Rawlinson collection of manuscripts preserved in the Bodleian Library at Oxford, there is a document, written about 1688, entitled "Proposalls made by Daniell Coxe propri-etary and Governor of ye provinces of East and West Jersey in America." One paragraph recites that "the above mencioned Daniell Coxe being resolved to sell his interest in Land and Government of the Colonies of East and West Jersey" has for sale land "Amounting unto one million of Acres." In the specifications we read:

Itt is believed a thousand pounds per Annum cleere of all charges the said Daniell Coxe hath likewise at Burling-ton two houses and kill with all necessary materialls and implements with divers servants who have made a greate progresse in a Pottery of White and China ware about 1200 li worth being already made and vended in the Country neighbour plantations and the Islands of Bar-bados Jamaica &C and well managed will probably bee very Advantagious to ye Undertakers D: C: haveing ex-pended thereon to bring it to perfection allmost 2000 li.

American Potteries Before the Revolution

Another document, an inventory of the Burlington property, says: "I have erected a pottery att Burlington for white and chiney ware, a greate quantity to ye value of 1200 li have been already made and vended in ye Country, neighbour Colonies and ye Islands of Barbados and Jamaica where they are in great request. I have two houses and kills with all necessary implements, diverse workemen and other servants. Have expended thereon about 2000 li."

In the records of New Jersey there is the report of a court of sessions held in December, 1685, which contains the account of a suit involving this old pottery. One James Budd was the plaintiff in the action, the defendant being one Edward Randall, a potter. The action was for payment of a bond of two hundred pounds, the said Randall having agreed to forfeit that sum if he failed to discharge certain duties to the satisfaction of the plaintiff, Budd. It would seem that Budd had been sent out from England to manage the pottery for Coxe, the proprietor, and that he had engaged and brought with him Randall, the defendant, to be foreman of the works.

Randall had failed to give satisfaction, and the

question confronting the jury was whether his failure was due to his fault or to conditions and circumstances outside of his control. For the defendant one William Winn, a potter, testified "that hee can finde noe Clay in the Country that will make white ware; And further sayth that Edward Randall, the def't, is as good a workman as James Budd ye plaint can finde in England." On the other hand, Mary Budd, who may have been the wife of the plaintiff, gave evidence tending to prove that Randall was not a competent potter: "Shee being at London before ye Def't came away shee was told by an honest woman there who had some concerne amongst ye Potters at London that shee feared ye Pott works here would come to nothing, for that the said def't Randall & ye other p'sons who were to come to manage ye same works had not skill to p'fect it."

We know that Dr. Coxe sold part of his Burlington property before 1690, and that in 1691 he sold all the remainder to the West New Jersey Society, of London. He sold his entire interest in the province at that time for the sum of nine thousand pounds sterling, the property sold including "the pottery house." This is virtually all that we know of the pottery. Meager as it is, it is more than we know of any other seventeenth-century American pottery. We know the owner, the approximate location, and the names of the manager and at least two of the potters. We know, too, that there were two kilns, that the ware made was what was called "white and chiney ware," and that the output was considerable enough to permit an export trade in it. One of the most extraordinary things about this pottery is the fact that in the conditions and circumstances then prevailing it should have been found possible to produce ware for export to Barbados and Jamaica.

There seems to be no room for reasonable doubt that the ware produced was the salt-glazed white stoneware of fine texture already described. It is difficult to suggest any other significance of the use of the terms "white ware," "chiney ware," "White and China Ware," and the like. These terms were never used to describe ordinary earthenware. On the other hand, it is certain that it was not a translucent ware, such as we now understand by the word "china." No fact in ceramic history is better established than that the ware which John Dwight patented in 1671, and repatented in 1684 because so many potters were copying his methods, was a fine white stoneware, salt-glazed. By 1684, the year when that great English potter took out his second patent, the manufacture of a white stoneware of fine texture, salt-glazed, had become fairly common in Staffordshire. When all the facts are taken into account, it is hardly thinkable that the good Coxe could have had any other ware in mind.

It will be recalled that in the civil suit referred to above, the witness Winn, who testified on behalf of the defendant Randall, said that he could "finde noe Clay in the Country that will make white ware." Barber has suggested that when the clay in the immediate vicinity proved unsatisfactory for the making of white ware, clay from South Amboy was used. The fact that Coxe owned a great deal of land in that vicinity lends plausibility to the suggestion, to say the least. Upward of a century and a half later the fine white clay of South Amboy was much in demand for the making of stoneware of a fine quality.

It is well within the bounds of possibility that reposing on the shelves of some collectors to-day are specimens of white salt-glazed stoneware, attributed to seventeenth-century England, and so classi-

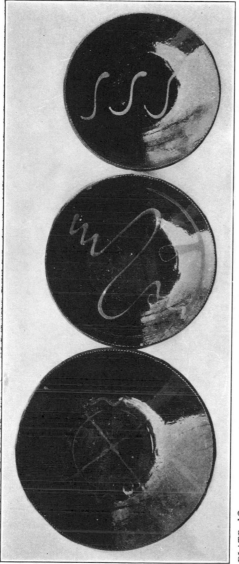

PLATE 10

Slip-decorated ware made at Huntington, Long Island

fied, which were actually made in the Coxe pottery at Burlington, New Jersey.

Reference has already been made to the fact that there were potteries in Virginia as early as 1650. By the middle of the next century considerable progress seems to have been attained. In 1745 William Cookworthy, one of the great figures in the history of the pottery industry in England, wrote a letter to a friend in which there is a clear reference to the manufacture of "china ware" in Virginia.

I had lately with me the person who hath discovered the china-earth. *He had samples of the china-ware of their making with him, which were, I think, equal to the Asiatic.* 'Twas found in the back of Virginia, where he was in quest of mines; and having read Du Holde, discovered both the petunse and kaolin. 'T is the latter earth, he says, is the essential thing towards the success of manufacture. He is gone for a cargo of it, having bought the whole country of the Indians where it rises. They can import it for £13 per ton, and by that means afford their china as cheap as common stoneware.

In 1744 Edward Heylyn and Thomas Frye, of the Bow pottery, took out a patent for the manufacture of "china ware." In the specifications they stated that the material used was "an earth, the produce of the Chirokee nation in America, called by the natives *unaker*." It is generally accepted as true that the famous Bow pottery was founded upon that patent. We are fortunate in knowing exactly what that "unaker" was, for there was in the old color-room at Wedgwood's factory at Etruria until a few years ago, and perhaps still is, a small wooden box of it, with a description on a slip of paper in the handwriting of Josiah Wedgwood. It was for years in the charge of that scholarly ceramist, William Burton, F.G.S., who examined it many times. He says that he found it to be nothing more or less than a sample of china clay, of no especial merit, rather poorly washed. From all that can be gathered about its use, it seems that this Virginian clay was shipped into England and sold to various potters who were interested in making porcelain and fine pottery, but that the cost of transportation made it too expensive for general use. The discovery of an abundant supply of china clay of superior quality in Cornwall, in 1768, gave the manufacture of porcelain its greatest impetus.

We know nothing of the Virginia potteries whose wares had in this manner influenced the development of the pottery industry in England. Some writers have questioned whether there was any ware made in Virginia, other than the coarsest type of red earthenware. They argue that the "samples of the china-ware" referred to by Cookworthy in his letter were probably made in England, from clay brought from Virginia. That seems to require a forced and unnatural construction of a very clear and forthright statement. It also seems to be unlikely that the clay would have attracted attention in such manner as to induce any man to buy it and ship it to England in quantities, unless wares actually made from it were available as positive evidence of its suitability for manufacture.

We know that in 1765 the Worcester and Bristol manufacturers imported clays from South Carolina. At first, the results were rather disappointing. The quality of the clay was not good; the cost of transportation, and the inevitable irregularity of supply, combined to make the experiment anything but a brilliant success. We know that there was the beginning of a pottery industry in South Carolina contemporaneously with the exportation of clay, and that fact tends to confirm our belief that much the same sort of thing occurred in

Virginia. A Staffordshire potter named Bartlem, who had been unsuccessful in England, emigrated to South Carolina and started a pottery. Soon he induced a number of workmen from his old home to follow him. Wedgwood, it is amusing now to recall, was genuinely alarmed. He believed that the South Carolina potteries indicated that British manufacturers would soon find the American markets lost to them.

The great bulk of the wares produced in the British potteries was for export trade. This was particularly true of the better class of goods. The domestic market for these was of little consequence. Much white stoneware was sent to the Continent, while the American colonies took an amazingly large share of the finer and more expensive wares. It will surprise most Americans to-day to learn from no less an authority than Josiah Wedgwood himself that the colonies in 1765 were such a market for the more costly wares made at the British potteries, yet such is the fact. "We cannot make anything too rich and costly," wrote Wedgwood with reference to this market. He continued:

This trade to our Colonies we are apprehensive of losing in a few years, as they have set on foot some Pott-

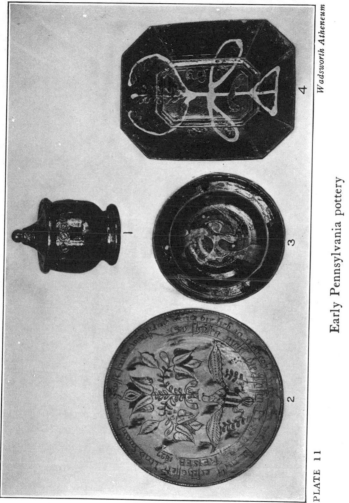

Early Pennsylvania pottery

PLATE 11

works there already, and have at this time an agent amongst us hiring a number of our hands for establishing new Pottworks in South Carolina; having got one of our insolvent Master Potters there to conduct them. They have every material there, equal if not superior to our own, for carrying on that manufacture; and as the necessaries of life, and consequently the price of labor amongst us are daily advancing, it is highly probable that more will follow them, and join their brother artists and manufacturers of every Class, who are from all quarters taking a rapid flight indeed the same way! Whether this can be remedied is out of our sphere to know, but we cannot help apprehending such consequences from these emigrations as make us very uneasy for our trade and Posterity.

How ill founded and vain the fears of the great English potter were, we know. We smile at the vast gulf that yawns between the scared fancy and the sober fact. The South Carolina potteries were small, and their owners eked out a precarious existence for a few years, when they disappeared altogether. One result they had which Wedgwood was not far-sighted enough to foresee: the migration of the potters to the New World brought to the Old World new supplies of kaolin. For several years Wedgwood used considerable quantities of South Carolina clay. Subsequently he used clay from the

Pensacola district of Florida instead, finding it of superior quality. It is interesting to know that the oldest specimens of old Bow china, the earliest in England, were made from American clay, and that American clay also went into the making of Wedgwood's finest wares.

Virtually nothing is known of these mid-eighteenth-century potteries of South Carolina beyond what is here set forth. We do not know that any of the wares made were marked with the makers' names, nor do we know if any specimens have survived until now. Here, as in the case of the seventeenth-century pottery at Burlington, New Jersey, there is at least a possibility that some specimens may still survive and are either classified as "early English" or not classified at all.

As already noted, there were potters in New Amsterdam as early as the middle of the seventeenth century. In 1735 we find the first John Remmey conducting a stoneware pottery in New York City. It was located on what was called Potter's Hill, near the Fresh Water Pond, not far from the site of the old City Hall. On a map purporting to show the city of New York as it was in 1742-44, though not published until 1813, and drawn from memory, there is a legend which would seem to imply that in 1742-44 there was only one pottery on Potter's Hill, operated by Remmey & Crolius. On the strength of that map apparently, Barber, in "The Pottery and Porcelain of the United States," assumed that the above-named John Remmey had entered into partnership with Clarkson Crolius. As will presently appear, it was impossible that there should have been a partnership between John Remmey and Clarkson Crolius, for the good reason that Clarkson was not born until about nine years after John Remmey's death.

If there was a partnership at all, it must have been between the grandfather of Clarkson Crolius and John Remmey. The writer has taken a great deal of trouble to investigate the matter and is satisfied that there was no such partnership. He is convinced that there were two potteries on Potter's Hill, close together but quite independent. One of these was the pottery of John Remmey. The other was the Crolius pottery. In the roll of the freemen of the city of New York for 1737 appear the names of William and Peter Crolius, both of them described as potters. Dr. John E. Stillwell, whose researches on the subject have been published by the

New York Historical Society, identifies this William Crolius with the "William Croylas, Potter," who became a freeman of the city in March, 1729. Why the same man should have been twice granted the burgher right, with an interval of eight years, is not apparent. Dr. Stillwell agrees with the present writer that William and Peter Crolius, whose names appear on the roll for 1737, and are both described as potters, were brothers. These were contemporaries of the first John Remmey. Anna Christina Cortselius, wife of John Remmey, was the sister of Veronia Cortselius, wife of William Crolius. The properties of the Remmey, Crolius, and Cortselius families were contiguous and lay on Potter's Hill, sometimes called Pot-Baker's Hill.

The present writer has been unable to find any evidence of a partnership of the brothers-in-law, at any time. Not knowing of Dr. Stillwell's interest, and investigating the subject on his own account, he reached the conclusion that the Crolius brothers, on one hand, and John Remmey, on the other, at all times maintained separate and distinct establishments, and were never associated in partnership. Dr. Stillwell assumes the partnership, but solely on the strength of Barber's statement. Hutchin's

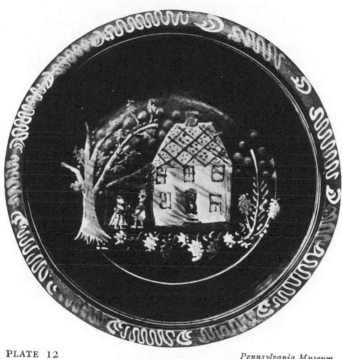

PLATE 12

Polychrome slip-decorated dish

map of the Collect Pond shows two potteries on the top of Potter's Hill. Collect Pond was filled in and leveled in 1812, so that Hutchin's map, which was published in 1846, must describe Potter's Hill as it was before 1812.

The first John Remmey died in 1762 and was succeeded by his son, John Remmey II. According to the Directory of New York, 1794, John Remmey II was then living at 9 Cross Street. He is described as a stoneware potter in business on Potter's Hill. John Crolius, son of William Crolius above referred to, is recorded as living at 215 Greenwich Street. His son, Clarkson Crolius, was then living at 10 Cross Street, next door to John Remmey II. Both John Crolius and his son Clarkson are described as stoneware potters in business on Potter's Hill.

This John Crolius was at that time a man of some importance in New York. He was born in 1733. He became a man of considerable substance, but, as an ardent Whig, he was forced to leave the city by the British in the fall of 1776. They seized his property, which was restored to him when they evacuated the city in 1783. He was active in municipal affairs and in 1799 was assistant alder-

[69]

man from the Sixth Ward. His son, Clarkson Crolius, who was born October 5, 1773, also became a man of considerable political influence, and, if we are to judge by the pretentious character of his Cross Street residence, a picture of which appears in "Valentine's Manual" for 1858, of some affluence also. He held for some time an important position in the custom-house, and his son, Clarkson Crolius II, was, like his grandfather, alderman from the Sixth Ward. Having hastily jumped to the conclusion that John Remmey I had been in partnership with Clarkson Crolius, and subsequently finding what seemed to him to be evidence that Crolius was not associated with any one, Barber had to suggest some explanation. He did so as follows: "John Remmey, one of the partners, having died in 1762, the second partner appears to have carried on alone, as indicated by a salt glazed stoneware jug or batter pot." The feature of the pot compelling Barber to evolve this hypothesis is the following inscription, which accompanies the floral ornamentation in blue cobalt on the sides of the pot:

NEW YORK, FEB'Y. 17TH, 1798
FLOWERED BY
MR. CLARKSON CROLIUS.

American Potteries Before the Revolution

As we have seen, Clarkson Crolius was not born until nearly ten years after the death of his supposed partner. The simple fact is that "Mr. Clarkson Crolius," who so carefully and precisely recorded that he "flowered" the jar, belonged to the generation of John Remmey's grandson. His grandfather, William Crolius, and John Remmey I were contemporaries. After the death of his father, John Crolius, the business was carried on by Clarkson, and when, in 1812, Potter's Hill was leveled and Collect Pond filled in, he moved the pottery to 65 Bayard Street, where the business was carried on until 1848, Clarkson Crolius II having in the meantime succeeded his father. From 1802 to 1805 Clarkson Crolius was assistant alderman from the Sixth Ward, as his father had been before him. He was a member of the New York Assembly in 1806-07 and again continuously from 1815 to 1825. In 1825 he was unanimously elected speaker of the House. An influential member of the Democratic party, as grand sachem of the Tammany Society, he laid the corner-stone of Tammany Hall, May 13, 1811. He served in the War of 1812.

Sometime before the death of Clarkson Crolius the business passed to the ownership and control of his son, Clarkson Crolius II. Stoneware jars with "C. Crolius, Manufacturer, New York," impressed into the clay have been ascribed—rather too hastily in the opinion of the present writer—to the period when the pottery was owned and conducted by Clarkson Crolius I. It is at least rather more than equally possible that they should be ascribed to the later period when the pottery was carried on by Clarkson Crolius II. At all events, in the absence of some positive evidence, such as the date on the piece "flowered" by "Mr. Clarkson Crolius," positive attribution to the father, instead of to the son of the same name, seems to be a violation of the rule governing the interpretation of historical data.

As already noted, John Remmey I died in 1762 and was succeeded by his son, John Remmey II. He, in turn, was succeeded by his son, John Remmey III, who was one of the most remarkable men ever associated with the pottery industry in this country. By all accounts, he was a good potter. He was likewise something of a literary man; he wrote articles for the newspapers on questions of the day, and in 1799 published a book entitled "Egypt as It Is." He conducted the pottery until 1820.

Merely noting here the fact that there is good

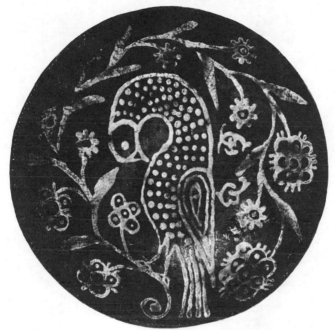

PLATE 13
Slip-decorated pie-plate by Benjamin Bergey, 1838

reason to believe that about the same time when the first John Remmey began to make stoneware in New York City, some unknown German potter had begun to make slip-decorated and sgraffito ware in Pennsylvania, and leaving to later chapters our sketch of those interesting wares, let us take note of some other early potters and their work. We are at once interested to observe that, as in Europe, the manufacture of glass and pottery very often went hand in hand.

Such was the case at the Germantown works, in Braintree, now part of Quincy, Massachusetts, begun in 1753. Joseph Palmer, a Devonshire man of good breeding and education, came to America in 1746, when he was in his thirtieth year. With him came his wife's brother, Richard Cranch, then twenty years old. Palmer purchased a large farm at Braintree and built for himself an elegant mansion. In 1752 he and Cranch leased a large tract of land and at once began to erect factory buildings. They must have had considerable capital, if we may judge from the variety and character of their undertakings. These included chocolate mills, glass and pottery works, spermacetti works, and salt factories. They hired a large number of German artisans, for whom they put up dwellings, the settlement acquiring the name "Germantown." Cranch withdrew from the business in 1760, selling out to his father-in-law. The Germans made glass bottles of all kinds in large quantities, and pottery on a lesser scale. Later on in the Revolution Palmer rose to enviable distinction. He was a member of the Committee of Safety and became a general in the Continental Army. Copley painted his portrait. He was the friend of Washington, Warren, John and Samuel Adams, and other leaders of the Revolution, and by the Provincial Congress was formally thanked for his "wisdom, fortitude and temperance."

Tradition says that glass quite similar to that associated with the name of Baron Stiegel was made at Germantown, together with much more of the coarser and commoner type. If that tradition is to be credited, it would be equally probable that the pottery that was made there included the slip-decorated and sgraffito types associated with the German potters of Pennsylvania. Yet this is pure conjecture and speculation, for so far as the writer can ascertain no authoritatively authenticated specimens of the pottery are known to exist. All that is known is that the son of Richard Cranch, many years after the works had closed, picked up on the site of the old works something of a collection of fragments of glass and pottery. The latter included some exceptionally heavy and coarse stoneware, and some that was very thin, apparently a fine cream-colored salt-glazed stoneware.

It is evident from the newspapers and the public records of the period that by 1765 there had developed a somewhat general movement to encourage the domestic manufacture of those articles which had hitherto been imported from England and continental Europe. Not only was there a growing feeling that practical support should be given to those disposed to undertake new branches of manufacture, but there was a developing national consciousness and sense of self-dependence, which led individuals to all sorts of adventurous undertakings. It was something of that spirit, doubtless, which led Baron Stiegel, the successful iron-founder, to undertake those experiments in glass manufacture which beggared him, but nevertheless made him famous long after his death.

Around the same time that Baron Stiegel was developing the enterprise that brought him both poverty and posthumous fame, and when he was building his flint-glass factory at Lancaster, Pennsylvania, another factory of equal interest and importance was being built in Philadelphia. A pottery for the manufacture of china was built in 1769-70, operations starting during the latter year. At the head of it, and its moving spirit, was a potter who had recently come from England, where he is said to have worked at the famous Bow pottery. His name was Gousse Bonnin, which would seem to indicate French or Flemish rather than British origin. One account says that he was a native of Antigua. There seems to be no doubt, however, that he had worked at Bow and migrated from there. With him was associated George Anthony Morris of Philadelphia, who appears to have subscribed most of the capital.

The factory was built in the Southwark section, on Prime Street, near the present navy-yard. What is believed to have been the first announcement made by the ambitious proprietors was published on December 1, 1769. It set forth that "the Proprietors of the China Works, now erecting in Southwark, have the pleasure to acquaint the public, they have proved to a certainty, that the clays of America are productive of as good Porcelain, as heretofore

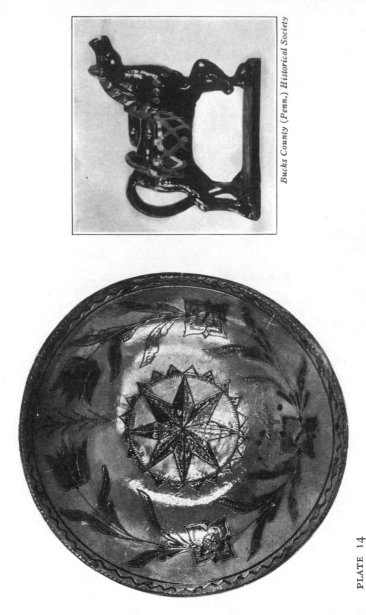

Pennsylvania slip-decorated and sgraffito ware

PLATE 14

manufactured at the famous factory in Bow, near London, and imported into the colonies and plantations, which they will engage to sell upon reasonable terms." The literary construction of this is not perfect, but it is not difficult to understand the intent.

The enterprising spirit of Messrs. Bonnin & Morris is clearly shown in the outline of their plans. They announced that all orders would be executed in rotation, on the principle of first come, first served. Dealers were assured of a square deal and told that "no goods under Thirty Pounds' worth, will be sold to private persons out of the factory, at a lower advance than from their shops." A bid was made for labor in these terms:

All workmen skilled in the different branches of throwing, turning, modeling, moulding, pressing and painting, upon application to the Proprietors, may depend on encouragement suitable to their abilities; and such parents, as are inclined to bind their children apprentices to either of these branches, must be early in their application, as only a few of the first offering will be accepted without a premium; none will be received under twelve years of age, or upwards of fifteen.

Soon afterward we find the announcement that

the principal part of the works was complete and in operation. At the same time the proprietors advertised for bones, offering twenty shillings per thousand pounds "for any quantity of beeves shank bones, whole or broken, fifteen shillings for hogs, and ten shillings for calves and sheep (a proportionate price for knuckle bones) delivered at the china factory in Southwark." An advertisement in 1771 materially aids us to form a trustworthy mental picture of the product of this pottery. The advertisement calls for "Zaffer or Zaffera" for making blue ware. Early in 1772 the firm was advertising for "apprentices to the painting branch, a proper person being engaged to instruct them," and for "several apprentices to the other branches, of equal utility and benefit to the children." The term of apprenticeship was seven years, the general practice of the trade. From an interesting address to the Legislature in January, 1771, we learn that the proprietors had "expended great Sums in bringing from London Workmen of acknowledged Abilities."

By the aid of these published statements and advertisements we are enabled to form a fairly definite idea of the sort of ware that was made at this early Philadelphia pottery. That some part of the ware must have been a soft-paste porcelain, or "bone-china," is evident from the large quantities of bones used. Kaolin was not mentioned, nor is there any other indication that hard-paste porcelain was made. The manner in which the proprietors referred to the Bow pottery as their standard, the fact that they brought their skilled workmen from London, taken together with the evidence of the use of quantities of bones, warrant us in concluding that the body of much of the ware was in imitation of that made at Bow. At the same time it seems quite certain that a good deal of ware was made which cannot by any stretch of imagination be likened to "bone-china." Perhaps this was made in the latter period, when the other ware had been found unprofitable. We know that in 1772 the firm advertised for "fifty wagon loads of white flint stone"; and we also know that the one example of their products that comes down to us with dependable attestation is "common white," an opaque ware.

We can go further than this: the emphasis laid upon painting, not merely in the preliminary announcement, but in the advertisements for apprentices during operation, affords conclusive evidence that the china was decorated, and we are justified in assuming that the style of decoration, like the body of the ware, was closely patterned after that made at Bow. In this connection the advertisements for "Zaffer or Zaffera" are worthy of note. It is well known that a great deal of the output of the Bow pottery at that time and previously consisted of blue and white china, zaffer being much used in colored decoration under the glaze. Whether other colors were used, and if so to what extent, is not known with any degree of certainty. The writer has seen plates and at least one tea-pot, elaborately decorated with flowers in natural coloring, which were said by the owners to have been made at the pottery of Bonnin & Morris. They bore absolutely no marks of identification, and the only feature at all distinguishing them from a good deal of cheap mid-Victorian decorated white earthenware was the extravagant price asked.

There is one well authenticated specimen in the Pennsylvania Museum, a broken fruit-basket. The body is white earthenware, of good quality, not china, and there is much in the general character of the piece suggestive of the Bow pottery of the period. The openwork sides are embellished with small floral ornaments in relief. The decoration is

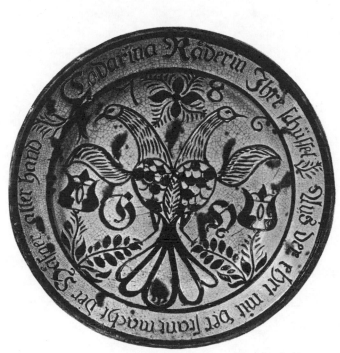

PLATE 15   *Pennsylvania Museum*

Sgraffito dish made by George Hubener, 1786

in zaffer blue under the glaze, with rosettes around the sides and a large rose with sprays of foliage on the bottom. There is a capital P in blue under the glaze on the under side of the bottom, but whether this was intended as a pottery mark or as the bench-mark of the decorator it is not possible to determine.

The authentication of the piece as a product of the Bonnin & Morris pottery seems to be complete. It takes the form of a letter from the original owner, Dr. James Mease, whose father was a friend of Bonnin and one of his strong financial backers. Dr. Mease, who in 1811 published an important work, "A Picture of Philadelphia," says in his letter that the fruit-basket was part of a dinner-set made for his father, and that the clay used at the pottery was brought from White Clay Creek, a few miles from Wilmington, Delaware.

All things taken into account, the writer of these pages is inclined to regard this early Philadelphia pottery as the most interesting, and also the most important, of all the potteries known to have existed in this country before the Revolution, of whose products we know anything definite. It is a great pity that only one sufficiently authenticated speci-men is known to exist. The impression given us is that we have lost a valuable chapter from our ceramic history. Gousse Bonnin was apparently too far in advance of his time, or rather, his ideals and his plans were unrealizable because too far ahead of the actual opportunities presented by the existing state of the country's development. Almost from the first the firm found itself in financial difficulties. Bonnin & Morris appealed to the Legislature in 1771 for financial support in the shape of a loan. In a petition, which appears to have been accompanied by an exhibit of the ware produced, the petitioners recited the facts of a great development of the industry accompanied by keen international rivalry, and continued:

America, in this general Struggle, hath hitherto been unthought of, and it is our peculiar Happiness to have been primarily instrumental in bringing her forward; but how far she shall proceed, in a great Measure, depends on the influence of your generous Support. We have expended great Sums in bringing from London Workmen of acknowledged Abilities, have established them here, erected spacious Buildings, Mills, Kilns, and various Requisites; and brought the work, we flatter ourselves, into no contemptible Train of Perfection. A sample of it we respectfully submit to the Inspection of your Honorable House, praying it may be viewed with a favourable Eye having

American Potteries Before the Revolution

Reference to the Disadvantages under which we engaged; if happy enough to merit your approbation we would not wish to aspire at the Presumption of dictating the Measure of your Encouragement, but with all Humility hint at the Manner.

In this stilted obsequious manner, which was the manner of the time, the petitioners proceeded to hint the sort of relief they desired: "We beg leave to point out the Propriety of a Provincial Loan, at the Discretion of your Honourable House, independent of Interest, for a certain Term of years." It is interesting to note, and not without significant bearing upon the state of the "infant industries" of the country at the time, that at the same session of the General Assembly Baron Stiegel was a petitioner, begging for assistance in much the same tone and manner. Whether the General Assembly was cynically skeptical or merely wedded to a program of economy, does not appear from the records, but neither the glass-maker nor the makers of pottery obtained anything. The Southwark pottery failed most disastrously and was closed in 1774. The proprietors made soul-stirring public appeals for charitable aid for the workmen who were now stranded. The lot of these workmen was indeed a pitiable one. Lured by promises that were golden, as such promises always are, they had left their employment and their homes in England, and were now without employment or likelihood of employment at their trade in a strange land. Bonnin returned to England, a sadly disillusioned adventurer.

There is ample evidence that the period when Baron Stiegel was starting his glass-factory and Bonnin and Morris their pottery was characterized by a considerable development of American industry. It was a time of expansion and progress generally, and nowhere was this more evident than in the ceramic industry. In Boston a pottery of some importance was established in 1769. From advertisements asking for samples of clay and sand, published in May, we learn that the enterprise was then being launched, and from an advertisement for four apprentices, dated October 16, 1769, we know that " the new Factory in New-Boston" was then in operation. From the same source we learn something of the wares they made: "Tortoise-shell, Cream and Green colour Plates, Dishes, Coffee and Tea Pots, Cups and Saucers, and all other articles in the Potter's Business." It is especially interesting to note that they were making "Tortoise-shell" ware

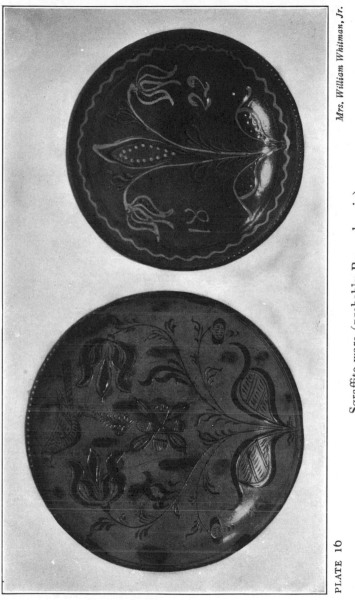

PLATE 16

Sgraffito ware (probably Pennsylvania)

Mrs. William Whitman, Jr.

in Boston at that early date. Presumably this was a mottled ware, an imitation of the tortoise-shell ware of Whieldon. It was probably a cream-colored earthenware body spattered with a glaze in which manganese was the principal coloring ingredient. In other words, it probably resembled what afterward was called Rockingham in this country.

Beyond what the advertisements indicate, virtually nothing at all is known of this early Boston pottery. No records of it can be found in any of the numerous archives of the city. From the fact that the name "New Boston" was formerly applied to the West End, we are reasonably certain that the pottery was in that section. It is interesting to recall that Anthony Haswell, the pioneer printer of Bennington, Vermont, was employed in a Boston pottery at about this time—perhaps the same pottery. The proprietors asserted that their wares were "equal to any imported from England," but in the absence of any authenticated specimens we are unable to judge how far the claim was justified. We do not know what the "Green colour" plates and other domestic utensils were like, whether green was used as a design contrasting with the lighter background of the body of the ware, or whether the entire surface was covered with a glaze colored by the use of oxides of copper. We do not know how long the pottery was operated nor what measure of success it attained.

Of course, that was not the first pottery in Massachusetts. For at least a full generation small potteries had existed in the province. As early as 1641 John Pride, of Salem, was registered as a potter; and soon after that we find William Osborne making pottery at Danvers, in a pottery which was continued in operation for several generations. In 1730 the manufacture of red ware and other simple types of earthenware began in Peabody, Massachusetts, the pioneer potters being Jonathan Kettle, Joseph Osborne, Joseph Whittemore, and Miles Kendall. In 1759 William Southwick made pottery at Peabody, the characteristic feature of which was the rich, almost black glaze which covered the red ware body. He made an interesting variety of simple domestic utensils. In 1765, at Weston, Massachusetts, Abraham Hews established a pottery and made milk-pans, bean-pots, jugs, pudding-dishes, platters, and so forth.

Among the early Connecticut potters first place must be given to John Pierce, who is known to have operated a pottery at Litchfield as early as 1753. Among his contemporaries were Jesse Wadhams and Hervey Brooks, both of whom operated small potteries either at Litchfield or in the vicinity. It is believed that these men made only the simplest red ware, except, possibly, some stoneware. No marked specimens of their work are known to exist, and although pieces are extant which have been attributed to them the attribution appears to be speculative. It is generally believed that John Norton, the pioneer potter of Vermont, learned his trade at the Litchfield potteries.

In 1774 and 1775 Jonathan Durell, who seems to have had a pottery in the city as early as 1753, when he was registered as a potter among the freemen, was again operating a pottery in New York City. From a contemporary advertisement we learn that his pottery was situated "about midway between the New City-Hall and the Tea-Water Pump, on the left hand side of the road as you go out of the city," close by "Kitechemet's Mead House." The same advertisement informs us that Durell, the proprietor of the pottery, had formerly been in Philadelphia, and it is not unlikely that he had been there for some years, employed perhaps in the ill fated Southwark pottery of Bonnin & Morris, though that is not definitely known.

Durell informed prospective customers that his ware was "far superior to the generality, and equal to the best of any imported from Philadelphia, or elsewhere." The list of articles made is impressive: "butter, water, pickle and oyster pots, porringers, milk pans of several sizes, jugs of several sizes, quart and pint mugs, quart, pint and half pint bowls, of various colours; small cups of various shapes, striped and coloured dishes of divers colours, pudding pans and wash basins, sauce pans, and a variety of other sorts of ware, too tedious to particularize." It would be interesting to discover an authentic example of the "striped and coloured" ware, but no such examples are known to exist, and we can only guess what they were like. We may hazard the guess that a body of common white earthenware was decorated by painting stripes or bands in zaffer and manganese, and then glazed.

This sketch is by no means a complete account of the pre-Revolutionary potters. It is sufficient to show that before the Revolution potteries were fairly numerous, and that in the decade preceding the fateful events of 1776 the industry had made substantial progress, particularly in the direction of improving the quality of the wares. The colonists were by no means as dependent upon British wares as we have commonly supposed. Numerous workmen from the English potteries, some of them most highly skilled, came to America, bringing with them the designs, formulas, and methods used in the best English establishments. It is true that many of the potteries that were established failed and were short-lived, but we should be careful to avoid misinterpreting that fact. We should bear in mind that what may be termed an excessive mortality rate was peculiarly characteristic of the pottery industry in the Old World as well as in the New. Furthermore a large percentage of failures invariably occurs in the early stages of every phase of industrial development.

CHRONOLOGICAL LIST OF COLONIAL POTTERS AND POTTERIES

NOTE: This list is admittedly incomplete. The compilation of anything approaching a complete list of potteries established during the colonial period would require a large amount of research and the expenditure of a great deal of money. It is too big an undertaking for a private individual.

Date	Place	Name	Types of Ware
1641	Salem, Mass.	John Pride	Unknown
1650	Virginia	Various potteries before that date	
1657	New Amsterdam	Dirick Claesen	Unknown; supposed to be red ware
1684	Burlington, N. J.	Daniell Coxe (proprietor) Edward Randall William Winn	Salt-glazed white stoneware
1698	New York City	Dirick Benson	Not known; supposed to be red ware
1698	New York City	William Croylas (Crolius)	Not known
1728	New York City	John Euwatse	Not known
1730	Peabody, Mass.	Jonathan Kettle	Red ware with black glaze
1732	New York City	Henry Bensing	Not known

Date	Place	Name	Types of Ware
1735	New York City	John Remmey I	Stoneware
1737	New York City	William Crolius	Not known
		Peter Crolius	Not known
1751	Huntington, Long Island	Adam States	Red ware and stoneware
1753	New York City	Jonathan Durell	Not known
1753	Braintree, Mass.	Joseph Palmer	Stoneware
		Richard Cranch	
1753	Litchfield, Conn.	John Pierce	Red ware and stoneware
		Jesse Wadhams	
		Hervey Brooks	
1759	Peabody, Mass.	William Southwick	Red ware with black glaze
1762	New York City	John Remmey II	Stoneware
1762 (circa)	New York City	John Crolius (son of Clarkson Crolius)	Stoneware
1765	South Carolina	—— Bartlem	Not known
1769	Weston, Mass.	Abraham Hews	Red ware
1769	Philadelphia	Gousse Bonnin George Anthony Morris	"Bone-china"; earthenware, white and decorated; fine stoneware

Date	Place	Name	Types of Ware
1769	Boston	Unknown	Tortoise-shell and other glazed earthenware
1769	New York City	Thomas Campbell	Not known
1774	New York City	Jonathan Durell	Decorated earthenware and stoneware
1775	East Greenwich, R. I.	—— Upton	Red ware and (?) white earthenware

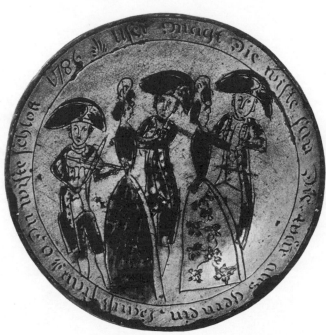

PLATE 17

Pennsylvania sgraffito plate

CHAPTER IV

POTTERS AND POTTERIES AFTER THE REVOLUTION

The Revolution greatly stimulated the manufacture of pottery in this country, and, at the same time, as greatly retarded its progress. Paradoxical as that statement undoubtedly is, its correctness as a summary can hardly be challenged by any who are familiar with the facts. War itself is a paradox, and its results and influences are frequently best expressed in paradoxical terms. When most abundantly justified—and history has indelibly stamped the War for Independence with full approval and justification—war achieves progress through reaction, freedom through despotism and servitude, and security for life and property through the wholesale destruction of both.

The outbreak of hostilities put a speedy end to

[93]

the importation of goods from Great Britain. This had the immediate effect of stimulating native industry, for two quite independent but complementary reasons of equal cogency. In the first place, it destroyed the formidable British competition which had caused so many American enterprises to fail. How important that was can best be comprehended from the light of the experience of Bonnin & Morris, whose ambitious efforts to imitate the Bow wares we have already noted. It seems to be clearly demonstrated that what brought them to disaster and irretrievable ruin was the competition of the manufacturers of the mother-country. No sooner was the American product fairly launched than the English manufacturers sent cargoes of wares to Philadelphia to be sold at prices which the local factory could not meet. That was by no means an isolated case.

In the second place, the stoppage of the importation of British goods had the effect of compelling the colonists to make extraordinary efforts to produce a supply at home. Either that, or they must needs resort to the use of substitutes. The non-importation of tea could not be offset by producing tea at home, and so substitutes had to be resorted to, such as "sassafras tea." Silk could not be produced at home, and so milady wore homespun linsey-woolsey or something of the sort. But when the supply of English earthenware failed, it was possible to replace it with home-made ware. True, it might not rival queen's-ware in quality, in color, or fine workmanship and the pleasant appearance derived therefrom, but it served the practical purpose. A cup made of slip-covered red ware might not be so pleasing to the eye as one of white earthenware glazed over a floral decoration, but it would meet utilitarian requirements quite as well. A coarse stoneware pitcher would hold cider or beer or water quite as well as one of Wedgwood's finest. There was a primary need to be met, and the essential factors were at hand to meet it. There was clay in almost every county which was capable of being potted. There was fuel for firing. There was enough labor sufficiently skilled at least to make simple wares that would serve.

If it were possible for us at this late day to compile anything even remotely approaching a complete list of the potteries that sprang up throughout the colonies during this period, we should find, doubtless, that the increase in their number was extraordinary and unprecedented. So much for the stimulus which had been given to the industry. On the other hand, could we gather together a thoroughly representative collection of the products of the potteries which sprang up during the Revolution, we should assuredly find an astonishing decline in the quality of their wares. The reasons for this are not hard to discover or to comprehend. Many of the most skilled workmen returned to England on the outbreak of trouble; the larger potteries engaged in making the finer wares went under in the general disruption of the time; the new establishments that sprang up were small, poorly equipped, operated by men of limited experience and skill in many instances, sometimes even as a side issue, incidental to some other occupation, such as farming or distilling.

Whoever has studied the effects of the War of Secession in this country upon the Southern States will fully understand the social process we are trying to describe, for it was repeated in the later struggle in all its essential features. There was the same incentive to local effort, leading to an increase in the number of small establishments catering to urgent needs no longer supplied by the old agencies,

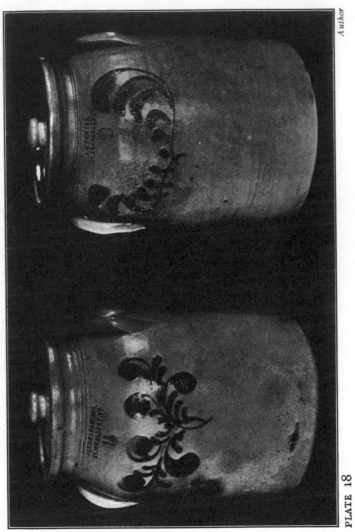

PLATE 18   Stoneware from St. Johnsbury, Vermont

and the same lowering of standards. Simple utility had to suffice. During the Revolution there was little opportunity to develop the manufacture of queen's-ware, for example, and people had to be content with simpler and cruder wares similar to those produced in the early settlements. The exceptions to this rule were few and comparatively insignificant.

As the great struggle neared its end the industry of the country began to revive, and the pottery industry was among the first to manifest definite signs of recovery. With the cessation of the war and the gradual return of normal ways of living came an era of great progress in all kinds of manufacture. It was an era characterized by a tremendous improvement in the quality of the products made and the standards of workmanship.

It is easy to discern the fact, and almost equally easy to explain it. Emerging from the great struggle triumphant, a nation in name and aspiring to the realization of its meaning, the dominant note in the psychology of the people was an overwhelming national consciousness. The sense of national independence was not confined to politics; it overflowed political channels and spread over the whole area of life. Independence, and its corollary, self-sufficiency, sought expression in industry and commerce and in culture.

There are two facts to be noted by the student of this phase of the development of American ceramics. The first is that the English manufacturers made desperate attempts to recover the important American market. The vast amount of transfer printed ware bearing the portraits of such leaders as Washington, Franklin, Jefferson, Hancock, and others, pictorical designs representing American triumphs in the Revolution, and mottos expressing American exultation and British humiliation, bear witness to the intensity of the new English competition. There has been much cynical comment upon the lack of patriotism thus shown by the English manufacturers, but with that we are not here and now concerned. Yet we may well be reminded that the war was not popular in England, that a large part of the English people sympathized with the American cause. This was especially true of the manufacturing and wage-earning classes. However we may regard the motives of the English purveyors of wares embellished with American patriotic sentiments and designs, the important fact is that it was a strong form of competition, which challenged

Potters and Potteries After the Revolution

American producers to exert themselves to the utmost.

The other fact is that the return of peace brought important accessions to the productive force of the country. The pottery industry in particular was greatly strengthened. Among those who had served under the British flag during the long struggle, both in the British regiments and those of the German auxiliaries, there were many skilled artisans, who elected to remain in this country rather than return to their own. Some of these men had been in America several years, either in active service or as prisoners, and had discovered for themselves opportunities which were alluring. This proved to be an important source from which the industrial enterprises of the country could draw the skilled labor they so greatly needed. Another source was the immigration which followed the making of peace, bringing from the Old World many of its best artisans.

The collector of early American pottery and china who regards his hobby seriously, and gives to it that enlightened intelligence without which its fullest enjoyment cannot be attained, will find his interest and pleasure in his hobby greatly enhanced by a study of the effects and influences of the Revolution along the lines indicated by this sketch. So studied, the individual specimens in his collection will acquire significance hitherto unsuspected. One of the most delightful things connected with the collection of any product of early American craftsmanship is the way in which it leads the collector into the by-paths of historical reading and research. Even a modest collection, properly understood, is a sort of historical outline. When the collector turns to the middle of the nineteenth century, for example, and notes the quite admirable wares made by potteries that failed, at the very time that English wares in no wise superior commanded a good market, a close study of his hobby will open an interesting chapter. He will find in the case of pottery after pottery that the greater part of the ware produced was unmarked. One specimen will be found marked, while others exactly like it, their origin amply attested and authenticated, are not marked. There is no obvious reason for this, and at first the collector is likely to be mystified by it. Study of his hobby, however, will soon bring him to face one of the most remarkable features of our national development.

The superb national consciousness which emerged

Burlington

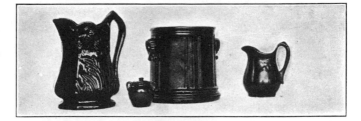

Middlebury
(frog is a
toy whistle)

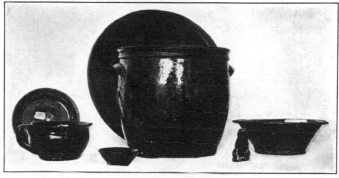

Fairfax

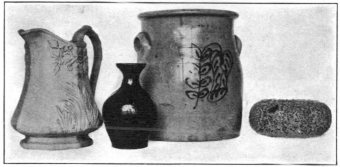

PLATE 19   *H. G. Rugg, Esq.*

Early Vermont pottery

from the Revolution was not long-lived. Scarcely a generation had passed when Americans seemed to be ashamed of American products. At least, they preferred those of Europe. In nearly all branches of manufacture, American products, even though they might be equal in every respect to those from abroad, were rejected and the foreign products taken by the most patriotic Americans. Often it was in self-protection that our American potters left their wares unmarked, since an American mark would have been a barrier to acceptance—a sort of stigma and an open invitation to rejection. When the United States Pottery at Bennington was at its zenith, it was not at all unusual for orders to be accompanied by the stipulation that the goods be unmarked. They could then be sold as English wares to people who prized them accordingly and openly despised American goods.

The supply of simple earthenware and stoneware utensils for domestic use was so important that even during the most trying and difficult days of the war, and in dangerous situations, small potteries persisted in some places. In New York the Remmey pottery operated during the Revolution. At Norwalk, Connecticut, a small stoneware pottery is known to have been started in 1780 and operated for some time. All over the country so far as it was then settled there were examples of this sort of enterprise. But it was not until some time after the termination of the war and the signing of the treaty of peace that anything like a revival of the pottery industry in America began.

It would be futile to attempt to present in these pages anything like a complete list of the numerous potteries that now sprang up in various parts of the country. In a great many instances there are no reliable records, and all that we have to rely upon is local tradition, notoriously undependable for dates and precise details. While a tradition current in a given locality concerning the existence of an early pottery may possess some value in that it keeps alive in the minds of some few persons the memory of a fact which might otherwise be lost in oblivion, it cannot be accepted for more than that. Time and again the writer of these pages has investigated such traditions regarding local incidents only to find that whatever substance of truth was back of them had been obscured by the most inexplicable and fantastic errors. All that can be profitably attempted in a handbook of this character is to cite such concrete examples, concerning which there is evidence fully authenticated, as will give the reader a fairly comprehensive picture of the revival of the industry after the Revolution.

Either in 1789 or 1790, the exact date not being known, Andrew Miller established an earthenware pottery in Philadelphia. This pottery, which was located on Sugar Alley, is of great interest because it was the beginning of one of the most significant and important chapters in the history of American ceramics, as we shall see later on. So far as can be learned, Andrew Miller marked none of his ware. Pieces have been vaguely attributed to him, but in no single case, so far as the writer has been able to discover, has there been any credible evidence to support such attribution. He made red ware, slip-covered, without decoration of any kind so far as is known, though it is possible that toward the end he resorted to simple decoration.

Andrew Miller seems to have carried on his little pottery until 1810 and then to have retired, leaving the business to be carried on by his two sons, Abraham and Andrew. They moved the business to a new location, at the corner of Seventh and Zane Streets, and carried it on until 1816 or 1817. Then

Andrew retired from the concern and Abraham Miller became sole proprietor. He was a potter of remarkable ability and made a vital contribution to the development of the industry in this country. Because his work extended over a long period, to the middle of the nineteenth century, any detailed account of it would take us too far in point of time from our immediate purpose of sketching the revival of the industry after the Revolution. So, promising to give due attention to Abraham Miller later on, we return to the last decade of the eighteenth century.

At the same time when the first Andrew Miller was making his bean-pots, porringers, tea-pots, jugs and jars of slip-covered red ware in his pottery on Sugar Alley—delightful name!—there was another potter in Philadelphia making ware of much the same sort. His name was John Curtis, and little is known about him except that he appears to have started his pottery at about the same time as Miller—1789-90—and that long after his time there was a tradition that he made pottery of good quality. From the fact that he was still carrying on the business as late as 1811, according to the city directory for that year, we may fairly conclude that the tradition referred to was based on solid fact. It is said that Curtis got the clay that he used from a clay-pit which was located about where, in the eighteen-nineties, the brewery stood at Tenth and Filbert Streets. There was a "china factory" in Philadelphia in 1800; that is to say, a factory which was producing fine white or cream-colored earthenware, glazed and resembling the English queen's-ware. We know that a murder which occurred there in August, 1800, was the occasion for a serious riot. Who operated it is not known; it may have been the Curtis pottery.

It is generally believed that Curtis was making a cream-colored earthenware similar to the English queen's-ware as early as 1791. This is tradition merely, and is to be accepted as such. There appear to be no marked specimens of his work, nor any which are otherwise authenticated beyond all dispute, upon which a more definite statement can be based. At the same time, it is not improbable that Curtis was making ware of the character described in 1791. For that matter, it is not improbable that his contemporary, Andrew Miller, was doing the same thing. In January, 1792, the Pennsylvania Society for the Encouragement of Manufactures and the Useful Arts, in a list of prizes offered in connection with their exhibition of that year, announced two premiums of great significance as showing the kinds of ware in which there was the greatest interest at the time. The first is "a plate of the value of fifty dollars, or an equivalent in money," to the person exhibiting the "best specimens of Earthenware or Pottery, approaching nearest to queen's-ware, or the Nottingham or Delft ware, of the marketable value of fifty dollars." The second prize, also "a plate of fifty dollars' value, or that sum in specie," is offered to the person exhibiting the "best specimen of stoneware, or that kind of earthenware which is glazed with salt, of the value of fifty dollars." One of the conditions laid down was that the ware must be made either in New Jersey or Pennsylvania. It seems to be a fair inference from this interesting announcement that those who were trying to encourage the development of the pottery industry in Pennsylvania and New Jersey were interested in fostering a branch of manufacture already existing. It is hardly likely that the prizes would have been offered unless some potters were actually known to be making such wares.

In 1789 one Samuel Dennis, a potter, petitioned

the Legislature of Connecticut asking for State aid
to establish a pottery in Connecticut, promising to
make stoneware of good quality and ware resembl‧
ing and equal to the Staffordshire queen's-ware. He
was unsuccessful, and there seems to be no record
of his having actually established a pottery. About
1790 Nathaniel Seymour established a pottery in
Hartford. He employed four men at the wheel.
His kiln was about ten feet in diameter and was
fired about fifty times a year, it is said. Seymour
was thoroughly convinced that from the Connecticut
clays alone pottery could be made as good as any
in the world. He used no clays from outside of
the State. He used a glaze made of lead oxides
mixed with local sand. Much of the stoneware that
was made at this pottery was decorated with rather
crude designs done in cobalt. Manganese, oxides
of copper, verdigris, and other coloring agents were
used. Nathaniel Seymour retired in 1825 or thereabouts, and the pottery was carried on by his grandson, Major Seymour, until 1842.

At the same time that Nathaniel Seymour started
his pottery in Hartford, another pottery was established in the same town by John Souter, an English-
man. He carried on the business until 1805, when

he sold out to Peter Cross and moved away. In 1792 Charles Lathrop was making salt-glazed stoneware and red ware at Norwich, Connecticut. A number of pieces marked "Norwich" and bearing various dates from 1794 to 1812 are attributed to him. In 1796 another pottery was started at Norwich by C. Pott & Son.

Several ring-shaped bottles made to be slipped over the arm have been attributed to this firm. These bottles, commonly called haymakers' bottles, are often said to have been intended primarily for use in the fields by haymakers, who carried them on the arm. Any one who has ever used a scythe, or watched a skilled mower use one, will be likely to smile at the suggestion. Anything more unlikely to be adopted it would be hard to imagine. It is far more likely that such bottles of this type as were made at Norwich were intended for the purpose for which such bottles have been made in many lands; namely, to be carried over the arm when riding or driving. The man who set out for a long ride on horseback, perhaps in cold and wet weather, found it a convenient way to carry a moderate supply of stimulant. He could refresh himself from such a bottle without dismounting. To a man wielding

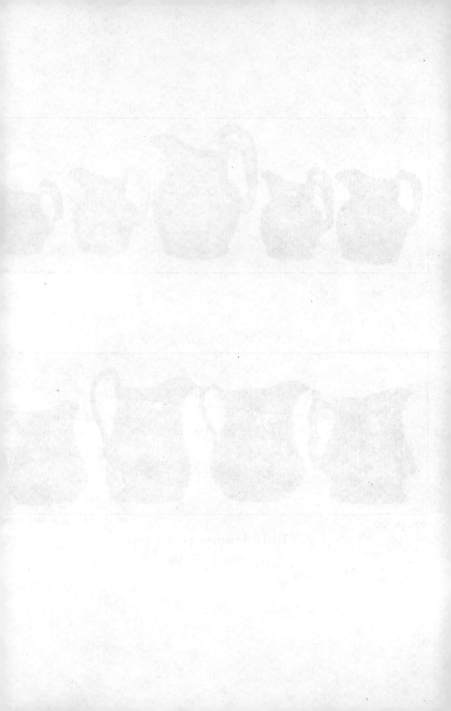

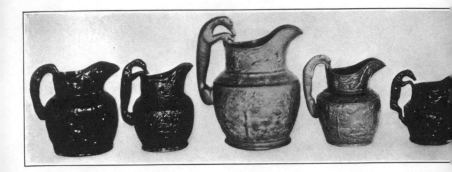

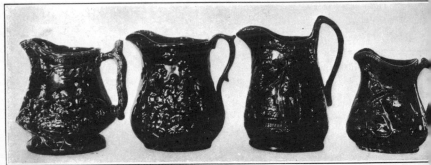

PLATE 20

Early American pottery jugs

scythe or sickle the bottle would be an encumbrance.

Because a few of these bottles have been found in and around Norwich, or with histories which pointed to Norwich as the place of their origin, the wholly unwarranted inference has been drawn by a number of writers that such bottles were made in large numbers at Norwich—an important "line," so to say. That is sheer nonsense, of course. The number of such bottles for which there would be a demand would necessarily be limited. As a matter of fact, bottles of this type have been made in potteries all over the world as occasional pieces, and it is doubtful whether they were made anywhere as a regular product for commerce. The writer has seen bottles of this type that were made in the Old World, and he has seen others made in Connecticut, Vermont, West Virginia, Maryland, Ohio, and South Carolina.

In 1793 the first pottery known to have existed in Vermont was started by Captain John Norton at the foot of Mount Anthony. Captain Norton, a Revolutionary soldier from Connecticut, had learned the pottery trade at Litchfield, Connecticut, which was the next town to Goshen, his home. In 1785 he settled in Bennington, the principal town in

Vermont, which State had not yet been admitted to the Union and was virtually an independent republic. Captain Norton conducted a distillery as well as a large farm, yet in 1793 he established a pottery on his farm in order to meet one of the most urgent demands of the community, a supply of such simple utensils as milk-pans, cider-jugs, butter-jars, platters and plates, and the like. He made red ware exclusively at first, some of it lead glazed and some of it covered with "Albany slip," in which some lead was mixed. Before long he added coarse stoneware salt glazed.

Captain Norton retired from the pottery business in 1823 and was succeeded by his sons. In the thirty years during which he carried on the pottery Captain Norton gained a splendid reputation as a potter, but he never attempted to make any other kinds of ware than those described. No pottery mark was used during his lifetime, but there are a number of pieces known to have been made at the pottery during the first few years of its existence. The little jug with the slip decoration shown in Plate No. 5 is of special interest as the oldest known piece of Vermont pottery. It was made between 1796 and 1798, at the Norton pottery, for a little girl named

Armstrong, the actual potter being one Abel Wadsworth, who had fought under Stark at the Battle of Bennington. It is a delightful bit of pottery. It is of red ware, fired very hard, and covered with nearly black Albany slip containing some lead. The crude floral design is brushed upon the almost black slip covering in a lighter yellowish slip in which ocher may have been used for the coloring.. The jar is red ware lead glazed, beautifully rich in its coloring. A milk-pan in the writer's collection is of red ware with a covering of yellowish slip inside. The Norton pottery was carried on by the descendants of the founder until 1894, a period of 101 years.

At Huntington, Long Island, a small pottery was established in 1751. Barber in his account of this pottery says that it was founded by "a man named Scudder for the manufacture of earthenware and salt glazed stoneware"; that Scudder operated it until 1775, "when the works passed into the hands of one Williams"; and that in 1812 "States & Scudder became the proprietors, the latter being the grandson of the founder." The present writer has been quite unable to reconcile this account with any known records and is compelled to believe that Barber was misled by inaccurate information. The account here given is based on the investigations made by Mrs. Irving S. Sammis, who has devoted much painstaking study to the subject, supplemented by information received from other local sources of a dependable character.

It seems that the founder of the pottery was Adam States, who started in 1751 with a single kiln. He made lead-glazed red ware at first; but after a few years, about 1758-60, he added salt-glazed stoneware, building an additional kiln for the purpose. He carried on the pottery until the outbreak of the Revolution. The pottery seems to have lain idle for a considerable time and then to have passed into the hands of one Jonathan Titus, who in turn sold it in 1805 to four men—Timothy Williams, Scudder Sammis, Samuel Fleet, and Samuel Wetmore. Later in the same year Timothy Williams sold his quarter interest to Moses Scudder for $65.25. For some time these men operated as Samuel J. Wetmore & Company. Moses Scudder, buying out his partners after a while, became sole proprietor and conducted the pottery until 1825, when he sold out to Benjamin Keeler. In 1827 Keeler sold out to Henry Lewis and Nathan Gardiner. The earliest pottery marks used belong to

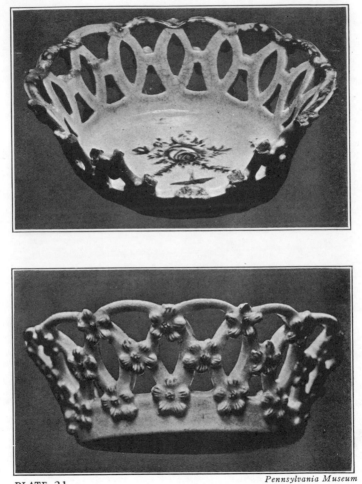

PLATE 21

White earthenware made in Philadelphia, 1770

this period, the mark being "Lewis and Gardiner."

In the Huntington Historical Society's collection there is a beautiful jar of a most unusual type. It is of red ware, lead glazed. It was apparently intended for use in growing bulbs. Mrs. Sammis calls it a crocus-jar, the idea being that the bulbs were to be so planted that they would bloom through the holes placed around the jar. Certainly against the rich red background the brilliant colors of the crocus would show to great advantage. And yet the jar somehow does not seem to have been intended for crocuses, and one is inclined to suggest rather some lovely trailing plant like the old-fashioned musk. Until a few years ago, certainly within the memory of the writer of these pages, English and Dutch potteries made jars akin to this one in shape, though not in color or type of ware, and they were largely used for growing the golden flowered pungent musk. (Plate No. 6.)

Fortunately we know approximately when this fine old jar was made. At least, we know that it was made before 1813. Inscribed in yellow slip that makes a striking contrast against the red glaze is the name of its original owner, Iantha Sammis. Now, Iantha was married, on August 26, 1813, to

Abner Chichester, and so we know that the jar was made for her before that time. It seems reasonably certain that it was made during the time when Moses Scudder owned the pottery, perhaps by Moses himself. Possibly it was Abner Chichester's gift to his beloved Iantha, and for that reason she preserved it with unusual care. Whether Abner was a potter is not known, nor does it matter much. Even if he was not, it may well have been his hand that incised her name. It is a great mistake to take for granted, as so many writers do, that the name or inscription incised on an old piece of pottery must have been incised by the same hand that shaped the piece itself.

Old diaries over which the present writer has pored, beguiling many hours away, throw an interesting light upon this subject. They show that it was the custom for men with an idle hour to spend to visit the local pottery to watch what is, after all, one of the most fascinating of all occupations. During such visits it was a common thing for a man seeing a jug or other utensil, which pleased his fancy or seemed well adapted to some need of the moment, to order it and to mark it as his fancy dictated while the clay was still wet. And on cold or wet evenings

[114]

the pottery was a gathering-place for young men especially when the kilns were burning ware. At such times many a "green" piece was selected and marked. It might be a mug to be marked with the initials of the youth newly conscious of the need of shaving, a cider-jug to be marked with the family name, or a pitcher to be inscribed with the name of mother, wife, or sweetheart, perhaps with a sentimental inscription in addition. Finally, many potteries advertised the fact that they would permit patrons to mark their wares.

It is to be regretted that we know so little about the pottery that was established at Morgantown, West Virginia, immediately after the Revolution. It appears to have been started in 1784 by a potter named Foulke, concerning whom there is a most extraordinary dearth of precise information. In the course of inquiries made several years ago with a view to obtaining some definite information about him, the writer of these pages elicited the most amazing medley of misinformation. He was a German according to one account, English according to another, and French according to a third. We know that he carried on the pottery at Morgantown until the beginning of 1800, and that he was a potter of very considerable ability. Foulke was succeeded in the ownership of the pottery by James W. Thompson, who had learned his trade under Foulke. The slip-decorated ware that was made here ranks with the best productions of the Pennsylvania German potters, but differs from the latter so greatly as to lend plausibility to the story that he was a Frenchman and that his name was originally spelled Foulque. In addition to the slip-decorated ware, Foulke and Thompson, his successor, made lead-glazed red ware, and plain gray stoneware, salt glazed. There are several examples of Foulke's pottery in the Smithsonian Institution, Washington.

To what extent the Revolution interrupted the operations of the potteries in New York City the writer of this volume has not been able to determine. From May, 1776, when the last session of the Common Council under colonial rule was held, to February, 1784, when the civil authority resumed functioning under Mayor James Duane, it is difficult to get precise information on such points. We know that John Crolius was dispossessed, but it is quite possible that the pottery was operated. The pottery of John Remmey II was operated, the writer believes, almost, if not quite, all the time. There is

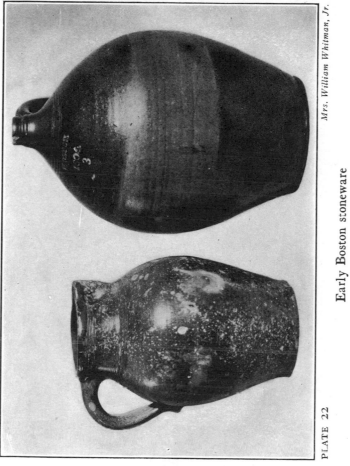

PLATE 22　　Early Boston stoneware

abundant evidence that when peace was at last restored these potters partook of the ensuing prosperity
and added to their substance.

It is evident from this brief sketch that during the
War for Independence the manufacture of pottery
in America sank to a very low state. That was
inevitable. It is no less certain that in the closing
years of the eighteenth century, from the signing
of the peace treaty to the very end of the century,
all the energies of the young nation were exerted
to repair the ravages of the years of destruction,
replenish stocks, and establish independence not
alone in the political sphere, as a national state, but
economically and culturally also. The ardent
national consciousness expressed itself in a passion-
ate desire and determination to equal the technical
achievements of the Old World, particularly of
England. But recovery from the war was then, as
in our more recent experience, much slower than
men's hopes and dreams. It was not until the dawn-
ing of the new century that the pottery industry in
America made any notable advances. The progress attained in various parts of the country in en-
grafting upon American industry the folk-culture
and folk-craft of European peoples, such as the

[117]

slip-decorated pottery made in various parts of the country, and the sgraffito ware that was produced mainly in Pennsylvania, may seem to controvert this generalization, but in reality it does not. After all, interesting as it is to the collector, it was a step backward from the point of view of a nation which had begun to make queen's-ware, and which in 1771 had attained to such excellence that it was reported in England of the wares produced in Philadelphia that "better china cups and saucers are made than at Bow and Stratford."

Before proceeding to survey the return to the ideals and aspirations which the great struggle had so ruthlessly interrupted, we may with profit and pleasure follow the development of that most delightful of all our folk pottery to which reference has already been made.

CHRONOLOGICAL LIST OF LATE EIGHTEENTH-CENTURY POTTERY

NOTE: From this list a number of potteries known to have been in operation between the close of the Revolution and 1799, which is the period covered, have been purposely omitted. This applies to those potteries which are known or believed to have made slip-decorated ware or sgraffito ware, and have been noted for that reason primarily. These potteries will be found listed among the makers of the types of ware named, following Chapter VI.

Date	Place	Name	Types of Ware
1784 (circa)	Huntington, Long Island	Jonathan Titus	Earthenware and stoneware
1784	Morgantown, W. Va.	— Foulke	Red ware, lead-glazed, slip-decorated ware, and salt-glazed stoneware
1789-90	Philadelphia	Andrew Miller	Slip-covered red ware
1789-90 to 1811	Philadelphia	John Curtis	Cream-colored earthenware, like queen's-ware
1790	Hartford, Conn.	Nathaniel Seymour	Lead-glazed earthenware and salt-glazed stoneware

Date	Place	Name	Types of Ware
1790	New York City	Clarkson Crolius	Salt-glazed stoneware
1790	Hartford, Conn.	John Souter	Earthenware and stoneware
1792	Norwich, Conn.	Charles Lathrop	Salt-glazed stoneware and red ware
1793	Bennington, Vt.	John Norton	Red ware and stoneware
1796	Norwich, Conn.	C. Pott & Son	Stoneware
1796 (circa)	Hartford, Conn.	Isaac Hanford	Stoneware
1798	In Kentucky across Ohio River from Lozantiville (now Cincinnati)	William McFarland	Earthenware
1799	Cincinnati	William McFarland	Earthenware

CHAPTER V

SLIP-DECORATED POTTERY

Of all the types of early American pottery, none merits the serious attention of the collector to a greater degree than the slip-decorated wares which form the subject of this chapter. The present writer has long felt a desire to make this a special hobby. No other type of American folk-pottery is quite so fascinating; none offers to the collector so rich a reward in quaintness of design, historical and genealogical allusion, and other manifestations of primitive art and craftsmanship.

In some respects, slip-decorated pottery holds a place in ceramics that is analogous to that held by the old-fashioned sampler in needlework. The sampler generally represents the work of juvenile fingers, to be sure, which is not generally true of slip-decorated pottery, though it should be remarked in passing that the aspiration of eager apprentices to the craft accounts for many a crudely executed design, and many a quaint inscription, in this type of pottery. Slip-decorated earthenware resembles the old needlework samplers in another respect, however. There are certain superficial objective characteristics common to both. The difference between a sampler and a slip-decorated pie-plate or platter is very often one of materials used rather than of feeling or manner of expression. One finds the same quaint and primitive designs, childishly drawn human and animal figures, wondrously impossible houses and landscapes. One finds, too, the same mottos expressive of naive piety, patriotism, courtship, and other emotions; the same fondness for recording simple autobiographical facts.

Fortunately from the point of view of the collector of modest means—and one is inclined to say that he is the only collector entitled to respect—this type of pottery, while scarce enough to give zest and interest to the quest for it, is not so rare as to be beyond the reach of any but the rich in purse. Good specimens are still to be found by the patient seeker, and to be bought at prices which are not excessive. This is a combination that approaches the ideal, and the amateur collector with a modest purse has a chance to acquire a collection in which he can take pride.

The credit of bringing the merits of this most interesting type of American folk-pottery to the attention of collectors belongs to the late Edwin Atlee Barber, one of the most industrious and learned students of American ceramic history. It may be doubted whether any of his other services to the fraternity of collectors equaled this. It is matter for regret that the practice prevails of designating all slip-decorated pottery as Pennsylvania ware or Pennsylvania Dutch Ware, as though its production were peculiar to that State. Although he did not himself make that mistake, Barber unintentionally contributed to its diffusion by the emphasis he placed upon the work of the German settlers in Pennsylvania and of their descendants, popularly called the Pennsylvania Dutch.

A great deal of the slip-decorated pottery that is offered by dealers—and quite honestly—as Pennsylvania pottery was actually made in Connecticut. Let the reader turn for a moment to Plate No. 9. Here we have grouped together five well authenticated specimens of slip-decorated pottery from

Connecticut potteries, selected by the present writer from the Pitkin Collection in the Wadsworth Atheneum for the express purpose of illustrating this important point. (The lion is not a slip-decorated piece, and is there simply because it was made at a Connecticut pottery.) The five pieces are good examples of Connecticut pottery of this type. It is doubtful whether there are five dealers in the whole of the United States who would hesitate to pronounce any one of them to be "unmistakably Pennsylvania ware, sir!" Many a collector, finding in Connecticut a good specimen of this ware, taking for granted that it was made in Pennsylvania, and never suspecting that it was made in the locality in which it was found, has missed the chance of adding to the interest of his find the facts of its history and the significance of the design or inscription.

A great deal of this slip-decorated pottery was also made in the New Jersey potteries. Even as late as the eighteen-sixties it was produced in that State in large quantities. At the old Red Ware Pottery of John Pruden at Elizabeth, some of the quaintest and most interesting slip-decorated ware that is now attributed to Pennsylvania was made from 1816 to 1876 or later. In 1879 or thereabouts, when L.

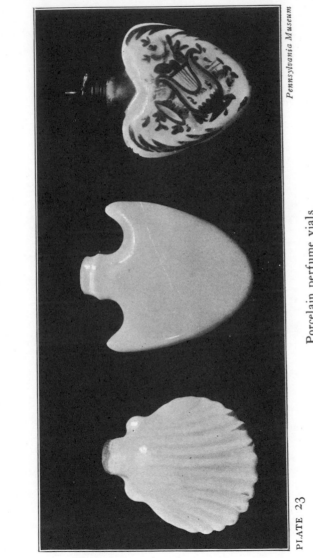

Porcelain perfume vials

PLATE 23

Slip-Decorated Pottery

B. Beerbower & Company took over the old Pruden works at Elizabeth, they found in the storehouse whole stacks of slip-decorated pie-plates, platters, bowls, and other utensils. These had been made by Samuel Dunham and were not at all distinguishable from similar articles made in Pennsylvania potteries. The writer has a small dish taken from the Pruden pottery from a pile of the same size and design, which he has been repeatedly assured was Pennsylvania Dutch ware. William G. Leake, who was the junior partner in the Beerbower firm, remembers in particular the stacks of platers and pie-plates inscribed "Shoo fly."

In some of the small New York potteries, slip-decorated utensils were made sixty or seventy years ago. The writer has seen a number of pie-plates and jars, with decorations in slip, which he is confident no human being could distinguish from pieces of the same sort made in Pennsylvania. They were indubitably made in Long Island potteries. It is certain that individual potters employed in the United States Pottery at Bennington, in the middle of the last century, made slip-decorated pieces for their own pleasure. The same general observations apply to Maryland and West Virginia; in both

States slip-decorated ware was produced in various small potteries. The collector who comes across a pie-plate of red clay, bearing a legend or design traced in slip and covered with a transparent yellow-ish lead glaze, should not jump to the conclusion that it was made in Pennsylvania. Even the dealer's attribution to the Pennsylvania Dutch should be regarded as tentative, not conclusive. The platter inscribed "Our daily bread," the bowl which pro-claims itself to be "Mary's dish," or the cookie-jar which has the initials of its original owner traced in slip, may never have been inside the boundaries of the great commonwealth that in its name perpetu-ates the fame of William Penn.

Indeed it is not impossible that the pie-plate, platter, or jar was brought across the Atlantic from the Old World. English and German potteries turned out such articles, in large quantities, not at all distinguishable from others of the same kind made in many parts of this country. It is quite clear, therefore, that to classify all ware of this kind in such a manner as to imply that its produc-tion was peculiar to Pennsylvania is misleading and not conducive to intelligent collecting. When we classify it as slip-decorated pottery, we are on firm and sure ground. Moreover, by such a classification we at once enlarge the interest of collecting. We no longer take a Pennsylvania origin for granted, but with every new specimen confront the problem of origin, of identification and attribution. Precisely the same fascination which there is in discovering the facts of the history of little Eliza, who worked the cross-stitch sampler, is attached to the discovery of biographical facts concerning the original owner of "Mary's dish."

Slip-decorated pottery is as easy to understand as it is to identify. Nothing in the whole range of ceramic products is simpler. The essential features of its manufacture can be described so easily that any novice can comprehend them and apply the knowledge to the work of identification and classification. "Slip" is the name given by potters to clay that is reduced by water to the consistency of cream. In making certain so-called cast or molded wares, notably porcelains made in molds of plaster of Paris, the entire body of the ware is of slip. With that we are not here concerned, however.

In the manufacture of common pottery slip is used for two purposes. For one thing, a local clay used for the body of the ware often presents a coarse or unattractive appearance. This may be overcome by giving it a coating of slip made from a finer clay of better appearance. The body clay used may be inferior not in appearance only, but from the standpoint of utility as well, and the application of the outer coating of a superior clay may be dictated by that consideration rather than that of appearance. This may be called the primary use of slip. A secondary use is for decorative effect. The use of clays of contrasting colors in order to obtain ornamental effects has been practised by potters in all lands and ages. The earliest method appears to have been the application of light clay ornaments to darker clay surfaces, or vice versa. If the potter desired to ornament the vessel he was making of red clay, let us say, by giving it a border of yellow clay, before the use of slip was discovered, this was his method: The design was actually formed in the yellow clay, either molded or shaped by the fingers. This was firmly pressed into the red clay body, which was less stiff than the yellow ornament and yielded to it. When the piece thus ornamented was dry, but before being fired, the surface was smoothed off by scraping or rubbing.

This process of ornamenting by the inlay of con-

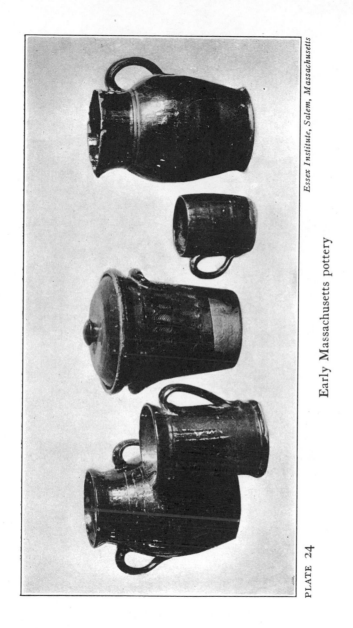

Early Massachusetts pottery

PLATE 24

trasting colors, analogous to the use of inlaid woods in cabinet-making, antedated the use of slip for decoration. Such inlaid ornament has been mistaken for slip decoration, and the resemblance is close enough to deceive almost any one on a superficial examination only. The point is worth noting in our discussion, but it is not likely to be of practical importance to the ordinary American collector. He is not likely to be much troubled by the early inlaid type.

Any one who has ever seen a pastry-cook trace an inscription or design on the icing of a cake, or who has gone into the kitchen and examined one of the handy little tools which the modern housewife uses for that same purpose, can visualize the whole process of slip decoration. The piece that is to be decorated has been fashioned from clay which, whatever its color before firing, will be red after that is done. No matter whether it was "thrown," that is made on the potter's wheel, or molded, or shaped by the hands without a mold; in any case, the clay had to be very wet and soft to permit its being worked into the desired shape. It cannot be placed in the kiln to be fired while in that condition, for the reason that it would crack to pieces. Before it can be fired at all it is necessary that a great part of the water in the clay be got rid of. This is done by evaporation, air-drying.

After some days it is dry enough to be handled without much danger of injury. In this state, which potters call the "green state," we may liken our piece of pottery to the cake ready for ornamentation. In pail or tub or vat the potter has his slip mixture—some lighter colored clay, generally either white or light yellow, mixed with water to the consistency of the cream on the top of the milk. He places some of the slip in a small earthenware container, called the slip-cup, which is fitted with one, two, or three small hollow pipes or tubes through which the slip can pass. An ordinary oiling-can, such as is used to oil the lawn-mower, illustrates the principle fairly well. Early potters used quills from feathers picked up around the barn-yard for this purpose. With the slip slowly passing through the quill, or through whatever sort of tube is used, the decorator literally writes or draws his inscription or design upon the "green" pottery he is to decorate.

The pottery, having been air-dried, absorbs the water in the slip-mixture so fast that the mixture does not run. The lines of the inscription or design stay much as the decorator draws them. The clay in the slip begins at once to set; in other words, absorbtion by the drier absorbent body of the ware, and also evaporation, cause the superimposed clay of the slip to dry quickly. The success of the design depends of course upon the artistic skill and manual dexterity of the decorator.

At this stage an interesting development takes place, including a division into two quite distinct categories. If the ware that has been decorated is primarily intended for a utilitarian purpose, with the ornamentation only incidental, it is given one treatment. If it is primarily intended for ornament, it is given quite another treatment. When the inscription or design has dried on, it is, of course, slightly raised above the surface of the body of the ware. The slip leaves a layer of perceptible thickness on the surface of the piece to which it is applied. Now, if the piece is intended to be used—a pie-plate or platter, for instance—the slip design or inscription is gently but firmly pressed and beaten down into the body until it is level with it. There may be need to rub it down, which is accomplished by rubbing with the hand or a simple tool. If the piece is intended for ornament only—as most of the elaborately decorated pieces were—the slip design is not smoothed to the level of the surface but left as it is, perceptibly raised above the surface level.

When the decorated ware is judged by the potter to be just right for glazing, the coat of glaze is applied. To do this successfully, the ware must be slightly warm; it cannot be done if the ware is cold. In summer-time it may be set out in the sun, on long benches, and will absorb sufficient heat in that manner. In winter-time the ware may be piled on top of a stove, or on the outside of a kiln, in order to make it warm enough for glazing. Each of these steps, simple as they all seem and in fact are, requires good judgment, the special sense that only experience can give. If the green ware is too dry or not dry enough, if it is too warm or not warm enough, when the glaze is applied, there will be trouble. Either the glaze will peel off or the ware will crack.

When all is ready for glazing, the glost-man performs his part. In a pail or tub he has his glaze all mixed, ready for use. Possibly he prepared it in secret, making a good deal of a mystery of it. Possibly, too, he has his formula written in some sort of cipher, probably based on the cipher used in the ritual of some fraternal organization. There has been a lot of nonsense talked about the lost art of this, that, or the other glaze, as we shall have occasion to note further along in this book. For the present it will suffice to say that there is no mystery about it, that the essential formulas are well known. Either galena or red lead, finely powdered, forms the principal element. Mixed with water, in proper proportions, this alone would suffice to form a glaze. As a rule, however, some clay, ground to great fineness, is added to give thickness to the glaze at a low cost.

For the sake of clarity in our present discussion, we shall continue to describe the process in the present tense, precisely as though we were describing an operation we were witnessing. This necessitates leaving the manner of glazing other wares for later discussion, and confining ourselves strictly to the method used in glazing the particular type of ware we have under consideration. In this manner we shall obtain a more definite understanding, and our collection will be made more intelligible to us.

Early American Pottery and China

Our glost-man has his wares ranged before him on long boards or benches, set upon trestles. We know enough about the "mysterious" mixture in his pail to follow his operations with intelligence. On one set of boards he has ranged pie-plates, platters, shallow dishes, and the like. On another he has cookie-jars, tea-caddies, small jugs, and so on. He begins with the first lot. Piece by piece he takes up, and, working as rapidly as he can, with a good-sized paint-brush he applies a coating to each, precisely as if he were applying paint. He applies the glaze only to the upper side, the side that is exposed and used. The under part he does not touch. He is careful to get well up to the edge, and we note that some glaze trickles over the edge to the under part, but this he does not mind.

As fast as he fills a board with glazed pieces, it is carried back to a drying-rack. Now we observe that he singles out some pieces for special attention. They are elaborately decorated ornamental pieces; we know by the elaborate character of the decoration that they are intended primarily for display, not for use. With a small piece of rag, or perhaps it is a piece of sponge, he applies little touches of green, apparently at random without any design, before applying the glaze. It is verdigris that he is using in this way. When the glaze comes to be fired, the verdigris will be carried in the fusion of the glaze and produce an effect which our glost-man highly approves. When he turns to the cookie-jars and the tea-caddies, we observe that he throws aside the brush and immerses the pieces in the pail, covering them completely and drawing them out quickly.

Now that we have seen the whole process of mixing the slip, applying it so as to form designs, mixing the glaze and applying it, we know as much as we are ever likely to know, or need to know, about the actual making of slip-decorated pottery. To complete the picture, we may as well let our imaginations play a bit, to anticipate the final stages through which the ware must pass before it is ready for the market. After being left in the rack for a while, the ware is again dry. The water is evaporated, and the particles of lead and clay have dried upon the surface. The ware is now placed in a store-room, where it is kept until there is a supply large enough to set the kiln; in other words, to fill the kiln and make firing economically profitable. The heat in the kiln, where the ware remains for a week or even more, not only bakes the clay hard, the primary purpose of firing, but it fuses the particles of the glaze mixture adhering to the ware, so that this becomes really a coating of thin glass, generally of yellowish tinge. When the fires are allowed to go out and the kiln is opened up, it will take perhaps forty-eight hours to cool the ware sufficiently to permit its being handled and removed to the stock-room.

The reader is asked to bear in mind that the foregoing detailed description is of a primitive form of industry, necessarily general, a composite picture, from which in practice there were incidental and varied departures. In its essential features, however, it is an accurate description of the methods which were used in Europe as early as the middle of the seventeenth century, and which still survive in small potteries in some places. Dated examples of slip-decorated ware believed to have been made by the German settlers in Pennsylvania go back as far as 1773. We may say then that, roughly speaking, from the end of the first quarter of the eighteenth century to the period of the Civil War slip-decorated ware was produced in this country in the manner herein described. In the Smithsonian Institution at Washington there is a collection of slip-

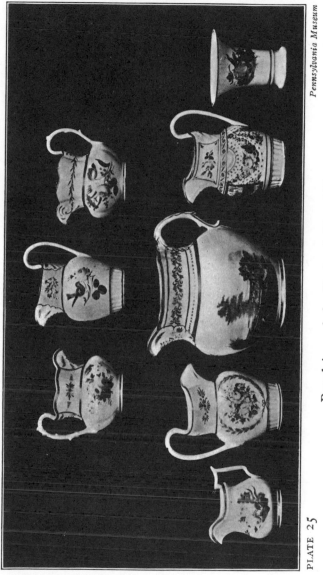

PLATE 25

Porcelain made by Tucker & Hemphill

decorated pottery made at Morgantown, West Virginia, at the beginning of the nineteenth century, together with the tools and implements used by the potters there. If the pottery itself were not regarded as sufficiently conclusive evidence of the fact, the tools used would prove beyond a shadow of doubt that the methods used there were identical with those used in Pennsylvania, precisely as the methods used in Pennsylvania are shown, by similar evidence, to be identical with European methods dating back to the middle of the seventeenth century.

For the benefit of the novice who is just aspiring to the making of a collection of American slip-decorated ware, no matter how modest, a few suggestions are here offered in the belief that their observance will materially contribute to eventual success, and greatly add to the interest of the collector:

1. The aim should be to secure well authenticated specimens from as many States as possible, and to make the attribution in each case as absolute as possible. Twenty-five pieces which represent five States will make a better collection than seventy-five pieces all from Pennsylvania, or believed so to be. The smaller collection will be richer in its

interest, which is the primary purpose of any hobby, and it will be of much greater significance than the larger one from the point of view of the student of ceramics.

2. Try to obtain pieces bearing names and dates, and to discover facts about the persons named. A good story, amply attested, will increase the interest and the value of the collection as much as an additional specimen will. The genuine hobbyist will rather discover a fact about his hobby that has been hitherto unknown than find a new specimen which merely adds to the numerical strength of his collection. He will even welcome the fact which compels him to discard a favorite piece, or to relegate it to a much lower position. There are people who act under the compulsion of a mere spirit of acquisitiveness and set possession of the material thing above everything else. They amass and hoard things like magpies. These are not collectors; they are not entitled to be counted among the hobbyists; they are slaves to a vulgar vice, not the devotees of a gentle sport, a recreation for philosophers.

3. Bear in mind that slip-decorated pottery is not confined to red ware with inscriptions and designs in yellow slip. That is the commonest type,

but there are many variations for which the collector should be on the watch. Sometimes the groundwork is green, against which a design in ivory slip shows to great advantage.

Such a piece is the pressed octagonal dish shown in Plate No. 11 (Fig. 4). This striking example of Pennsylvania slip-decorated ware is from the Pitkin Collection. It seems that the ware in its green state was given a coating of slip, colored either by oxide of copper or by verdigris, probably the former. When this had dried the decorator applied the design in white slip, the piece being subsequently given a covering of transparent lead glaze. In the Pennsylvania Museum there are several examples of polychrome slip decoration. The paste of the body seems to be ordinary red ware covered with a slip of rich chocolate color, obtained by the use of manganese. On this the design is worked out in slip of various colors—green, blue, amber, white—the colors being obtained by the use of metallic oxides. The use of a transparent lead glaze brings out the color-scheme quite admirably. An interesting example of this type of slip decoration is shown in Plate No. 12.

Still another type of slip-decorated pottery made

in this country calls for notice. Instead of the design being worked out in a slip much lighter in color than the general surface of the ware, its background, the latter is made light and the design worked out in dark slip. Ware of a dark body is heavily coated with a white slip. On this background the design is worked out in a slip that is red, probably made of the same clay as the hidden body of the ware. It is covered with transparent lead glaze. The technique here is very like the early Italian majolica, in which the surface of the body was covered with a slip composed of fine white clay. On this new surface the design was painted with colors derived from various metallic oxides, and then given a protective coat of transparent lead glaze. Except for the use of colored slip to make the design, instead of simple oxides applied with a brush, the process is similar to the one used by the makers of early Italian majolica.

4. It is nearly, if not quite, superfluous to urge the collector to add to his collection, whenever the opportunity occurs, specimens which bear designs of a historical character. In the Pennsylvania Museum there are a number of such pieces. One of these, a pie-plate, has a quaint representation of

Slip-Decorated Pottery

Andrew Jackson on horseback. It is believed to have been made by Benjamin Bergey in 1838 or thereabouts. Bergey is said to have conducted a pottery in Montgomery County, Pennsylvania, from about 1820 to 1845, but surprisingly little seems to be known about him. The writer of this volume spent a good deal of time and effort trying to learn something definite about Bergey and his pottery, but without any useful result. If the specimens in the Pennsylvania Museum which are attributed to him—upon what is admittedly a very slender body of evidence—are to be accepted as authentic and as typical examples of his work, it is a pity that so little is known about him. The writer is disposed to doubt that the same man produced the quaint and crude picture of Jackson, already referred to, and the really fine design of a pigeon-like bird standing on the branch of a conventionalized tree with blossoms and plucking its breast. As a design this is wholly admirable and vastly superior in every way to any of the other pieces.

No matter how crudely drawn a historical subject like the General Jackson design might be, as a collector's piece it would be a treasure. Any design of a historical character, or any allusion to a historical event, whether local or national, gives a piece of pottery special interest and value. Next in importance to the historical designs come those designed as gifts to individuals. These cover a wide range embracing the chief events of life from infancy to old age. "Baby's dish" often appears on pieces that were given as presents at christenings; sentimental mottos and humorous designs are found on a variety of engagement and wedding gifts; and so on. Rarely indeed are these pieces characterized by artistic design; their attraction is their quaintness. The collector who views them from precisely the same point of view as the old samplers are viewed will not go far wrong.

Of course, pieces which bear the maker's name are much more valuable than pieces of equal merit not so marked. It can do no harm and may do some good to warn the amateur collector against the quite common mistake of assuming that the name found on a piece of pottery, whether impressed in the clay by a stamp or incised, must be the name and mark of the maker. Many times the writer has found that the name impressed on the front of a stone jug was not that of the maker at all but of the distiller or merchant for whom it was made. Repeatedly, too, he has discovered that names scratched on pieces of pottery in the green state, before firing, were not the names of potters at all, but of the persons for whom the utensils were made. In the course of researches into the history of the Bennington potteries, for example, in diaries kept by local residents who were in no wise connected with the potteries, a number of entries were found recording the fact that the diarists while visiting the potteries inscribed their names on jugs, crocks, and the like.

Nothing approaching a check-list of the makers of slip-decorated pottery has ever been compiled. Barber, in his classic work, "Tulip Ware of the Pennsylvania-German Potters," and in other writings of his, has recorded the names of many of the Pennsylvania potters with much information concerning them. Fragmentary as Barber's record admittedly is, it is far more extensive than anything of the kind that has been done for any other State. The list which is given in this volume is based partly upon Barber's work, augmented by independent research and made as correct as possible by reference to local authorities. It is not offered as a complete list; as that would involve far more extensive research than the writer has been able to make. It is presented, with all its shortcomings, in the belief and hope that many a collector will find it useful.

CHAPTER VI

SGRAFFITO WARE

No apology is offered for dealing with this interesting type of pottery in a chapter by itself, rather than following the usual practice of writers on ceramics and dealing with it under the head of slip-decorated ware. The present writer holds the latter practice to be basically unsound. There is no more reason for distinguishing between slip decoration and molded decoration than there is for distinguishing between slip decoration and sgraffito decoration. The former method is the achievement of the desired effect by imposing upon the surface of the object to be decorated a pattern or inscription in slip of contrasting color; the latter method is the making of the desired design by a sort of carving, cutting away the surface of a slip-covered body in such a manner as to present the pattern or inscription in the color of the under body contrasted against the surface slip.

[145]

Literally, sgraffito means ware that has been scratched, from the Italian *sgraffiare*, to scratch. The same term is used by architects, but spelled "scraffito"—which is a better form etymologically and otherwise. Old English potters used the name "scrabble ware." The method is very simple and easy to understand. The body of the ware in its green state, before firing, is covered with slip of another color. Usually the slip is much lighter than the body, but occasionally this is reversed. When the slip covering is partially dried, the inscription or design is produced by scratching through the slip or scraping it off in such a manner as to show the color of the body beneath against the superimposed covering.

This method of decoration has been used from time immemorial. In crude forms it is found on the pottery of many primitive peoples. During the fifteenth century Italian craftsmen took this primitive process and developed it to a high degree of artistic excellence. Sometimes they combined the method with the application of molded flowers and figures in relief, achieving results which have probably never been surpassed. The sgraffito ware produced in Italy during the fifteenth century was later

[146]

Sgraffito Ware

copied by Swiss, German, and French potters, especially during the sixteenth century. Toward the middle of the seventeenth century it was made in England, and it is a remarkable fact that the designs used by the English potters at that time, and the ware itself, were practically identical with those made familiar by the work of our Pennsylvania potters during the eighteenth and nineteenth centuries. The tulip motive was as common in England as in Pennsylvania. In passing it may be worth while to note the fact that in seventeenth-century England, as in this country a century or more later, sgraffito was a folk-pottery made for common people, not a pretentious product intended for the rich and aristocratic few as the earlier Italian product was. But a few English potters in more recent times have used the method in a manner rivaling the great Italians of the fifteenth century. Toward the middle of the nineteenth century the great firm of Minton produced some wonderful sgraffito ware, quite worthy to be ranked with the masterpieces of the old Italian craftsmen.

The term "Pennsylvania ware" can be justified in connection with sgraffito decorated pottery. While, as we have already noted in the preceding

chapter, slip-decorated pottery was produced somewhat extensively in other places, the production of
sgraffito decorated ware was very largely confined
to Pennsylvania. Very little of it was produced in
other States, and that little was less elaborate in
its design than the Pennsylvania product. Through
the agency of the German immigrants who settled
in that State, the art as it was practised in Germany,
during the seventeenth century and the first part of
the eighteenth century, was transplanted in American soil and took root and flourished.

The earliest dated piece of pottery with sgraffito
decoration that has been discovered in Pennsylvania
is a barber's basin, dated 1733, and bearing a characteristic legend in German. As a considerable number of Germans had already settled in Pennsylvania,
is is probable that it was made there, though there
is a possibility that it was brought from the old
country. Within the memory of the present writer,
it was the custom for people who were leaving England for the purpose of settling in America or other
foreign countries to take with them articles embellished with the date, at least the year. Perhaps
there was behind this custom the feeling that it
would serve to mark the close of a chapter and

Fig. 56.

Fine example of Flemington porcelain

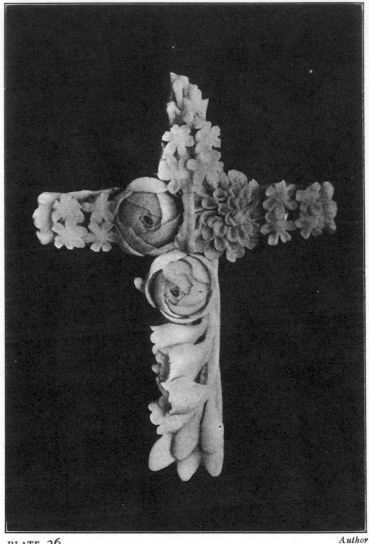

PLATE 26

Author

Fine example of Bennington porcelain

the opening of a new one. Children in school worked samplers with the date of the last day of their attendance; simple articles made by emigrants or their friends were likewise dated. In the pottery districts of Staffordshire it was the custom for workmen who were leaving the country to mark some piece of ware in this manner—a shaving-mug, perhaps, or a flask. Similarly, it was the custom to make gifts of mantel ornaments and other souvenirs, dated in the same way, to friends about to emigrate. That something like this custom prevailed among the Germans who came to Pennsylvania is not impossible or even unlikely. Nevertheless, having due regard to the subsequent history of the pottery industry in Pennsylvania, the balance of probability would seem to favor the theory that the barber's basin dated 1733 originated there and not in Europe.

Sgraffito decorated utensils were not made for general use as the ordinary slip-decorated utensils were. They were intended primarily for ornament. Most of them were made for gifts; potters made them for their sweethearts, wives, children, and friends. Births, baptisms, birthdays, betrothals, and weddings were marked by the presentation of such pieces, many of which represented a great deal of

labor. Because highly valued and carefully treasured, a larger proportion of these pieces survived
than of the ordinary utensils which were in daily
use. At the same time, the number made was so
small, by comparison with the utility pieces, that
good specimens are hard to find. The collector of
moderate means is not at all likely to find his collection of genuine old sgraffito growing too rapidly.
He will be fortunate indeed if he acquires three or
four good specimens at a moderate price, particularly those with interesting designs or inscriptions.
Finding a signed piece by one of the old potters,
such as George Huebener or David Spinner, is an
event to be celebrated. Even the acquisition of a
piece of sgraffito signed by one of the later potters—
such as Jacob Scholl or Samuel Troxel, who were
active in the eighteen-thirties—is an event of more
than ordinary interest in the life of a collector.

There can be no doubt that many of the German
immigrants who came to this country in the middle
of the last century, immediately following the
political disturbances in Europe in 1848, and for
some years thereafter, brought pieces of German-
made sgraffito decorated pottery with them. The
writer has seen several such pieces, concerning whose

history there could be no sort of doubt. At one time he numbered among his friends at least half a dozen Germans who possessed such pieces which they had brought with them from their native land. Some of these pieces of German-made sgraffito he has handled and examined closely many times. With all deference to those authorities who have believed that they could distinguish between the wares made in Germany and those made in Pennsylvania, he confesses that he could detect no difference, and, furthermore, that he doubts whether any human being could do so.

To begin with the color of the clay: in discussing this point Barber notes the fact that in the case of a sgraffito dish known to have been imported from Germany the clay as shown by the back was "of a lighter and brighter red color than any of the Pennsylvania ware." It would be a great mistake to infer from this fact that the German pottery can always or generally be distinguished from that made in Pennsylvania by means of a marked difference in the color of the clay. That is not the case. Assuming the entire correctness of Barber's statement concerning the particular piece of German-made ware, it does not follow that all German-made sgraffito ware is of the same color. As a matter of fact, variations of color-tones are common, both in the case of the American and of the European product. Every practical potter knows that pottery made by the same men from clay taken from a single pit, but at different times, will vary considerably in color. This applies to accidental variations only. The fact that one batch of clay has been more thoroughly refined and cleansed than another will affect the result. Then there are variations due to differences in the temperature of the kilns in the firing process, to say nothing of accidental mixing of clays. Then, too, we have variations of color deliberately brought about. It was a common occurrence in most potteries for the mixer—a most important figure, by the way—to change his mixture from time to time, aiming now at a lighter and now at a darker body.

Barber seems to have attached a good deal of importance to the treatment of the edges of their plates and platters by the Pennsylvania potters, who used a tool called a coggle, a small-toothed wheel, to make a band of regular indentations around the edge of the piece. Such edges, made in precisely the same manner, with exactly the same sort of

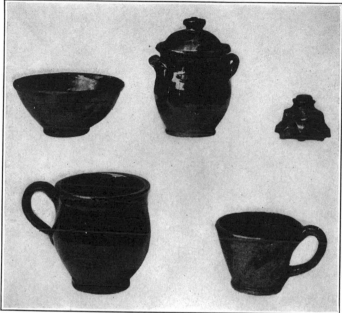

PLATE 27   *Homer E. Keyes, Esq.*

Pottery playthings from Pennsylvania

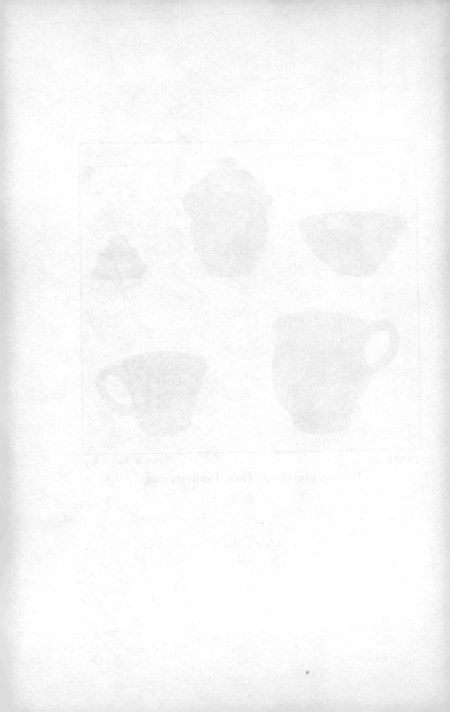

tool, are common in the German-made ware, so common in fact as to be the rule. Neither in the color of the body or the glaze nor in any other feature does the sgraffito ware of the German potters of the middle of the nineteenth century differ from that of the earlier German potters who settled in Pennsylvania. The late Albert W. Pitkin told the present writer that he had examined two sgraffito plates, both brought from Germany within twenty-five years, which were identical with one in his collection made by Troxel, in Montgomery County, Pennsylvania, bearing his name and date. In every respect, except for the name and date on the American piece, the three specimens were identical. After hours of examination of the three side by side he could detect no difference whatever.

The writer of these pages believes that Pitkin's conclusion in the case of this single experiment would have been the same if the experiment had embraced three thousand pieces instead of three. He has handled, scores of times, a large round platter with a sgraffito design of tulips and a German inscription to the effect that potters rejoice when dishes are broken. It was made in Germany and brought to this country by the owner; in Reading,

Pennsylvania, where he had worked as a cigar-maker, this German found another so exactly like it that the only means of telling which was the German-made and which the American was the fact that a small chip had been broken from the edge of the former.

These facts are set down in the interest of the hobby of collecting, and for the benefit of its devotees. The collector need not be discouraged by the fact that there is ever present the possibility that the cherished specimen of Pennsylvania Dutch sgraffito ware may have been made in Germany. The knowledge should add to his interest in his hobby and to his respect for it; he will probably find himself keener in his quest for marked pieces and for authentic pedigrees.

While it is true, as previously observed, that in this country the making of sgraffito ware, unlike that of slip-decorated ware, was virtually confined to Pennsylvania, very little being produced anywhere else, it is well to warn the collector to remember that "exception proves the rule" in this as in everything else. Although I have never seen a piece of sgraffito decorated ware that was made at the Bennington potteries, there is a well supported local tradition that William Burtleman (or Bartleman), a German, Stephen Theiss, a Belgian, Jacob Merz, a German, and Peter Steinbach, a German, while working at the United States Pottery, made a number of sgraffito plates and platters. According to the story, these four men vied with one another in the making of these, each trying to excel the other. Burtleman went from Bennington to Pennsylvania to work in a pottery there. According to the late Dr. S. R. Wilcox of Bennington, who as a young man worked in the United States Pottery, Burtleman was dissatisfied at Bennington because he had no opportunity to display his talent for the German style of decoration. Later on when he was operating a small red ware pottery on his own account at Bennington, doing all the work himself, Jacob Merz occasionally made sgraffito pieces on order, it is said. Similarly, individual pieces of sgraffito ware are known to have been made at the Pruden pottery in Elizabeth, New Jersey, where a great deal of slip-decorated ware was made. Knowing something of the ways of old-time potters, working in small potteries, not subject to the rigid rules and discipline of the great factories of to-day, the writer is inclined to believe that careful and patient local researches would disclose the fact that in many, and perhaps a majority, of the potteries in which earthenware was made in this country, during the latter half of the eighteenth and the first half of the nineteenth centuries, individual workmen experimented in sgraffito decoration in making pieces for themselves or their friends. Potters in all parts of the world have been noted for their fondness for indulging in experiments of all sorts, a fact amply attested by the odd and whimsical specimens of individual workmanship surviving in every pottery center.

This opens an entirely new and virgin field to the American collector. Instead of confining his quest in the neighborhood of any old pottery to the typical things, specimens of the regular product, he will do well to search out the unusual things, mere trifles many of them, in which individual workmen found amusement and recreation. Among these, in many cases, there is good reason to believe will be found specimens of sgraffito ware, which will not only delight the soul of the collector, and add to the charm of one of the most interesting of hobbies, but materially enlarge our knowledge and understanding of American ceramics.

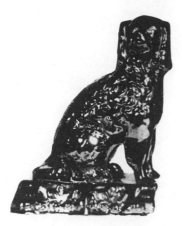

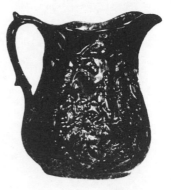

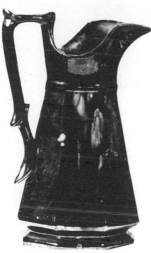

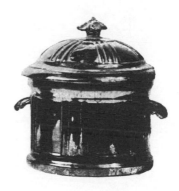

PLATE 28

Mrs. Rhea M. Knittle

Rockingham ware from Ohio

A Chronological List of Potters Known or Believed to Have Made Slip-Decorated and Sgraffito Wares

NOTE: This list has been compiled with great care and is the result of much painstaking research and investigation. No part of this book has involved greater labor. While it is not positively known that some of the potters whose names are included made slip-decorated or sgraffito wares, there has seemed to be in every case sufficient evidence to justify the belief that they did. It is not suggested that the list is complete; doubtless there were many potters who made slip-decorated and sgraffito wares whose names have not been handed down, nor is it likely that the author of these pages has covered all the records extant. With all its limitations it is believed and hoped that the list will be of assistance to many collectors.

Name	Location	Date	Marks
States, Adam	Huntington, Long Island	1751	None
Stout, Abraham (or Isaac?)	Between Gardenville and Point Pleasant, Montgomery Co., Pa.	Began about 1760; continued a number of years—to 1775 or later	No marked pieces known

Name	Location	Date	Marks
Mumbauer, Conrad	Haycock, Montgomery Co., Pa.	Started in 1760; carried on by him a few years; he was succeeded by John and Milton Singer; how long they continued not known	No Marks
Smith, Joseph	Wrightstown, Bucks Co., Pa.	Established 1763 and known to have been operating in 1799; about 1800 the pottery was taken over by his son, Thomas Smith, who ran it a number of years	Pieces marked with his name and date; one has date 1799
Klinker, Christian	Bucksville, Bucks Co., Pa.	Circa 1772-92; not positively known; he was operating in 1792; he died in 1793	Jar in Pennsylvania Museum "C.K."
Drach, Rudolf	Bedminster, Bucks Co., Pa.	Started about 1780 and operated by him until about 1800; exact year not known	Sgraffito dish in Field Museum, Chicago, bears his name and date, 1792
Kintner, Jacob	Nockamixon, Bucks Co., Pa.	Established about 1780 and run to about 1840	No marks

[158]

Name	Location	Date	Marks
Foulke, ——	Morgantown, W. Va.	1784	None
Hersteine, Cornelius	Nockamixon, Bucks Co., Pa.	Established about 1785; continued by son, Daniel, and grandson, David, to about 1875	No marks
Huebener, George	Montgomery Co., Pa.; exact location not known	About 1785-98	A number of pieces bearing his name have dates ranging from 1785 to 1798
Titus, Jonathan	Huntington, Long Island	1784 (*circa*)	None
Miller, Andrew	Philadelphia	1789-90	None
Curtis, John	Philadelphia	1789-90	None
Seymour, Nathaniel	Hartford, Conn.	1790	None
Souter, John	Hartford, Conn.	1790	None
Crolius, Clarkson	New York City	1790	Full name accompanying design in slip, 1798
Lathrop, Charles	Norwich, Conn.	1792	None

Name	Location	Date	Marks
Taney, Jacob	Nockamixon Township, Bucks Co., Pa.	1794	Marked with initials and date
Goodwin, Seth	Hartford (West Division), Conn.	1795	None
Pott & Son	Norwich, Conn.	1796	None
Leidy, John	Franconia, near Souderton, Montgomery Co., Pa.	Started in 1796 (Leidy was sixteen at the time); how long continued is not known; the best available information points to 1815 (*circa*)	No mark; a number of well authenticated pieces bear the date 1796
Nessz, Johannes (also "John Nase")	Tyler's Port, Montgomery Co., Pa.	Exact date not known; probably started about 1798 and continued to about 1828-29, when he was succeeded by his son, who anglicized his name to "John Nase."	No marks

Name	Location	Date	Marks
Spinner, David	Willow Creek, Milford, Bucks Co., Pa.	Established 1800 and operated to 1811, the year of Spinner's death	Pieces bear his name in full
Headman, John (also Peter Headman)	Rock Hill, Bucks Co., Pa.	Established about 1800; exact date not known; he carried on the work for a good many years and was then succeeded, *circa* 1830, by his son, Peter Headman, who continued it until about 1870	No marks
Thompson, John W. Cross, Peter Scudder, Moses	Morgantown, W. Va. Hartford, Conn. Huntington, Long Island	1800 1805 1805-06	None None None
Headman, Andrew (also Charles Headman)	Rock Hill, Bucks Co., Pa. (near that of his brother)	Established about 1806; carried on by Andrew to 1840 or thereabout, then by his son Charles until about 1870	Pieces marked "Andrew Headman" and dated 1808

Name	Location	Date	Marks
Vickers, Thomas Vickers, John Kline, Philip	West Whiteland, Chester Co., Pa. Carversville, Bucks Co., Pa.	Established 1806; moved to Lionsville, 1822 Established about 1808; not known how long in operation	Marks "T.V." and "V." Puzzle-jug in Pennsylvania Museum, marked with his name and date, 1809
Seymour, Israel	Troy, N. Y.	1809	Stoneware pieces bear his name; said to have made slip-decorated plates during 1809-12
Roudebuth, Henry	Montgomery Co., Pa., location not known	Started about 1810 and believed to have been operated up to 1820 or later	Pieces marked with his name, and some with his initials, bear dates ranging from 1811 to 1816
Mullowny, Captain	Philadelphia	Started about 1810 and operated to 1817 or later	No marks

Name	Location	Date	Marks
Scholl, Michael (also Jacob Scholl)	Tyler's Port, Montgomery Co., Pa.	Established about 1810 and operated by him until 1828-30, then carried on some years by his son, Jacob Scholl	Used floral factory mark pressed in ware; earliest dated piece known, 1808
Haig, Thomas	Philadelphia	Established 1812 and carried on by founder many years; pottery operated to 1890 or later	No marks
Stofflet, Heinrich	Berks Co., Pa.	1814; not positively known whether he was proprietor or journeyman potter	His name and date, 1814, on dish; the inscription indicating he was the maker of it
Groff, Joseph	Franconia, Montgomery Co., Pa.	Succeeded John Leidy about 1815; carried on business a number of years—probably around 1832	No marks

[163]

Name	Location	Date	Marks
Albert, Henry	Allentown, Lehigh Co., Pa.	Established in 1816 and operated for some years	No marks
Pruden, John	Elizabeth, N. J.	1816	None
Sanders, John	Connecticut; (location not known)	1817	Lion marked with his name; slip-ware pieces have been attributed to him
Nash, ——	Utica, N. Y.	1818-20	No marks
Herring, John	Nockamixon, Bucks Co., Pa.	Established 1818-20; conducted for several years; date of closing, 1866	No marks
Goodwin, Thomas O.	Hartford, Conn.	1820	None
Vickers, John, & Son	Lionsville, Pa.	1822-65	No marks
Troxel, Samuel	Upper Hanover, Montgomery Co., Pa.	Established 1823 and continued to about 1835	Pieces bear his name

Name	Location	Date	Marks
Weaver, Abraham	Nockamixon, Bucks Co., Pa.	Established 1824-25; operated continuously until 1844	Many pieces bear names of different members of the Weaver family; one plate with turtle-dove and tulips bears inscription: "When this you see, remember me. Abraham Weaver, Noxamixon County Bucks Township May 4th 1828"
Keeler, Benjamin	Huntington, Long Island	1825	None
Hildebrand, Frederic	Tyler's Port, Montgomery Co., Pa.	1825 (*circa*)	No marks
Cope, —	Frederick, Montgomery Co., Pa.	1825-45 (*circa*)	No marks

Name	Location	Date	Marks
Horn, Samuel	Allentown, Pa.	1826-35 (*circa*)	No marks
Neisser, Jacob (also spelled Niezzer)	Carversville, Bucks Co., Pa.	Established about 1827; operated until 1850, perhaps later	No marks
Moore, Richard	Carversville, Bucks Co., Pa.	Established about 1828 and known to have been in operation several years	No marks
Nase, John	Tyler's Port, Montgomery Co., Pa.	Succeeded father, John Nessz, 1828-29, and carried on the business several years	No marks
Harring, David	Nockamixon, Bucks Co., Pa.	Established 1828; operated continuously until 1865, when he retired from business	No marks
Johnson, Joseph	Attleboro, (Langhorne), Plumstead Co., Pa.	Established about 1830 and in operation during Civil War	No marks
Toomey, Helfrich	Plumstead, Bucks Co., Pa.	Established about 1830; in operation until 1850, perhaps later	No marks

[166]

Name	Location	Date	Marks
Diehl, George	Near Rock Hill, Bucks Co., Pa.	Established about 1832; continued by him and son, William, to 1894	No marks
Ranniger, Conrad K.	Montgomery Co., Pa.; exact location not known	In operation about 1835-45	No marks
Bergey, Benjamin	Montgomery Co., Pa.; exact location unknown	1835-45 (*circa*)	No marks
Spiegel, Isaac	Philadelphia	1837	No marks
Bartleman, —	Plumstead, Bucks Co., Pa.	1840-50 (*circa*)	No marks
Moore, —	Quakertown, Bucks Co., Pa.	1840-50 (*circa*)	No marks
Kinzie, —			
Bell, Solomon	Strasburg, Va.	1840-45	Name stamped in clay
Miller, Christian	New Britain, Bucks Co., Pa.	Established 1845; how long operated not known	No marks
Schrumm, —	Plumstead, Bucks Co., Pa.	Established 1845-6 and operated until 1850-51	No marks

Name	Location	Date	Marks
Bitting, —	Near Pennsburg, Montgomery Co., Pa.	Established 1847 and in operation up to 1852	No marks
Greber, —	Upper Hanover, Montgomery Co., Pa.	1848-55 (*circa*)	No marks
Wolfe, William	Blountiville, Tenn.	1848	Said to have made slip-decorated and sgraffito wares while employed at United States Pottery (see text); no mark on these types
Merz, Jacob	Bennington, Vt.	1850-58	
Steinbach, Peter	Bennington, Vt.	1850-58	
Theiss, Stephen	Bennington, Vt.	1850-58	
Burtleman, William, (or Bartleman)	Bennington, Vt.	1850-58	
Mehwaldt, Chas. A.	Bergholtz, N. Y.	1852	No marks

[168]

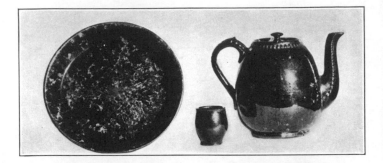

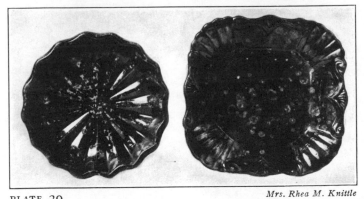

PLATE 29

Ohio wares often taken for "Bennington"

CHAPTER VII

EARLY NINETEENTH-CENTURY POTTERS
AND POTTERIES

In a general way the progress that was made in the pottery industry in the early part of the nineteenth century was similar to that which occurred in other directions, and the character of the wares made in any given locality was to a great extent determined by the general social conditions there existing. Where there was no class distinction, where all were simple hard-working people, the potteries of the locality turned out utensils of earthenware and stoneware, with only the crudest ornamentation.

Like all such historical generalizations, this one needs to be applied with intelligence and caution if it is be helpful and illuminating to the student, and not confusing and misleading. It is only too true that in the field of American ceramic history we have had a great many generalizations which

[169]

crumple up as soon as they are subjected to the criteria of exact and well informed scholarship. They are the products of uncritical minds working with inadequate and untested data. On the other hand, it is equally true that the most careful generalization, embodying the results of patient research and sound scholarship, can be so misused as to be an obstacle instead of the aid it was intended to be. There are no fool-proof rules which can be applied to the study of this hobby of ours.

Let us take the case of the early Vermont potteries, for example, and consider them in the light of the generalization formulated above. The first settlers in Bennington, its oldest town, arrived in 1761. Soon they were involved in the great controversy over their land-titles, which led to the long and bitter struggle against the claims of New York. The Revolution came while that issue was still unsettled, and, as an independent republic, though an ally of the United States, Vermont was inevitably involved in the greater conflict. Naturally its development was greatly retarded. Whoever is familiar with the essential facts, even in the most elementary outline, will understand that at the beginning of the nineteenth century, and for a long time thereafter, its economic life was of the simplest. True, some of the inhabitants were richer than others, just as some were more industrious than others, some more virtuous and some less. In the main, however, the greater wealth of some individuals was mainly represented by the ownership of more land. Practically all the people were poor in the sense that they had no money. There was no marked class division, no considerable class distinguished by its wealth and its leisure and by a manner of living that was distinctive.

Because life in Vermont was what it was, we do not find any attempt to make china, or even the finer and more costly forms of earthenware, until almost the middle of the nineteenth century. By that time there had developed, in Vermont as elsewhere, marked class distinctions. Moreover the great improvement of highways and the development of new methods of transportation had expanded the markets accessible to most of the potteries, with the result that production was no longer limited by the demands of the locality in which a pottery was situated, nor to the supplying of the more primitive needs. Thus, when Christopher Webber Fenton and his associates entered upon

the manufacture of porcelain and the more ornamental and costly earthenwares at Bennington in
the middle of the century, the demands of the
locality were insignificant; the market extended to
points as far distant as Montreal, Buffalo, Boston,
and New York.

Quite different was it when the new century
opened and for a full generation thereafter. Captain John Norton had operated his little pottery
at the foot of Mount Anthony for seven years when
the century began. He was succeeded in 1823 by
his son, Luman Norton; and in 1833, when the
pottery was moved to a new location, to what was
then called East Bennington, it was operated by
Luman Norton and his son Julius. Yet in all that
time, the third part of a century, there was no
attempt to make anything except common utensils
of red earthenware, usually lead glazed, and the
coarse stoneware crocks, jars, churns, and jugs which
have survived in such large numbers.

What was true of this pioneer pottery is equally
true of every other pottery that existed in the State
of Vermont during that period. Jonathan Fenton
established a pottery at Dorset, Vermont, in 1801.
He was a good potter and came from Connecticut.

His ink-well, marked with his name impressed in the clay, long owned by a gentleman in Connecticut is one of the prized pieces in the collection of the present writer. It is of a very dark, almost black, earthenware body, fired extremely hard, and covered with a greenish lead glaze. It was certainly not made in Vermont, and we may safely conclude that it was made not far from Windham, Connecticut, Jonathan Fenton's birthplace, where it was found. To 1834, or thereabouts, the Dorset pottery was operated by Jonathan Fenton or his sons, Richard Lucas Fenton and the famous Christopher Webber Fenton. During all that time only common red ware and coarse stoneware were made. There is not the slightest evidence that anything finer was ever attempted. The same thing may be said of the pottery operated at Burlington, Vermont, by Norman L. Judd, 1806-09. Judd was a splendid potter, a nephew of Captain Norton of Bennington, under whom he had learned the trade. He moved to Rome, New York, in 1810 and carried on a successful pottery business for thirty years or more.

At about the same time at which Jonathan Fenton started his little pottery at Dorset, his brother Richard Webber Fenton settled in St. Johnsbury,

Vermont, where he started a pottery about 1808. He was succeeded by his son, Leander W. Fenton. The pottery was operated continuously from 1808 to 1859. Father and son were admirable potters, as the marked examples of their work prove, but in all that half-century of continuous operation nothing was ever attempted in the way of porcelain or even fine earthenware.

The writer of these pages has examined with painstaking care every scrap of available evidence concerning every one of the early Vermont potteries of which any record has been preserved, no matter how insignificant it might be. He has unearthed the main facts concerning Samuel Woodman's pottery at Poultney, and he came into possession of Timothy Crittenden's shaving-mug, which was undoubtedly made there. Woodman operated his pottery from 1800 until about 1820. He made earthen milk-pans and plates and stoneware jugs, jars, and other simple utensils. His work is cruder than that of the Nortons and the Fentons. He seems to have prospered at the business during a score of years, but he never made any of the finer or more expensive wares. The same thing is true of the pottery which Caleb Farrar established at

[174]

Middlebury, Vermont, in 1812, and which was operated by him until 1850. He made coarse red earthenware utensils, and after 1820, common white tableware, but nothing finer was ever attempted by him or even by his successor, James Mitchell.

The same thing must be said of the several potteries at Fairfax, Vermont. There was a pottery there in 1831, how much earlier is not known. Although there is some uncertainty in this regard, since no local records appear to mention the industry, it is believed that it was conducted by a man named E. L. Farrar, who had previously owned a small pottery at Burlington, Vermont. The Fairfax pottery passed from the elder Farrar to two of his sons, who for a number of years made earthenware at North Fairfax. Sometime prior to 1850 the brothers separated, one continuing in business on his own account, and the other joining partnership with a man named Stearns. With the later developments of the industry in and around Fairfax we are not now concerned. Our sole interest at present lies in the fact that a careful study of every scrap of evidence bearing upon the subject, and of all the authenticated specimens known to exist—the most notable of these being owned by that indefatigable collector, Harold G. Rugg, Esq.—reveals that only common red earthenware and coarse stoneware were made here until at least the middle of the century. The same thing is true in every case of the potteries known or reputed to have been operated at Bradford, Fairlee, Cavendish, Corinth, Newport, and other places in the State. In no single instance do we find any manufacture of china, or of the finer grades of decorated earthenware, during the first third of the nineteenth century.

This fact cannot be accounted for otherwise than as the natural expression of a phase of social development, a supply conditioned and circumscribed by the local demand. It was not due to lack of skill, for the surviving work of such potters as the Nortons, Fentons, and Farrars shows that they were competent workmen, craftsmen of the finest type. It was not due to lack of business enterprise and resourcefulness, for these men proved themselves capable business men, resourceful, ambitious, industrious, energetic. It was not due to lack of materials suited to the production of finer wares; the subsequent development of the industry at Bennington proved that. When all the facts have been duly considered there appears to be no other ex-

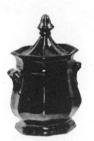
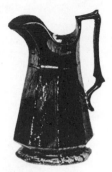
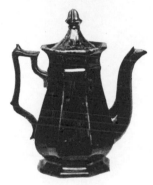
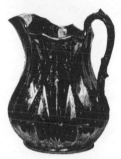
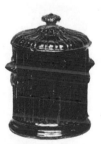
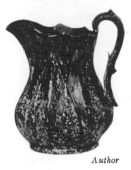

PLATE 30

Typical Bennington pottery

planation than the one offered for the uniformity
with which the potters of Vermont kept to these
crude and coarse wares.

When we turn to the more highly developed and
complex civilization of Philadelphia we are at once
confronted with a most remarkable contrast. Just
as in the years immediately preceding the Revolution, so when the nineteenth century opened, Philadelphia was the principal center of the manufacture
of the finer and costlier ceramic wares. This is not
at all difficult to understand. In many respects,
Philadelphia was the social capital of the nation.
There was a class of well-to-do cultivated people,
commanding a supply of what many other parts of
the country must have considered impossible
luxuries.

It is a great pity that we do not possess more
definite information about the "china factory" that
was the scene of the murder and riot in 1800,
already referred to in our sketch of the pottery
industry in the years immediately following the
Revolution. It may have been that John Curtis,
who was in business at that time, was making
queen's-ware in 1800, and that it was at his pottery
that the trouble occurred. On the other hand, there

is much to be said for the theory that it was a pottery conducted by Alexander Trotter, an almost forgotten and little known potter of great ability, who contributed as much as any man of his day to the development of the industry in this country. He made queen's-ware that is said to have been a great improvement upon any that was made by any of his contemporaries. We do not know for a certainty that this notable potter was in business as early as 1800, for it not until 1808 that we find him mentioned prominently among the leading manufacturers of the city. In that year he was at the head of an extensive establishment called the Columbian Pottery. It is not positively known whether he was the sole proprietor or whether others were associated with him, but the latter is presumed to be the case. The pottery was located on South Street between Twelfth and Thirteenth, and was the most extensive establishment of its kind in the city. An exhibit of its products constituted one of the attractions of Peale's Museum in 1808, and it was said that the quality of the ware and the workmanship were equal to the best that Staffordshire produced. At the great dinner held on July 4, 1808, in celebration of the anniversary of the declaration of American independence, part of the table service used consisted of "an elegant jug and goblets from the new Queensware manufactory of Trotter & Co." In his message to the Pennsylvania Legislature in December, 1809, the governor referred to the fact that there had been "lately established in Philadelphia a Queensware pottery on an extensive scale."

So far as known, none of the ware produced at the Columbian Pottery was marked with any distinctive mark enabling its present identification. Pieces have from time to time been attributed to this pottery, but in every case known to the writer there has been a complete absence of reliable evidence, or even of credible tradition, supporting such attribution. At one time and another he has had submitted to him perhaps as many as a dozen pieces of early queen's-ware with requests for his opinion whether they could be identified as Alexander Trotter's work, but in no instance has there been any evidence to warrant even so much as a presumption of a Philadelphia origin. In every case the kindest conclusion was that "the wish was father to the thought." It is so easy to conclude that because a piece of early queen's-ware came "from one of the oldest families" in the city, it "must be," or "very probably is," a specimen of the work of Bonnin & Morris, of Trotter, or of some other notable potter.

Alexander Trotter retired from business in 1812 or 1813. One of the many evidences of the rapid progress that was being made in the manufacture of ceramics at that period is the fact that the work of the Columbian Pottery had already been out-classed. Daniel Freytag, who had a pottery on South Fifth Street, Philadelphia, in 1810 or 1811, made a fine earthenware, the paste resembling queen's-ware, much of it being quite elaborately decorated. He used silver and gold ornamentation and other designs in bright colors, over-glazed. He is also believed to have made bone-china, or soft-paste porcelain, though evidence on this point is not so conclusive as one could desire. Freytag seems not to have remained in business long. He used no pottery mark, and positive identification of his wares is almost impossible.

Much the same may be said of another Phila-delphia potter, David G. Seixas, who, from 1816 or 1817 to 1822 or 1823, operated a small pottery where he made a cream-colored earthenware in

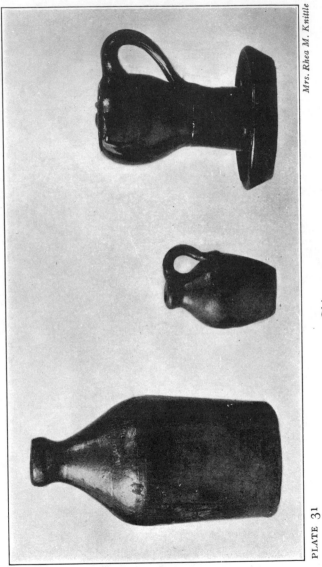

PLATE 31

Ohio pottery

imitation of Liverpool ware, and, it is said, not to be distinguished from it. He appears to have used principally, if not exclusively, clay obtained from the neighborhood of Wilmington, Delaware, and to have "pirated" the English designs systematically and so successfully that the most expert could not tell the English ware from the American.

At this state we may well consider at some length the work of another great Philadelphia potter of the period, to whom reference was made in a preceding chapter, Abraham Miller. He was the most remarkable member of a family of potters. His grandfather, Andrew Miller, had conducted a pottery on Sugar Alley, Philadelphia, from about 1789 to 1810, when he gave way to his two sons, Andrew and Abraham. The two brothers carried on the business in partnership until 1816, when Andrew retired, leaving Abraham, as sole proprietor, to make that great contribution to the development of the American pottery industry which gives him such a unique place in our ceramic history.

Abraham Miller was a remarkable man. He was an ardent social reformer, in some respects a radical; but he did not permit his zeal for reform to interfere with his business, in which he was eminently successful. He took an active part in the political affairs of the city and the State, and was at one time a member of the State Senate. He was one of the leading members of the Franklin Institute, to the development of which he gave a great deal of time and service.

Of course we are concerned mainly with his work as a potter, and only incidentally with his activities in other directions. That he was widely regarded as one of the most progressive potters in the country there can be no doubt whatever. He would be entitled to a conspicuous and honored place in these pages if for no other reason than that there is good reason for believing that he was the first potter in America to make silver lustered ware, which had come into vogue in England and this country. He exhibited a silver lustered pitcher at the exhibition of the Franklin Institute in 1824, so we learn from the report of the judges, which says that Miller's exhibit consisted of "red and black glazed teapots, coffee-pots, and other articles of the same description. Also a sample of platinated or lustre pitchers with a specimen of porcelain and white ware, all of which exhibited a growing improvement in the manufacture, both in the quality and form of the articles." The report of the judges goes on to say: "It is but a few years since we were under the necessity of importing a considerable proportion of this description of ware for home consumption, but since our potters have attained the art of making it equal, if not superior, to the imported, and as cheap, they have entirely excluded the foreign ware from the American market." This last statement needs to be received with considerable reserve. It can only be taken to mean that the importation of the cheaper earthenware for ordinary table use had largely ceased. Certainly a considerable amount of luster and porcelain was being imported from England at that time.

We find Miller again a prominent exhibitor at the Franklin Institute exhibition in 1835. According to the official report, on that occasion he had a notable exhibit illustrative of all the stages of pottery manufacture, from the crude raw materials to the finished product. Again in 1842 we find him exhibiting fine earthenware, the exhibit consisting of decorated plates, vases, and ornamental flowerpots. We know that Miller originated and made the famous Tam O'Shanter mugs in Rockingham ware which were so popular in the decade from 1840 to

1850. They were apparently never marked; at least the writer has never seen one that was marked. Mugs of this type can be attributed to this pottery, and to the period named, with a fair measure of confidence.

Abraham Miller is said to have made many successful experiments in the manufacture of porcelain. It will be recalled that in the report of the judges of the Franklin Institute exhibition for 1824 mention was made of the fact that he exhibited "porcelain and white ware." The fact that the two terms were used in this manner is significant. Evidently "porcelain" was not applied by the judges of the exhibition to ordinary white ware. By that time the word "porcelain" was being restricted in ordinary usage to the transclucent ware, the manufacture of which was making some headway. But although Abraham Miller succeeded in his experiments in porcelain-making, it is said that he never placed any of it on the market. He confined himself to earthenwares, producing a large variety of these, ranging from what in the trade are known as common white and common yellow, to highly decorated tableware, Rockingham, and silver luster.

Miller possessed considerable ability as a modeler, according to tradition, and for his own pleasure and recreation he modeled a great many figures which were made in white earthenware biscuit. These he gave away to his friends, and it is both notable and regrettable that they were generally, and perhaps always, unsigned. He was fond of employing "lace-work" on these figures. This he produced by copying a method long familiar to European potters. A piece of lace was first thoroughly saturated in white slip, and was then attached to the ware to form the decorative effect desired. When the piece of ware thus treated was fired the threads in the lace were consumed, leaving the clay stand exactly in the pattern of the original. The method is an old one, and the claim occasionally advanced that Miller invented it is absurd.

Abraham Miller died in harness in 1858, the business then passing into the hands of his superintendent, Charles J. Boulter. Within the span of his lifetime Miller had seen an enormous change come over the industry with which he was so long and so honorably connected. His lifetime encompassed a veritable revolution in the ceramic industry in this country. Before his death porcelain was being made in America equal to the best that was being produced in England, and yet it was true that many of the best potters in the country were finding to their chagrin and their bitter cost that it was contrary to their best interest to have their wares known for what they were, American made.

Our account of the work of Abraham Miller, though no more than a mere outline, has taken us to the middle of the nineteenth century. It becomes necessary for us to retrace our steps and to return to the first quarter of the century, in order to take note of some other potters meriting the attention of collectors and students. Among these, place must be given to Captain John Mullowny, who had a pottery on Pine Street, Philadelphia, from 1810 to 1816, and perhaps somewhat later. Captain Mullowny, a soldier in the Revolution, called his works the Washington Pottery, and his ware Washington ware. It is doubtless due to the fact that the captain used this name in advertising the products of his pottery that something of a legend grew up that in the early part of the nineteenth century a kind of ware was made in Philadelphia the manufacture of which had become a lost art.

The legend varies with the telling. One version

is that Captain Mullowny used a peculiar glaze. This is sometimes said to have been a metallic luster and at other times a "wonderful coloring." Another version is that the characteristic feature of the good captain's ware, from which it derived its name, was the use of Washington's portrait for ornamentation. It may seem to be a pity to be guilty of such iconoclasm as the smashing of such interesting legends, but the simple truth is that there is not the least scrap of evidence that Captain Mullowny made any ware that was unusual or in any degree notable or uncommon. He was a good potter. So much we are justified in believing from the number of his apprentices who became good potters. He made red ware, lead glazed, ordinary yellow ware, known to the trade as common yellow, and "black ware." The latter must not be confounded with *basalt* or *Egyptian black.* It was simply red earthenware, of a rather fine texture, heavily glazed with a glaze containing a very large amount of manganese. In these simple wares the Washington Pottery turned out large numbers of tea-pots, coffee-pots, pitchers, and similar domestic utensils.

There is one feature in an advertisement of Captain Mullowny's pottery which merits attention for the light it throws upon our hobby. The advertisement appeared in the "Aurora-General Advertiser" in May, 1810. After announcing the address and the character of the goods offered for sale, the notice informed the readers that they could have "any device, cypher, or pattern put on china or other ware at the shortest notice, by leaving orders at the ware-house as above." Here is an explanation of the frequency with which the collector of to-day finds pieces of pottery and china bearing names, inscriptions, and designs obviously not intended for general commerce. There was a definite catering to that sort of thing, not alone by Captain Mullowny but by potteries in general, and it is a mistake to infer from pieces so inscribed or decorated that they bear witness to any sentimental attachment on the part of some potter to the individual to whom they were presented. Just as we go into a jewelry store to-day and buy a gift on which we have engraved the initials or name of the recipient, so a century ago men and women ordered mugs and pitchers and cuspidors inscribed for their friends. There was as little personal feeling on the part of the pottery decorator as there is on the part of the jewelry engraver.

[188]

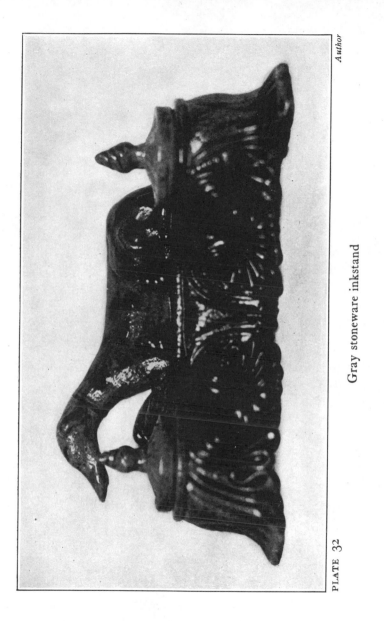

PLATE 32

Gray stoneware inkstand

Author

Early Nineteenth Century

This same custom has an important bearing upon the study of slip-decorated pottery and its attribution. The writer of this volume is confident that there were few of the potteries at which the customary range of earthenware objects was made in which slip-decorated presentation pieces were not made on order. Practically every pottery making common earthenware used slip to a greater or lesser extent, so that the materials for making slip-decorated pottery were constantly on hand. The work required no special tools; any ordinary bottle with a piece of quill or even a bit of hollow reed passed through a hole in the cork would make a workable "slip-cup" or "quill-box," the simple vessel used to hold the slip for tracing patterns on the ware. If he wanted a better instrument than such a makeshift, any potter could make a good one in five minutes or less.

With tools and materials ready at hand, a potter who desired to try his hand at slip decoration could do so. It required no special artistic talent or training to trace the crude designs or inscriptions, nor did the firing of the ware so decorated present any special problems. The average apprentice working in an earthenware pottery was certain to try his hand at this sort of decoration; the same impulse that leads boys, and men too for that matter, to write their names or draw figures on walls, carve their initials on trees and fence-posts, and the like, would inevitably lead to such experiments, the materials and the tools being so temptingly accessible.

For these reasons, the present writer holds in light esteem all attributions of ware of this sort to particular potters *unless there is some specific record of the actual maker's name*. Virtually all other attributions are mere guesswork, of no real value. These guesswork attributions do no particular harm, however, provided the collector understands the limited sense in which they are to be accepted. At the same time when Captain Mullowny started making earthenware at his Washington Pottery on Pine Street in 1809, there was another pottery not far distant, on South Street, where Messrs. Binney & Ronaldson made the same class of goods in the same sort of ware. In the absence of some inscription which enables us to place the matter beyond reasonable doubt, or some other equally positive evidence, it is pure charlatanry for anybody to pretend that he can tell from which of the two potteries a slip-decorated plate came. It is often equally impossible to distinguish between the products of potteries in different towns or even different States.

Thomas Haig, a Scotchman, was another Philadelphia potter whose work, begun early in the century, extended over a considerable period of time and contributed greatly to the progress of the industry. His pottery, which was located at Northern Liberties, Philadelphia, was established in 1812, and the product was earthenware. In the familiar red and black varieties of earthenware common to all the potteries of the period, Haig made tea-pots, coffee-pots, milk-pans, cake-molds, pitchers, strainers, bowls, mugs, plates and platters, and similar articles for domestic use. At the exhibition of the Franklin Institute in 1825, he exhibited a selection of his wares, which he appears not to have sent in time to qualify for the competition, for the judges in commenting upon them say that "if they had been sent in time [they] might have entitled him to the silver medal." The judges note that the ware was made "from clay taken in the city," and they award the potter high praise. "These articles are considered of very superior quality, and are in the opinion of the judges better than goods of the same kind, brought from England. The body of the ware is perfectly burned and deprived of all absorbent qualities. The glaze is good and free from cracks and the workmanship is neat." In 1826 he received the bronze medal of the Franklin Institute for the best red ware displayed.

Thomas Haig carried on the business until 1833, and was succeeded by his two sons, James and Thomas, who carried it on for another half-century. Within the lifetime of the founder, in addition to the wares already described, a good deal of Rockingham was made, and it is believed that Haig made the Rockingham pitcher with the full-length figure of Washington as a master mason, wearing his regalia and in the act of presiding over his lodge. This account of the pitcher is given here with great reserve, for it has been vaguely attributed to at least three other potters, namely Abraham Miller, Philadelphia, M. Perrine, Baltimore, and James Carr, of the Swan Hill Pottery, South Amboy. All that the writer knows of this pitcher is that the one in his collection was purchased in Philadelphia by a dealer, who was told that it was made at the Thomas Haig pottery before 1830.

With the year 1825 the era of porcelain manu-

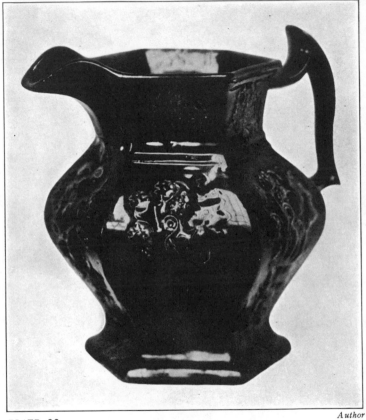

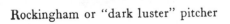

Author

PLATE 33

Rockingham or "dark luster" pitcher

facture in America may be said to have opened.
This statement must not be taken too literally, however, or too narrowly interpreted. Porcelain had
been made in this country, to some extent, a number
of years before 1825. Loosely as we know the word
to have been used in the early days, certain as we
are that it was applied to common earthenware, both
within the trade and outside of it, we know that
Bonnin & Morris made artificial, or soft-paste, porcelain as early as 1772. We also know that around
1815 Abraham Miller was making natural or hard-
paste porcelain in an experimental way, and that as
early as 1816, at least, hard-paste porcelain of good
quality was made in New York City by Dr. Mead.
Interesting as these examples of early porcelain-
making are, they are significant mainly as showing
that there was a period of tentative groping, of
intermittent experiments, preceding the introduction
of porcelain manufacture on any large scale.

Even though it necessarily involves a break in the
chronological sequence of our sketch of the development of the pottery industry, and also the need of
some repetition, we shall probably gain a clearer
view by leaving our account of the early American
porcelain factories to a later chapter, devoting the

remainder of this one to a hasty summary of the other ceramic developments of the early part of the nineteenth century. Not much need be said, or can be profitably said, of the products made at the numerous small potteries where ordinary earthenware and coarse stoneware were made. The general character of these wares, which were common to practically all of the potteries of the period, has been sufficiently described in connection with the wide range of potteries already dealt with.

Let us take the potteries of South Amboy, New Jersey, and the surrounding neighborhood, by way of illustration. It will be recalled that at the Burlington pottery of Daniel Coxe, in the seventeenth century, clay from South Amboy is believed to have been used. In 1800 Van Wickle's stoneware pottery was started at Old Bridge, later known as Herbertsville, New Jersey, the clay used being drawn from South Amboy. In 1802 another stoneware pottery was started at Roundabout, later called Sayreville, on the Raritan, also using South Amboy clay. In 1807, and perhaps earlier, a stoneware pottery was operated at South Amboy by Warne & Letts. Practically all that is known of this pottery is the testimony of a single marked crock owned by William Goedecke, Esq., of Richmond Borough, New York City. It is a rather crudely potted vessel, of good shape. In color and general appearance it does not differ from other early stoneware vessels found in New Jersey. But for the fact that it bears a date and the name of the pottery firm, it might have been ascribed either to Van Wickle or to John Hancock, who came on the scene twenty years after it was made. Impressed into the clay, apparently by wooden types, the crock bears on one side the inscription, "Warne & Letts, 1807." On the other side, impressed in the same way, is, "Liberty For Ev S. Amboy. Ne Jer'sy." It is evident that the issues which led to the second war with Great Britain were agitating the mind of the maker of this humble stoneware crock.

Ceramically speaking, the crock which was inscribed with the name of the firm of Warne & Letts, and with the patriotic sentiment quoted, is of little interest. It does not differ in quality or any technical distinction from numerous other contemporary pieces. Yet the individuality given to it by the inscription does endow it with great interest, and even with importance. It is, in the first place, a valuable contribution to our knowledge of the history of the pottery industry. It is a historical document of a sort. Incidentally, the general historian may find it of interest to note the evidence of the foment that led to the War of 1812.

In 1828 John Hancock, an English potter, who had been manager for James Clews at Cobridge, England, and later held a similar post at the famous Cambrian potteries, at Swansea, South Wales, started a pottery at South Amboy. He made stoneware and yellow ware. In 1849 Thomas Locker was making yellow ware at South Amboy, in the Swan Hill Pottery. In the absence of definitely marked pieces or other positive evidence, there is no way of telling whether early stoneware found in this locality was made by John Hancock or by Van Wickle. Similarly it is impossible to tell whether an unmarked piece of yellow ware was made by Locker or by Hancock. Not only is that the case, but it is impossible for any human being, no matter how expert, to tell with certainty whether an unmarked piece of yellow ware was made at South Amboy or elsewhere. Knowledge of the simple facts already set forth, that these potteries existed at the times indicated and made wares of the types

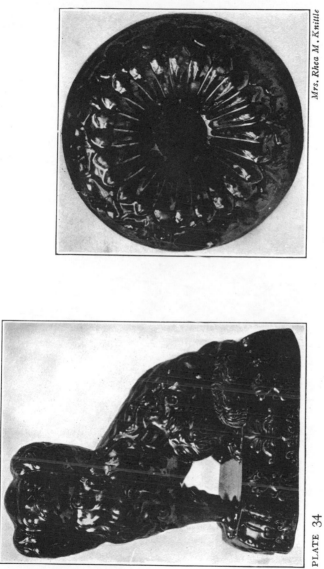

Mrs. Rhea M. Knittle

PLATE 34 Ohio Rockingham ware

described, may be helpful to the collector. Beyond that is romance, not history.

In 1827 Jabez Vodrey, an English potter of great ability, with a partner named Frost, started a pottery at East Liberties, Pennsylvania, now part of the city of Pittsburgh. They made earthenware and stoneware. So far as is known, that was the first pottery established west of the Allegheny Mountains; by the white man, that is. We do not know definitely what wares Vodrey & Frost made. Or perhaps it would be better to say that we know very little about the wares they made, for we do know that they made yellow ware. It is believed that they also made coarse salt-glazed stoneware utensils and some white earthenware. The writer has never seen a piece of ware so marked as to definitely establish the fact that it was made at this pioneer pottery of the vast region west of the Alleghenies. Some years ago he was shown a pitcher in Rockingham ware of good quality and color with an imperfectly impressed pottery mark. The first word, "Vodrey," was plain enough; the character "&" could be guessed at with some assurance. Beyond that there was nothing but an undecipherable blur. The owner of the pitcher had bought it from a Pittsburgh dealer, and, the wish no doubt fathering the thought, had jumped to the conclusion that here was an authentic specimen of the ware made at the first Pittsburgh pottery. Of course if that were certain the importance of the specimen to the student of our ceramic history would be very great. It is more than likely, however, that the pitcher was not made at Pittsburgh at all but in East Liverpool, Ohio, and that the mark was really that of Vodrey & Brother, sons of Jabez Vodrey.

There was nothing about that Rockingham pitcher, other than the partly legible mark, which gave the least clue as to when, where, or by whom it was made. There was nothing in the glaze or the color or texture of the body underneath, so far as these could be noted, to enable the most expert connoisseur to form any opinion on the subject. A less learned and experienced person might do so, for little learning and great assurance often go together in this field, as in many others. Except for the mark, so tantalizing by its inconclusive character, that pitcher could have been attributed to any one of a dozen places with perfect assurance that no man or woman living could have proved the attribution wrong. It was not in any manner distinguishable from Rockingham pitchers of the same type known to have been made at Bennington, at South Amboy, at Zanesville, at Baltimore, at East Liverpool, and so on through a long list of places where Rockingham ware was extensively made in the middle of the nineteenth century.

Let us take another example. In 1802 Thomas Crafts, of Whately, Massachusetts, started a small pottery making coarse red earthenware. It appears that until 1821 no other kind of ware was made at the little pottery and that Crafts never employed more than one or two assistants, usually one man and one boy. In 1821 he seems to have been joined by a partner or partners, and from that time until 1832, in addition to the red ware, black tea-pots were made in fairly large quantities, as many as seven or eight men being employed. In 1833 the pottery was enlarged, Crafts having taken on a new partner, according to the best account attainable. By the enlargement the manufacture of stoneware was added to the business, and from that time until 1847 or 1848, when the pottery closed, black tea-pots and coarse salt-glazed stoneware jugs, crocks, churns, and other domestic utensils of the same general character were made.

Now, there was nothing about the red earthenware that was made by Thomas Crafts and his associates to distinguish it from other red ware made by scores of other potters in as many places. From time to time pieces of old red earthenware have been picked up in this part of the Connecticut Valley which have been rather vaguely ascribed to "the old pottery." In no case, so far as the writer has been able to learn, has any of these pieces been accompanied by authentic evidence of its origin. Assuming some or all of them to have been made at the Whately pottery, it has not been possible to tell whether they were made as early as 1805 or as late as 1840, for example. Nor could the most careful examiner point to a single feature of the ware, whether a quality of the material used or a marked individuality of workmanship, demonstrating that they could not have been made anywhere else. In other words, even if it could be proved beyond a shadow of doubt that any particular piece of this ware was made at the Crafts pottery, the fact could not be of any particular interest or importance, ceramically speaking. It might have some interest historically, as a historical fact that could endow it with special interest to students of local history.

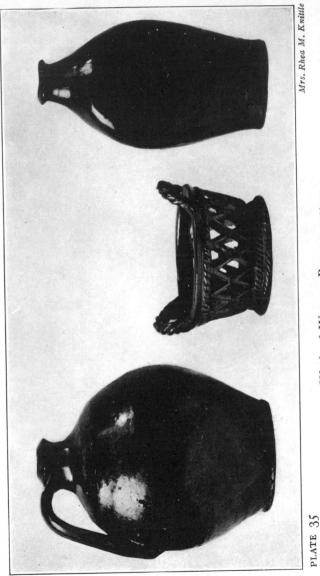

Work of Western Reserve potters

PLATE 35

Early Nineteenth Century

The same thing might be said of the stoneware that was made at Whately from 1833 to 1847. So far as can be learned, it was as undistinguished, and as undistinguishable from the product of scores of contemporary potteries, as the red ware. But when we come to a specimen of the work produced at such pottery, bearing unmistakable evidence of its origin, marked and dated, and of such marked individuality of workmanship that we learn from it something of the craftsman who made it, we are stirred by interest of a wholly different kind. Take, for instance, the extremely interesting old cider-pitcher illustrated in Plate No. 56. Presumably this grotesque jug was made to hold cider. It was found in 1924 by Frank MacCarthy, Esq., then living at Northampton, Massachusetts, but now in business in Cheshire, Connecticut. The jug is slightly over seven inches high and is of about the same width across the front at its widest part. It seems to be made of the same clay as the light stoneware of the period, but to have been fired at the lower temperature of ordinary earthenware. The face is in the light gray stoneware color, but other portions are decorated with color and gilt, the latter almost certainly applied long after it was made.

The colors used are red and dark green, and were apparently applied to the biscuit, which was then refired.

The grotesque face is crudely enough modeled, to be sure, yet it suggests a certain native talent for sculpture. Whoever made it was not aiming at a likeness, but rather at a caricature, a brutal satire perhaps. Somehow it does not seem to be American, or Anglo-Saxon, in conception or execution. Yet it bears some resemblance to others so numerous as to constitute a type. It will be noted that the side and back views show a jug of good shape, well proportioned, with sprays of rose, thistle, and shamrock in relief, quite admirably modeled. What are we to make of the union of the graceful design along conventional lines with the crude passion of the caricature?

It seems quite clear to the writer that originally this was a graceful jug, copied from an English model beyond any doubt, a fact evidenced by the use of the rose, thistle, and shamrock. After the Act of Union linking Ireland to Great Britain in 1801, the use of these three emblems in pottery decoration was fairly common. It is quite likely that it was used by the early Lambeth potters, for example. Whatever the history of the original design, it seems quite clear that some one had made a jug from a good model, and that, while the clay was still wet and plastic, the front of it was changed, deliberately distorted into a satire. It may have been the potter himself who, mastered by some impish impulse, changed what was meant to be a graceful jug into a grotesque jest. It is easy to imagine that some accident occurred to spoil the front of it, and that he had permitted himself to play with it before returning it to the clay-pile.

It is even more probable that some other person than the actual potter who made the jug was responsible for its ultimate shape; perhaps some apprentice was led to try his hand at modeling, evolving a design as he went along. Every old-time potter could tell of strange things made by themselves or their friends in apprentice days. In every pottery town where the industry goes back to the days when old methods prevailed, before the disciplines of modern systems of management, one will find evidence of the habit of playing with the clay, of modeling queer, fantastic, and sometimes obscene things according to individual fancy. It would be quite a natural thing for an apprentice to make a figure of this sort.

Unfortunately the photographs do not show clearly the rather elaborate inscription. Across the forehead, impressed in the clay, is this legend: "A. Friend. To. My. Countrey." On the left cheek, also impressed in the clay, are the words, "E. G. Crafts, Whately, Mass." On the right cheek, likewise impressed, is the political sentiment, "O. The. Dimmocratick. Press." Across the chin and lower lip, impressed in the same manner, is the proverb, "United Wee Stand. Divided. Wee Fall." Beneath the handle, on the back, is the date, 1833, not impressed in the clay but, significantly, in gilt. We may hazard the guess that this date was an afterthought; otherwise it would have been impressed; possibly it was added years after the jug was made, when it had become a matter of some interest to record it.

That the jug was made at Whately, in the Crafts pottery, either by E. G. Crafts or by some other person who placed his name upon it, is certain. That the date now on it is correct can be taken for granted, whether it was placed there at the time or not until long after. It seems fairly certain that the political

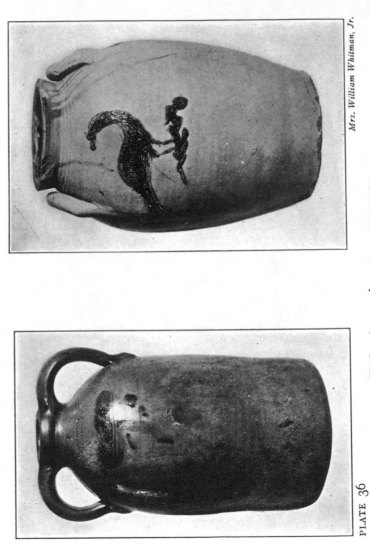

Mrs. William Whitman, Jr.

PLATE 36

Early nineteenth-century stoneware

sentiment expressed has some reference to Jackson's second election, since the Crafts group were noted Jackson Democrats. The name on the jug is that of Elbridge Gerry Crafts, son of Thomas Crafts, the owner of the pottery. This son was nineteen years of age in 1833. Like his father he was a potter, and he learned his trade in the Whately shop. That he made the grotesque face and inscribed it, seems to the present writer altogether likely.

This view is not shared by some other collectors whose views are entitled to respect, nor is it shared by members of the Crafts family now living. They say that tradition credits Thomas Crafts with being a potter of exceptional ability, while his son, Elbridge Gerry Crafts, is reputed to have been simply an ordinarily good potter. So far good and well. They next assume that only a potter of extraordinary ability and skill could have made this jug. With all deference to those who hold this view, it should be said that it is quite baseless. Granted that the back and sides display good workmanship, even that does not attain a height beyond the reach of a "good potter." The front is crude, and there is nothing in the modeling which an apprentice might not achieve. Even if we were to admit the exaggerated view of the merits of the conventional parts of the jug, and the skill required to make it, that would not militate against the theory that young Crafts fantastically changed a piece which had been made by an older and abler potter, perhaps his father. That the father made it, that he did work of such excellence on one side and of such crudity upon the other, does not seem to be tenable as a theory.

We must not forget, in trying to estimate this strange piece of craftsmanship, that grotesqueries of the same general character were commonly made in the small potteries of an earlier day. We shall have occasion in a later chapter to discuss the whole subject of caricature and lampooning by our early potters. For the present we can only ask the reader to compare the three examples illustrated on Plate No. 61 with the Whately jug.

Mention has already been made of that famous English potter, James Clews. There are few names that are better known than his among the Staffordshire potters of the early part of the nineteenth century. He has been long regarded, especially by American collectors, as a great and extraordinarily gifted potter, but a somewhat critical modern scholarship tends to modify that estimate considerably. His great reputation arose largely from the extraordinary popularity and vogue among collectors of his extensive series of earthenware plates decorated with deep blue transfer prints. His Syntax and Quixote series are sought and prized by collectors on both sides of the Atlantic. Among American collectors the designs depicting notable American historical events, scenery, and buildings are perhaps still more highly prized. Neither the quality of the ware itself nor the rich coloring and excellent printing of the transfer-printed decorations were surpassed by any similar product of his time. When so much has been set down to his credit, however, it should be noted that Clews did not originate this type of decoration. The four Adamses, the Woods, and the elder Stevenson had all preceded him in this field. They had all produced American views in blue transfer-printed earthenware. When James Clews succeeded Andrew Stevenson at Cobridge in 1818, he had to continue an established business, with an extensive market. In reality he originated very little.

Although he was credited by his contemporaries with being a resourceful and highly successful business executive, Clews was compelled to close the Cobridge works in 1829. He came to America and made a new start. At Louisville, Kentucky, a pottery had been established by the Lewis Pottery Company, in 1829, for the making of cream-colored earthenware of a good quality. The original incorporators were joined by Vodrey and Frost, who for some two years had been in business in Pittsburgh, Pennsylvania. After two or three years, the other proprietors having withdrawn, the business was carried on by Jabez Vodrey and Jacob Lewis. They were operating the business, successfully, though on a modest scale, when Clews arrived on the scene in 1836.

He was a man of considerable charm of manner, notably well educated, and a good talker. Added to these qualities there was the great prestige he possessed on account of the extraordinary popularity of his blue transfer-printed wares. That such a man should have inspired the confidence of enterprising capitalists is easily understood, and there is nothing surprising in the fact that he soon succeeded in obtaining financial backing for the establishment of a new pottery on a large scale at Troy, Indiana. The Indiana Pottery Company was incorporated by special act of the Legislature of that State on January 7, 1837. The Lewis Pottery Company was absorbed in the new concern, though Vodrey withdrew from the latter at this time and remained at Louisville, carrying on the pottery.

The history of the Troy pottery is perhaps the principal reason for challenging the long accepted estimate of Clews as a potter of extraordinary ability amounting to genius. He had confidently asserted that from the Troy clay he could produce white ware, including stone china, of a high quality equal to the best produced in England. The nearest approach to this standard was a rather muddy white earthenware of low grade, not equal to that which Vodrey was making at Louisville. So unsatisfactory was this result that in a little while the manufacture of this type of ware was abandoned and that of common yellow and Rockingham substituted therefor. Plate No. 51 shows a specimen of the early white ware made at Troy under the management of Clews. It is owned by Mrs. Rhea Mansfield Knittle, of Ashland, Ohio.

None of the Rockingham that was made at Troy was marked, so far as the writer has been able to discover. He has seen pie-plates, soap-dishes, and cuspidors which were said to have been made there, but there was not in any case sufficient evidence to make the attribution authentic beyond cavil or question. It can only be said that if the articles in question were made at Troy, and were fairly typical, the standard set there was astonishingly low, for the quality of the ware, both in body and glaze, was decidedly inferior to that of the average American pottery of the period. After about two years Clews gave up and returned to England. A great deal of money had been lost in the enterprise, and his financial backers were dissatisfied. Jabez Vodrey was then persuaded to close his pottery at Louisville and assume the management of the Troy concern in the place of Clews. Vodrey moved to Troy in the spring of 1839, taking his best workmen with him. He carried on the business until 1846, and then it was abandoned for lack of capital.

Thus ended the ambitious experiment of the famous English potter. What were the reasons for a failure so complete and an achievement so trivial? Many excuses are offered: the workmen were incompetent; they were intemperate and unreliable; the clay was not good enough by itself, and the cost of transporting other clays to improve the quality of the paste proved excessive. These and many other explanations of the failure are offered. Summed up, they amount to a demonstration of the fact that Clews was not big enough for the job he had undertaken. It was one thing to enter an established business and continue it, even to improve it, and quite another thing to undertake a new enterprise under wholly different conditions. In Cobridge Clews had worked with materials which had been tested by many years of actual experience; in Indiana he found the English formulas and methods impracticable, and he lacked the ability to make the necessary changes.

With the exception of the great and epoch-marking achievements in porcelain-making which have been barely hinted at, we have outlined the principal features of the advance made in the ceramic industry in this country during the early part of the nineteenth century. The porcelain makers and their contribution to the development of the industry we shall consider in a chapter devoted to the subject. Even then the total result will not be a complete history. Some collectors will seek in vain for names they have encountered, for detailed information concerning local potteries of which they have heard, or which are represented in their collections. We have not attempted to write a detailed history of the pottery industry in America, however. The historical sketches given are intended simply to help the collector to comprehend the general development of American ceramics, so that he may understand his hobby better and derive greater pleasure from it.

If the reader will take this broad sketch of the main lines of the development of American ceramics during the first half of the nineteenth century, and the special chapters embracing the achievements of the same period, supplementing these with the data contained in the chronological lists, he will find the task of classifying his collection, and of determining the probable origin of many specimens, greatly simplified. And that, the writer believes, is all that can be successfully undertaken in a handbook of this character.

CHRONOLOGICAL LIST OF EARLY NINETEENTH-CENTURY POTTERS

Date	Place	Name	Types of Ware
1800	Willow Creek, Milford, Bucks Co., Pa.	David Spinner	Slip-decorated and sgraffito wares
1800 (circa)	Rock Hill, Bucks Co., Pa.	John Headman (also Peter Headman)	Slip-decorated and sgraffito wares
1800	Morgantown, W. Va.	John W. Thompson	Slip-decorated and sgraffito wares
1800	Old Bridge (now Herbertsville), N.J.	—— Van Winckle	Stoneware, salt-glazed, made from So. Amboy clay
1800	Poultney, Vt.	Samuel Woodman	Red ware and stoneware, queen's-ware
1800	Stonington, Conn.	Adam States	Red ware
1800	Hartford, Conn.	Isaac Hanford	Stoneware
1801 (circa)	Cincinnati, Ohio	Jas. & Robt. Caldwell	Earthenware
1801	Dorset, Vt.	Jonathan Fenton	Red ware and stoneware
1801	Burlington, N. Y.	Jacob Fenton	Red ware and stoneware
1802	Whately, Mass.	Thomas Crafts	Stoneware

[213]

Date	Place	Name	Types of Ware
1802	Roundabout (now Sayreville,) N. J.	— Price	Salt-glazed stoneware from South Amboy clay
1804	Boscawen, N. H.	Jeremiah Burpee	Stoneware
1805	Hartford, Conn.	J. C. Fisher	Salt-glazed stoneware and red ware
1805	Steubenville, Jefferson Co., Ohio	Peter Cross	Red ware and slip-decorated ware
1805-06	Huntington, Long Island	Moses Scudder	Slip-decorated and sgraffito wares
1806	Hillsboro, Highland Co., Ohio	Richard Illif	Stoneware
1806	Burlington, Vt.	Norman L. Judd	Red ware and stoneware
1806 (circa)	Rock Hill, Bucks Co., Pa.	Andrew Headman (also Charles Headman)	Earthenware
1806	West Whiteland, Chester Co., Pa.	Thomas and John Vickers	Earthenware
1807	Steubenville, Jefferson Co., Ohio	Thos. Fisher	Red ware and slip-decorated ware
1807	South Amboy, N. J.	Warne & Letts	Stoneware

[214]

Date	Place	Name	Types of Ware
1808	St. Johnsbury, Vt.	Richard Webber Fenton	Red ware and stoneware
1808 (*circa*)	Carversville, Bucks Co., **Pa.**	Philip Kline	Earthenware
1808	Philadelphia	Alexander Trotter	Queen's-ware
1808	Zanesville, Ohio	Samuel Sullivan	Red and yellow earthenware, slip-decorated ware
1809	Philadelphia	Captain Mullowny	Red and black glazed earthenware
1809	Philadelphia	Binney & Ronaldson	Red and black glazed earthenware
1809	Troy, N. Y.	Israel Seymour	Salt-glazed stoneware
1809 (possibly 1807)	Albany, N. Y.	Paul Cushman	Stoneware
1809	Downington, Chester Co., Pa.	Thomas Vickers & Sons	Queen's-ware
1809	Montgomery Co., Pa.; location not known	Henry Roudebuth	Earthenware
1809	Greensboro, Pa.	Alexander Vance	Earthenware

[215]

Date	Place	Name	Types of Ware
1810 (circa)	Tyler's Port, Montgomery Co., Pa.	Michael Scholl (also Jacob Scholl)	Earthenware
1810	Philadelphia	Abraham & Andrew Miller	Earthenware
1810	Rome, N. Y.	Norman L. Judd	Stoneware
1810-11	Philadelphia	Daniel Freytag	Fine decorated earthenware and, possibly, "bone-china"
1812	Philadelphia	Thomas Haig	Red and black glazed earthenware, Rockingham
1812	Middlebury, Vt.	Caleb Farrar	Common red and white earthenware
1814	Jonathan Creek, Ohio	Joseph Rosier	Stoneware
1814	Berks County, Pa.	Heinrich Stoffler (not positively known whether a proprietor or journeyman potter)	Earthenware
1815	Franconia, Montgomery Co., Pa.	Joseph Groff (succeeding John Leidy)	Earthenware
1815 (?)	Whately, Mass.	Daniel Goodale	Stoneware

Date	Place	Name	Types of Ware
1815 (circa)	St. Johnsbury, Vt.	William Hutchinson	Earthenware
1816	Elizabeth, N. J.	Original proprietor not known; pottery later acquired by John Pruden	Earthenware
1816	New York City	Dr. Mead	Hard-paste porcelain
1816	Philadelphia	Abraham Miller	Queen's-ware, silver luster ware, Rockingham
1816	Philadelphia	David G. Seixas	Cream-colored earthenware in the imitation of Liverpool ware
1816	Allentown, Lehigh Co. Pa.	Henry Albert	Earthenware
1817	Jaffrey, N. H.	Potter unknown	Red earthenware and white ware
1817	Connecticut; location not known	John Sanders	Earthenware
1819	Utica, N. Y.	— Nash	Stoneware
1818-20	Nockamixon, Bucks Co., Pa.	John Herring	Earthenware

Date	Place	Name	Types of Ware
1820 (circa)	Philadelphia	Wm. Ellis Tucker	Decorated imported white ware up to 1825
1820	Lionsville, Pa.	John Vickers & Sons	Earthenware
1820	Putnam, Ohio	Solomon Purdy	Red and earthenware, slip-decorated ware
1823	Upper Hanover, Montgomery Co., Pa.	Samuel Troxel	Earthenware
1823	Bennington, Vt.	L. Norton & Co.	Stoneware and earthenware
1824-25	Nockamixon, Bucks Co., Pa.	Abraham Weaver	Earthenware
1825	Huntington, Long Island	Benjamin Keeler	Earthenware
1825 (circa)	Tyler's Port, Montgomery Co., Pa.	Frederic Hildebrand	Earthenware
1825-45 (circa)	Frederick, Montgomery Co., Pa.	—— Cope	Earthenware

[218]

Date	Place	Name	Types of Ware
1825	Jersey City, N. J.	Jersey Porcelain & Earthenware Co.	Earthenware, stoneware, and hard-paste porcelain
1825	Philadelphia	Wm. Ellis Tucker	Hard-paste porcelain
1825	Mount Sterling Ohio	—— Burley	Stoneware
1825	Hartford, Conn.	T. Harrington	Stoneware
1826	Utica, N. Y.	Justin Campbell	Earthenware
1827	Utica, N. Y.	Brayton, Kellogg & Doolittle	Earthenware
1826-35	Allentown, Pa.	Samuel Horn	Earthenware
1827	Carversville, Bucks Co., Pa.	Jacob Neisser (also spelled Neizzer)	Earthenware
1827	Baltimore, Md.	M. Perrine	Stoneware
1827	Pittsburgh, Pa.	Vodrey & Frost	Earthenware
1827	Near Putnam, Ohio	Prosper Rice	Stoneware
1828	Jonathan Creek, Ohio	A. Ensminger	Stoneware, red ware, slip-decorated ware
1828	Springfield, Ohio	Fiske & Smith	Stoneware
1828	Utica, N. Y.	Noah White	Stoneware
1828	Philadelphia	Tucker (Wm. Ellis) & Hulme (Thomas)	Porcelain and other wares

Date	Place	Name	Types of Ware
1828 (circa)	Carversville, Bucks Co., Pa.	Richard Moore	Earthenware
1828-29	Tyler's Port, Montgomery Co., Pa.	John Nase	Earthenware
1828	Bennington, Vt.	L. Norton	Stoneware and earthenware
1829	Jersey City, N. J.	D. & J. Henderson	Porcelain, earthenware, and stoneware
1829	So. Amboy, N. J.	John Hancock	Yellow ware
1829	Louisville, Ky.	Lewis Pottery Co.	Cream-colored earthenware
1830	Philadelphia	Smith, Fife & Co.	Porcelain resembling the Tucker & Hemphill ware
1830	Rahway, N. J.	John Mann	Earthenware
1830 (circa)	Attleboro, (Langhorne), Pa.	Joseph Johnson	Earthenware
1830 (circa)	Plumstead, Bucks Co., Pa.	Helfrich Toomey	Earthenware
1831	West Troy, N. Y.	Sanford S. Perry	Stoneware
1831	Philadelphia	Tucker (Wm. Ellis) & Hemphill (Judge Joseph)	Porcelain and other wares
1831	Fairfax, Vt.	E. L. Farrar (?)	Earthenware and stoneware

Date	Place	Name	Types of Ware
1832	Philadelphia	Joseph Hemphill	Porcelain and other wares
1832	Near Rock Hill, Bucks Co., Pa.	George Diehl	Earthenware
1833	Jersey City, N. J.	American Pottery Mfg. Co.	Porcelain, earthenware and stoneware
1833	Philadelphia	James and Thomas Haig	Earthenware, including Rockingham
1833	Bennington, Vt.	L. Norton & Son	Stoneware and earthenware
1834	Near Putnam, Ohio	Thomas Wilbur	Stoneware
1835 (circa)	Near Putnam, Ohio	—— Mootz	Stoneware
1835 (circa)	Near Putnam, Ohio	J. Bodeen	Stoneware
1835	Springfield, Ohio	Edwin H. Merrill	Stoneware
1835 (circa)	Bridgeton, N. J.	George Hamlyn	Earthenware
1835 (circa)	Doylestown, Wayne Co., Ohio	S. Routson	Brown ware, slip-covered
1835–45	Montgomery Co., Pa.; exact location not known	Conrad K. Ranniger	Earthenware

[221]

Date	Place	Name	Types of Ware
1835-45 (circa)	Montgomery Co., Pa., exact location not known	Benjamin Bergey	Earthenware
1836	Norwich, Conn.	Sidney Risley	Stoneware
1836 (circa)	Near Putnam, Ohio	Samuel Havens	Stoneware
1837	Philadelphia	Thomas Tucker	Porcelain and other wares
1837	Philadelphia	Isaac Spiegel	Rockingham and other earthenware
1837	Troy, Ind.	Indiana Pottery Co.	Earthenware
1838	Near Putnam, Ohio	Joseph Bell	Stoneware
1839	Cincinnati, Ohio	Uriah Kendall	Stoneware, yellow ware, and Rockingham
1839	East Liverpool, Ohio	James Bennett (with Anthony Kearns)	Yellow ware
1840	Louisville, Ky.	John and Frederick Hancock	Stoneware
1840	Cleveland, Ohio	— Higgins	Stoneware
1840	Zanesville, Ohio	Howson & Hallam	Stoneware
1840 (circa)	Cincinnati, Ohio	Kendall & Sons	Stoneware, Rockingham and yellow
1840	Philadelphia	Charles J. Boulter	Soft-paste porcelain

Date	Place	Name	Types of Ware
1840	East Liverpool, Ohio	Benjamin Harker	Yellow ware and Rockingham
1840-50 (*circa*)	Plumstead, Bucks Co., Pa	— Bartleman	Earthenware
1840-50 (*circa*)	Quakertown, Bucks Co., Pa.	— Moore and — Kinzie	Earthenware
1841	East Liverpool, Ohio	Salt & Mear	Yellow and Rockingham
1841	Bennington, Vt.	Julius Norton	Stoneware and Earthenware
1842	Cincinnati, Ohio	Wm. Bromley	Stoneware, yellow ware, and Rockingham
1842	Strasburg, Va.	Solomon & Samuel **Bell**	Salt-glazed stoneware
1844	East Liverpool, Ohio	John Goodwin	Yellow and Rockingham
1844	Birmingham (now included in Pittsburgh), Pa.	Bennett & Bros.	Yellow ware and Rockingham
1844 (*circa*)	Philadelphia	R. Bagnall Beech	Rockingham and other types of earthenware
1844	East Liverpool, Ohio	Croxall Bros. (Samuel, **Jesse**, Thomas, and John)	Yellow ware and Rockingham

Date	Name	Place	Types of Ware
1845	Norton & Fenton	Bennington, Vt.	Earthenware and stoneware
1845	Henry McQuate	Near Myerstown, Lebanon Co., Pa.	Red glazed earthenware and slip-decorated earthenware
1845	Christian Miller	New Britain, Bucks Co., Pa.	Earthenware
1845 (circa)	Adam A. and Adam L. Shorb	Canton, Stark Co., Ohio	Stoneware
1845-46	— Schrumm	Plumstead, Bucks Co., Pa.	Earthenware
1846	George Scott	Cincinnati, Ohio	Stoneware, yellow ware, and Rockingham
1846	S. Routson	Wooster, Wayne Co., Ohio	Brown ware slip decorated
1846	Lazelier Burley	Crooksville, Ohio	Stoneware
1846	Edwin Bennett	Baltimore, Md.	Queen's-ware, yellow and Rockingham, and colored earthenware
1847	Edwin H. and Calvin J. Merrill	Middlebury, Ohio	Stoneware and tobacco-pipes
1847	Walter Orcutt (with Eleazur and John Gilbert)	So. Ashfield, Mass.	Stoneware

Date	Place	Name	Types of Ware
1847	Near Pennsburg, Montgomery Co., Pa.	— Bitting	Earthenware
1848-55 (circa)	Upper Hanover, Montgomery Co., Pa.	— Greber	Earthenware
1848	Blountiville, Tenn.	William Wolfe	Earthenware
1848	Baltimore, Md.	E. & W. Bennett	Queen's-ware, yellow and Rockingham, and colored earthenware
1848	East Liverpool, Ohio	Woodward & Vodrey	Yellow and Rockingham
1848	New York City	Salamander Works	Earthenware of Rockingham type
1848	Green Point, Long Island	Chas. Cartlidge & Herbert Q. Ferguson (as Chas. Cartlidge & Co.)	Porcelain buttons
1849	South Amboy, N. J.	Thomas Locker	
1849	Akron, Ohio	Hill, Foster & Co.	Stoneware
1849	Zanesville, Ohio	George Pyaitt	Rockingham and yellow

[225]

Date	Place	Name	Types of Ware
1849	Cincinnati, Ohio	George Scott & Sons	Rockingham, common yellow, cream-colored, and white granite
1850	So. Amboy, N. J.	— Cadmus	Rockingham ware
1850	So. Ashfield, Mass.	Hastings & Belding	Stoneware
1850	West Troy, N. Y.	George Walker	Rockingham
1850	Virginia (near Wilson's Landing)	Moro Phillips	Stoneware
1850	Bennington, Vt.	J. & E. Norton	Buttons in Rockingham ware
1850	So. Norwalk, Conn.	Asa Hill and L. D. Wheeler	Stoneware
1850	Atwater, Ohio	Gordon B. Purdy	Salt-glazed stoneware
1850	Greensboro, Pa.	Alexander Boughner	Rockingham and yellow ware
1850	Middlebury, Ohio	Enoch Raleigh and Herbert Baker	

CHAPTER VIII

THE PIONEER PORCELAIN MAKERS

IN a preceding chapter reference was made to the year 1825 as the opening of "the era of porcelain." That phrase may be challenged by some meticulous critic, and so it may be well to anticipate the challenge and disarm the critic by admitting that the phrase is not scientifically accurate, being something in the nature of a compromise with reality. There was no transition such as the phrase might seem to indicate; earthen wares of the old type were not displaced by the new translucent ware. In point of fact the manufacture of the new type of ware, and its general use, occurred simultaneously with great progress in the manufacture of the opaque wares. All that is meant is that beginning with 1825 there was a period in which the manufacture of porcelain in America passed from the stage of laboratory experiment and became an important factor in the ceramic industry.

It is said that early in 1825 some French artisans began to make porcelain at Jersey City, but diligent inquiry has failed to elicit anything concerning these men. Even their names are unknown. In 1878, when Miss Jennie J. Young wrote her really great book, "The Ceramic Art," she possessed a small bowl with a gold band round the outside of the rim, which she said was made by them. The present writer believes that her bowl is the same one that ultimately found its way into the Trumbull-Prime Collection, with the attribution, "Jersey City, 1825."

If French artisans were the pioneers, it seems certain either that they were simply employees and not owners, or that their connection with the enterprise must have been exceedingly brief. The first owners of whom there is any record were not Frenchmen. They bore good old American names suggestive of New England. On December 10, 1825, under an act of the New Jersey Legislature, the Jersey Porcelain and Earthenware Company was incorporated, the incorporators being George Dummer, Timothy Dewey, Henry Post, Jr., William W.

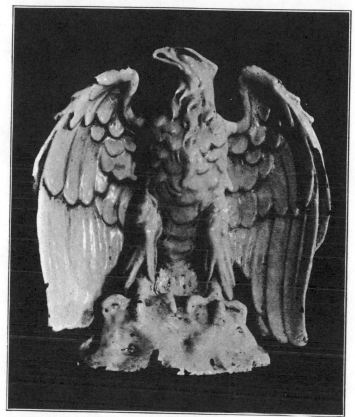

PLATE 37

Pottery eagle made at Phœnixville, Pennsylvania

The Pioneer Porcelain Makers

Shirley, and Robert Abbatt. There is no evidence that any one of these men was a potter. It is fairly safe to assume that had any of them been potters their names would have been encountered in connection with some pottery or other during the ensuing half-century. For this reason the writer believes that they were connected with the enterprise solely on its financial side, as owners, and that the actual potters were the French artisans already referred to. It appears that the pottery had been in operation some time when the incorporation took place. Probably the Frenchmen found themselves obliged to secure financial backing, as so often was the case.

In 1826 the silver medal of the Franklin Institute, Philadelphia, was awarded to the Jersey Porcelain and Earthenware Company for its exhibit as "the best china from American materials." That is evidence that the pottery was turning out a product of high quality, at least equal to the best made in America at that time. Philadelphia was the principal center of the industry, and the award of the Franklin Institute proves that the Jersey City establishment successfully met the competition of the best Philadelphia potters, such as Abraham Miller.

Early American Pottery and China

The product of the Jersey City concern at this time included earthenware, both common white and common yellow. Its specialty, however, was a hard-paste porcelain, of excellent body and glaze, decorated with gold as a rule. As we have seen, hard-paste porcelain had been made in this country before that time, but it was now for the first time turned out in quantity as a commercial product. There has been some question whether the credit for first making porcelain on a commercial scale belongs to the Jersey City concern or to Tucker of Philadelphia, but all the evidence favors the claim of the former, though the latter was a close second as we shall see.

From a technical standpoint the manufacture of porcelain at Jersey City was an immediate and a decided success. Things did not go well with the concern, however. There was trouble with the workmen, and there was financial trouble also. It was hard to meet the competition of the English wares. Sometime early in 1828 the manufacture of porcelain was discontinued and production limited to earthenware only.

In the meantime, William Ellis Tucker, a Philadelphia Quaker, had achieved notable success in the manufacture of porcelain in that city. Few figures in our ceramic history are of greater interest or importance to the collector than William Ellis Tucker. He was the son of Benjamin Tucker, a prominent member of the Society of Friends. A teacher by profession, and by all accounts a good one, in 1815 or thereabouts Benjamin Tucker opened a china-shop at 324 High Street, later called Market Street. His shop stood near where the post-office building now stands. He carried on the china business until 1822 or 1823, when he gave it up and established what was called a "select academy."

A man of parts was this Quaker educator and merchant. During the period when he was in business as a china merchant on High Street, he built a small kiln in the back of his shop for his son, William Ellis Tucker. The son thought—without much reason—that he had some talent for painting, and believed that the decoration of the white china imported from England and sold by his father offered the possibility of a pleasant and profitable occupation. He painted floral and other designs upon the white china and fired the pieces in his small kiln, to fix the decoration. There is no evidence that he had any special ability as an artist, or that his china decoration was at all notable or praise-worthy. On the contrary, there is plenty of evidence that he was as bad an artist as it was possible to be. There was an engraver of the same name living in Philadelphia at the same time, and some confusion has resulted. Mistakenly assuming the engraver and the potter to have been the same person, some writers have attributed to the latter artistic attain-ments he did not in fact possess. The two men were apparently wholly unrelated.

The china decorating led the younger Tucker to experiment in potting. Using clays obtained in and around the city and from Delaware, he made simple earthenware utensils at first, and, later, a fairly good quality of queen's-ware. Then he began to experiment with kaolin and feldspar, aiming at making hard-paste porcelain. He appears to have known, in a general way at least, the methods employed almost half a century earlier by Bonnin & Morris in making their bone-china, or soft-paste porcelain. His ambition, however, was to make natural, or hard-paste, porcelain. Failure crowded upon failure, but he persisted until he succeeded in producing porcelain of good quality, which, while it was not so hard as the best European, he was fairly

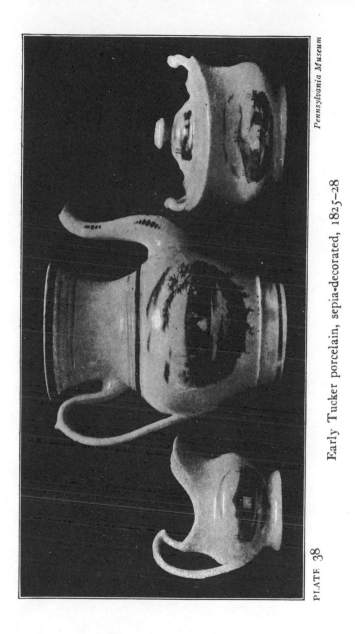

PLATE 38

Early Tucker porcelain, sepia-decorated, 1825–28

Pennsylvania Museum

entitled to classify as hard paste. He used bone-dust and flint with the kaolin and feldspar, but not enough of the former to remove the product from the hard-paste category.

What he had succeeded in producing was in fact a good white ware of considerable translucence, good glaze, medium hardness, and capable of standing great changes in temperature. In other words, it was a fairly good hard-paste porcelain. Having accomplished so much in his small experimental pottery, Tucker decided to embark upon the manufacture of porcelain as a commerical undertaking. Perhaps he was influenced in that decision to some extent by the new enterprise at Jersey City. He acquired from the city of Philadelphia the old waterworks near the Schuylkill Permanent Bridge, about where the junction of Chestnut and Twenty-third Streets is at present. He began to erect his kilns early in 1826, according to the best accounts available, and in October of that year he acquired a tract of land containing a large feldspar deposit, in Newcastle County, Delaware. Although Barber published, in his "Pottery and Porcelain of the United States," under a picture of the old waterworks, a legend to the effect that it was "Used as a

China Manufactory in 1825," his text does not quite bear out the statement, and the present writer believes it was not until 1826 that the pottery was acually started there. The exact date is only of importance in so far as it bears upon the question whether Jersey City or Philadelphia is to be credited with priority in producing porcelain on a commercial scale.

What appears to the writer to determine this point is that whereas we know that the Jersey Porcelain and Earthenware Company exhibited its wares at the Franklin Institute in 1826, Tucker did not. He did exhibit there in 1827, however, and was awarded the silver medal of the Institute. There is no evidence of any kind to justify belief that Tucker placed any porcelain on the market before 1827. It would seem to be clearly established that the Jersey City establishment was first in the field.

Tucker was not very successful in the beginning. Kiln after kiln was fired without success, and the ware that was turned out was cracked or misshapen and wholly unsalable. This was due partly to bad firing and partly to improper mixing of the paste. Thomas Tucker, a younger brother of the enterprising founder, who became his apprentice and, later on, his partner, has given a graphic account of his brother's difficulties at this period, in a paper read in 1868 before the Historical Society of Pennsylvania. He attributes the greater part of the difficulties to the malice of "some interested parties in England." In plain words he charges that English manufacturers hired a man to obtain employment in Tucker's factory and deliberately to spoil the ware. This man is alleged to have surreptitiously cut around the handles of pitchers, mugs, cups, and the like, while in the green state, before they were placed in the kiln to be fired, so that they dropped off during the firing process. Another piece of sabotage which he is alleged to have practised was the secret covering with feldspar of the inside of the saggars in which the ware was placed to be fired, and of the rings which were used to keep the ware off the bottom of the saggar. The feldspar melted, and thus the greater part of the ware stuck to the rings and the saggars, and could not be removed except by breaking.

With all due respect and deference to the author of this story, and to Barber, who appears to have believed it implicitly, the present writer believes it must be taken with a liberal amount of salt. He agrees with W. P. Jervis, author of "The Cyclopedia of Ceramics," that "the story must be taken with much reservation." What is most likely is that some workman, rebuked for bad workmanship and perhaps given notice of dismissal, in his resentment resorted to sabotage in order to "get even." It is not difficult to comprehend how, in seeking for a motive for such conduct, a suspicious mind might either evolve or accept from others the theory of a conspiracy by competitors.

At the annual exhibition of the Franklin Institute in 1827 a silver medal was offered for "the best specimen of *porcelain*, to be made in Pennsylvania, either plain white or gilt." Tucker was awarded the silver medal for his exhibit of gilt-decorated china. The judges said in making their award, "the highest credit is due to Mr. Wm. E. Tucker for the degree of perfection to which he has brought this valuable and difficult art." They went on to say: "The body of the ware appeared to be strong, and sufficiently well fired, the glaze generally very good, the gilding executed in a neat and workmanlike manner. Some of the cups and other articles bear a fair comparison with those imported."

Of course the judges shared the desire of the

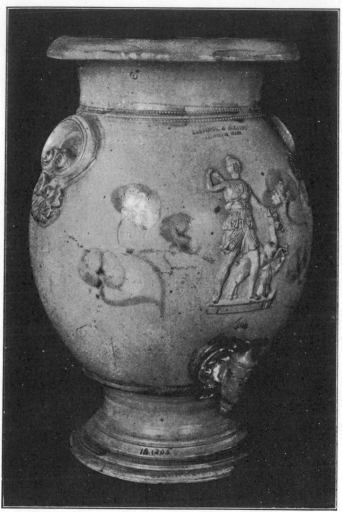

PLATE 39

Stoneware water-cooler, Ashfield, Massachusetts

The Pioneer Porcelain Makers

Franklin Institute to foster local industrial enterprise, and full allowance must be made for their mental attitude. It would be a mistake to accept too literally their statement that the ware exhibited by Tucker bore "a fair comparison with those imported." The collector who makes that mistake is sure to be disappointed and disillusioned. Such examples of Tucker's early work as have survived are far inferior not merely to the best English porcelain of the period, but to any known to have been made by any of the reputable English potters of the time. The body and glaze are not inferior to the average of the English ware, perhaps, a fact which shows that Tucker had attained success in his experimenting. But the workmanship displayed in these early pieces is as poor as the ware itself is good. Having in mind the fact that Tucker had started with ambitions as a china decorator, and had given some time to work along that line, it is surprising to discover how very bad the decoration of his wares was at this time.

It was as thoroughly bad as anything can well be imagined. Amateurishness and crudity were its distinguishing features. Where gilt was used it was applied without taste, the borders being badly proportioned and clumsily executed. Other pieces were decorated—"marred" would be a more fitting word —with what even Barber calls "rough brown daubs intended for embellishment, but execrable to a degree." In view of the extent to which coarse, commonplace, and even ugly wares of all kinds are called "beautiful" and "artistic" by people of debased and perverted taste, it would perhaps be going too far to say that nobody will ever value Tucker's early pieces for esthetic reasons; it is quite safe, however, to say that nobody of cultivated taste will ever do so. From the collector's standpoint the piece may of course be a "beautiful specimen" notwithstanding the fact that it is irredeemably commonplace or even ugly.

By the year 1828, at the very time when the manufacture of porcelain at Jersey City was being abandoned, great improvement was attained by Tucker. At the exhibition of the Franklin Institute in that year he again received the silver medal. It is worthy of note that this time the medal was not offered for the best porcelain made in Pennsylvania, as in the previous year, but for the "best porcelain made in the United States, gilt, painted and plain." True, there was at the time of the exhibition no other pottery in the United States in which porcelain was being made, so far as can be discovered, though it is probable that at the time of the announcement of the conditions the Jersey City pottery was still making it. The terms of the announcement indicate at least an enlargement of the ideas and ideals of the promoters of the exhibition with respect to this ware. Tucker's exhibit also reflected a great advance. He exhibited one hundred pieces, some pure white, some quite admirably decorated with gold bands, others with designs of flowers and fruits in natural colors, showing good taste in design and skill in execution.

In large measure this great advance was due apparently to the fact that Tucker had been joined early in 1828 by a partner, who brought considerable capital to the business. His name was Thomas Hulme. He was a highly respected resident of Philadelphia. Although the partnership lasted not much more than a year, it proved of immense importance to the development of American porcelain manufacture through the increase of the financial strength of Tucker's enterprise at a critical juncture. The wares made during the period of this partnership are generally marked with the name of the firm, "Tucker & Hulme, Philadelphia, 1828," in a three-line inscription, penciled in red beneath the glaze. Sometimes the inscription is in four lines, the words "China Manufacturers" following the firm-name.

When Hulme withdrew from the firm, which was sometime in the later part of 1829, Tucker was considerably embarrassed by lack of capital to carry on the business. We find him trying to secure government aid in the form of a subsidy. He asked that Congress vote him twenty thousand dollars as a reward for his discovery of the secret of successfully making porcelain and to remunerate him for making the process public and free to the world. At the same time he wanted Congress to impose protective duties, particularly on French porcelain. In this strain he wrote to many of the leading public men of the time, including President Andrew Jackson, to whom in March, 1830, he sent a present of his ware. "I was not apprised before of the perfection to which your skill and perseverance had brought this branch of American manufacture," wrote Jackson. "It seems to be not inferior to the finest specimens of French porcelain."

At the exhibition of the American Institute of

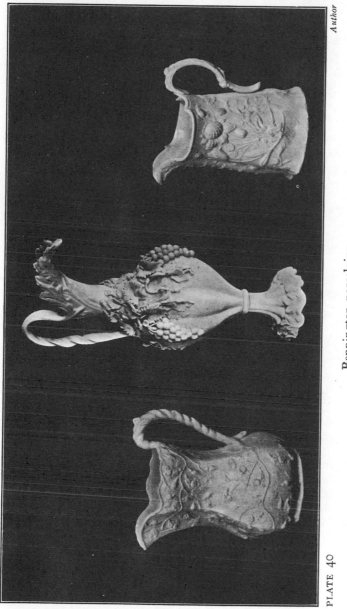

PLATE 40

Bennington porcelains

The Pioneer Porcelain Makers

New York in 1831 Tucker was awarded a silver medal for an exhibit of his porcelain ware, but although he was maintaining the standard of excellence reached during the partnership with Hulme, if not improving upon it, he was greatly distressed. In the first place, a strong local competitor had appeared on the scene. Moreover he was increasingly hampered by lack of funds. Congress did not come to his aid as he had suggested. Silver medals and such prize awards were very gratifying, of course, but they were of no use in paying wages. For a time it looked as if the Tucker factory would have to go the way of its Jersey City rival. Tucker manfully struggled along until the early months of 1832, when he was joined by a new partner, Joseph Hemphill, a former judge of the district court in Philadelphia and a representative of that city in Congress for three terms. A man of sixty-two, highly respected for his character and ability, Judge Hemphill brought new capital into the concern. More important than that, however, was the fact that he brought a better capacity for business and a larger vision than Tucker had. Within a few months from the consummation of the new partnership William Ellis Tucker died. The concern passed into the hands of Judge Hemphill, who a short time later took his son, Robert Coleman Hemphill, into partnership with him.

Before proceeding with the story of the Philadelphia enterprise under Hemphill, let us take notice of the competitor who had appeared, to whom reference has already been made. At the exhibition of the Franklin Institute in 1830, according to the report, "two beautiful porcelain pitchers" were exhibited by a new firm, not previously mentioned in our ceramic annals, Smith, Fife & Company. We know very little about this firm, and the record of its exhibit of the two pitchers at the Franklin Institute is almost the only contemporary reference to its work. It is said that a well known Philadelphia merchant, one Jason Fennemore, furnished most, if not all, of the capital of the new firm. Of Smith and Fife we know nothing at all, but it is supposed that they were potters who had been employed by Tucker. Because of the fact that a lady friend to whom Fennemore sent a representative collection of the firm's products had the good sense to preserve them carefully, we know exactly what kind of ware they made, and how closely it resembled the ware made by Tucker. The new firm

[242]

marked its ware very much as Tucker did, the name of the firm penciled on the bottom in red, under the glaze. It is thus possible to place the wares of the rival producers side by side for comparison.

The Smith & Fife ware sent by Jason Fennemore to his careful lady friend included two pitchers, a smelling-bottle, two leaf-shaped pickle or preserve dishes, and a small heart-shaped perfume-vial. They were of hard-paste porcelain decorated with gold and colors in a manner almost identical with that of Tucker's wares. More remarkable even than that is the fact that the shapes and patterns are absolutely identical in both cases. It is not simply a case of close similarity but of that absolute identity which could only result from the use by both parties of the same or duplicate molds. Special emphasis is laid upon this incident, because the present writer believes that it holds for the collector of American pottery and china one of the most important lessons he will ever have occasion to learn. To learn it fully will insure against many a blunder and heart-ache.

Except for the fortunate circumstance that the known examples of the wares made by Smith, Fife & Company are marked, it is probable that no human being would ever have distinguished them from the products of the Tucker pottery. Had they been unmarked, the chances are as a million to one that the most expert connoisseurs would have classified them as Tucker porcelain. When one finds an unmarked piece of pottery or china so nearly identical with the marked piece of a well known maker, clearly made either from identical or duplicate molds, it is the most natural thing in the world to jump to the conclusion that both pieces came from the same pottery. The writer of these pages has listened to hundreds of demonstrations proving the unprovable in somewhat this fashion: this piece bears the mark of the potter and is undoubtedly his handiwork; here is another piece, indistinguishable from the marked piece except by the absence of the mark, and obviously made from the same pattern in the same or a duplicate mold; beyond all possible doubt, therefore, the two pieces must have been made at the same pottery.

Such reasoning is fallacious and misleading because it is based on faulty premises. One of the most important factors in the problem is omitted in the search for its solution. Mold-making was often carried on as a trade by itself, by men who

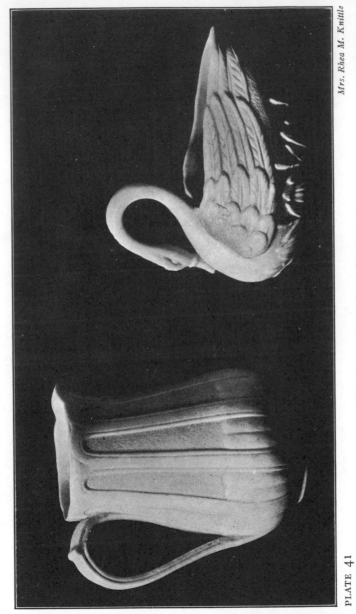

PLATE 41

Biscuit porcelain from Cincinnati

kept their own shops and who sold their molds to anybody that cared to buy. It was a common enough practice for even rival potters to buy molds from the same mold-makers, and there was no thought of obtaining exclusive use of a design. When a mold-maker shifted from town to town he took his patterns with him, further multiplying duplicate molds of popular patterns and making futile and foolish every attempt at identification by the method described. The small potteries employing only two or three men did not keep mold-makers but purchased such molds as they wanted. Sometimes they purchased from men who made and sold molds as a business. At other times they purchased the molds of defunct potteries. Both these practices led inevitably to the perplexing condition which so baffles the collector of this later day. For example, the American Porcelain Company of Gloucester, New Jersey, went out of business in 1859 or 1860. Some of its best molds were later acquired and used by the Phœnixville Pottery, Phœnixville, Pennsylvania, for making Parian. In the same way, when the United States Pottery at Bennington was given up many of its molds were bought by other potteries. So we find a certain type of pitcher that was undoubtedly made at Bennington in large numbers, made from duplicate molds at other Vermont potteries in Burlington, Fairfax, and Middlebury for example, and in other potteries outside of the State. Similarly, in Ohio one soon discovers that the so-called Daniel Boone pitcher was made contemporaneously in several places, doubtless by reason of the fact that duplicate molds were distributed in the manner described. The identification of an unmarked piece of pottery or china, in the absence of positive and credible evidence supplementing whatever is suggested by the specimen itself, can never be more than tentative.

How long the firm of Smith, Fife & Company continued in business we do not know. The fact that the firm does not again appear among the exhibitors at the Franklin Institute exhibitions, and the absence of any further mention of it, taken in connection with the remarkable scarcity of specimens bearing its mark, warrant the conclusion that it was short-lived. It is doubtful whether it endured more than a year at most. The few known marked pieces made by Smith, Fife & Company are slightly inferior in workmanship to those made by the Tucker and Hemphill concern.

The Pioneer Porcelain Makers

The ware is somewhat less white and more cream-tinted, presumably, because of a large admixture of bone-ash. It is exceedingly doubtful, however, if we are warranted in drawing any conclusion from such a small number of examples. The collector who gets a piece of porcelain bearing the mark of Smith, Fife & Company may well celebrate the event.

Now let us return to the older concern. On the death of its founder the works passed into the control of Judge Hemphill, as has already been explained. He was not a practical potter, as we know, and the practical side of the undertaking was supervised by Thomas Tucker, the younger brother of the founder. It was due to the energy and enterprise of Judge Hemphill, however, that artists and skilled workmen were brought from France, England, and Germany to improve the quality of the product. A deliberate attempt was made to follow the forms as well as the decorations of the best productions of the famous Sèvres factory. Artists who had worked in the Sèvres factory produced more or less close copies of the elaborate floral designs in vogue there, especially borders of roses, forget-me-nots, and tulips. The Sèvres practice of decorating pieces with elaborate monograms, coats of arms, and other designs of a personal nature, usually in a floral border, was copied and soon became something of a vogue. Portraits of noted men were painted in colors on pitchers and vases, Washington and "Mad Anthony" Wayne being among the most successful of these portraits. Judge Hemphill or his advisers had the good sense to use only acknowledged masterpieces of portraiture for reproduction in this manner, such as the Vaughan portrait of Washington by Stuart, and Charles Wilson Peale's portrait of Wayne. One of the most notable pieces produced is the magnificent vase with the fine picture of Napoleon watching the burning of Moscow.

Much of the work of this period is plainly marked with Hemphill's name in red under the glaze. But a great deal of the ware produced, including some of the very finest, bore no mark at all. It was left unmarked because there was a distinct prejudice against American made wares. Perhaps it would be fairer to say that a great many Americans were unable to believe that any fine wares could be made in this country to equal those made in France or England. It is one of the amusing ironies which the collector encounters as he rides this hobby that no little of the "genuine old Sèvres" sold to American collectors until a few years ago was actually made at the Hemphill factory in Philadelphia between 1833 and 1837. Nowadays good Hemphill specimens are so valuable that there is no temptation to the dealer to knowingly offer them as anything else, not even as "genuine old Sèvres." Yet there is good reason for believing that from time to time vases and other objects made at the Hemphill pottery are sold as Sèvres.

In 1833 Hemphill received honorable mention for his exhibit of American porcelain at the exhibition of the Franklin Institute, the judges calling attention to the great improvement made since the previous year's exhibition, especially in molding and glazing. He also received that year a diploma and silver medal from the American Institute of New York. It is not too much to say, in the opinion of the present writer at least, that some of the best specimens of Hemphill porcelain are as fine as any produced in France, and that they have never been excelled in this country.

In 1836 Judge Hemphill was again an exhibitor at the Franklin Institute, but for the last time. He sold out his interest in the concern and retired from it some time in 1837, being succeeded by Thomas Tucker, who leased the works for a period of six months. Tucker carried on the manufacture of porcelain for a short time only, until he had filled a store, when he retired from the manufacturing end and closed the pottery. Much of the machinery and most of the molds were purchased by Abraham Miller and used by him. Tucker went into the business of selling china, just as his grandfather had done. It is a rather pathetic commentary upon the development of our nation and its lack of national consciousness that Thomas Tucker at once began importing china from France and England to supply American needs.

In the Tucker, Tucker & Hulme, Tucker & Hemphill, and Tucker terms of ownership and management were embraced twelve of the most fruitful years in our ceramic history. If splendor of achievement and its fundamental importance are to be the criteria upon which our judgment is based, it may be asserted with a large measure of confidence that in all the history of our ceramic development no other period of equal length approaches it. Beginning with the rather poorly made tableware of the first period, decorated over the glaze with clumsily painted butterflies, flowers, or landscapes, done by hand in sepia and dull brown, we pass through the second period, that of Tucker & Hulme, with its greatly improved workmanship both in making and decorating the ware, and the brief Tucker & Hemphill period, to the rich Hemphill period with its careful workmanship and its opulent splendor of design and ornament. The final period, under Thomas Tucker's brief lease of the business, was an anti-climax, a dismal ending for so brilliant a chapter.

The kaolin used during the twelve years the pottery was in operation was obtained in Chester County, Pennsylvania. The feldspar came from Newcastle County, Delaware, about six miles from Wilmington. It was packed in barrels, carted to Wilmington, and from there shipped to Philadelphia by vessel. A great deal of blue clay from Perth Amboy, New Jersey, was used.

The writer is frequently asked to tell how the Tucker & Hemphill porcelain can be identified when it is not marked. By one of those curious coincidences which attract our attention and incite us to philosophical speculation and reflection, as this account of the Tucker & Hemphill wares is being written a letter on the subject comes from a genial fellow-hobbyist. "Please tell me in simple language," he writes, "by what signs or characteristics you are able to identify the unmarked Tucker & Hemphill porcelains, and tell them from any others? B—— assures me that you can do this with as much precision as I can tell a cat from a camel." In one form or another that same question has been addressed to the writer of these pages many times. He wishes that it were possible to give a more encouraging reply. It is candor, not modesty, that makes him reply invariably that he knows no way of making such attributions with any degree of certainty, and, further, that he firmly believes there is not a soul on earth who does. What is the use of pretending in such matters?

Any collector who will take the trouble to examine with care a number of representative specimens of the wares made at the Tucker & Hemphill works, embracing pieces made at each period, will very soon perceive that there are some signs which can be identified with a fair measure of confidence. This is particularly true of William E. Tucker's early work. The poor workmanship of the potter and

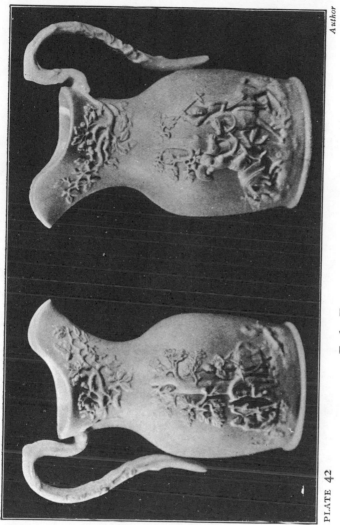

PLATE 42

Early Fenton porcelain pitcher

the childlike crudity of the decorator combine to produce a result that one can recognize without great trouble or the fear of making a mistake. When we come to the wares made during the Hemphill period, however, we are confronted with a wholly different condition. While it is true that some of the unmarked pieces produced during this period are so distinctively associated with this pottery, either by their form or by some quality in the decoration, that identification and attribution can be undertaken with a close approach to certainty, it is also true that by far the greater part of the marked wares are of such a character that only the mark makes identification possible. If the marks did not exist, identification would be impossible. No matter how expert the connoisseur may be, in many cases he will be utterly unable to tell whether the particular unmarked specimens he is called on to examine were made at Sèvres or at the Hemphill pottery.

How could it be otherwise? Hemphill brought from France the most expert workmen he could obtain from the Sèvres factory. They copied the Sèvres models. They used the formulas of Sèvres. They reproduced the designs they had been accustomed to make at Sèvres. All their energies were bent upon copying the Sèvres ware, and all their training and experience inevitably contributed to that result. Let us grant that a chemist in his laboratory could discover differences in the chemical composition of bodies and glazes, it is unthinkable that it could be done by any amount of observation, no matter how expert and careful the observer might be. The writer knows of a vase which has been pronounced to be "Hemphill without the least shadow of doubt" by some of the most competent judges in this country. Yet that vase was purchased at Sèvres, and its present owner possesses not only the receipted bill showing when and by whom it was purchased and the price paid for it, but the letter which accompanied it when its original purchaser sent it as a gift to the lady he later married.

It is difficult for the student of to-day to discover any satisfactory explanation of the failure of the Philadelphia porcelain industry, which Judge Hemphill had raised to such a high plane. All that we know is that the enterprise, while a great success from the point of view of its technical and artistic achievements, was a failure from the financial point of view—a splendid failure. After the

The Pioneer Porcelain Makers

abandonment of the enterprise in 1838, there was a lull in the industry so far as the manufacture of porcelain was concerned. For several years only fitful and relatively insignificant experiments are known to have been made. For example, at the exhibition of the Franklin Institute, in 1843, "two porcelain baskets" made by Bagaly & Ford were exhibited and rather cautiously praised by the judges as "a well finished article for American manufacture." Who Bagaly & Ford were, or where their works were located, the writer of this volume has been unable to discover. It is certain that however interesting or meritorious their experiment may have been, they made no notable contribution to the industry.

CHAPTER IX

SOME LATER PORCELAIN MAKERS

THE manufacture of porcelain in America was practically extinct from 1838 until 1847, when it was resumed at Bennington, Vermont, in the pottery directed by Christopher Webber Fenton. As early as 1843 Julius Norton, Fenton's brother-in-law and at that time his employer, was greatly interested in the subject of porcelain manufacture. We may well believe that Fenton was to a large extent responsible for his brother-in-law's keen interest in the subject, though we ought to remember in that connection that Norton was one of the best American potters of the time, and a man of progressive spirit and ideas. Whether of his own initiative, or because he was spurred on by Fenton, early in 1843 Norton sent to England and engaged John Harrison, an expert modeler employed by Copeland, to come to America for the purpose of

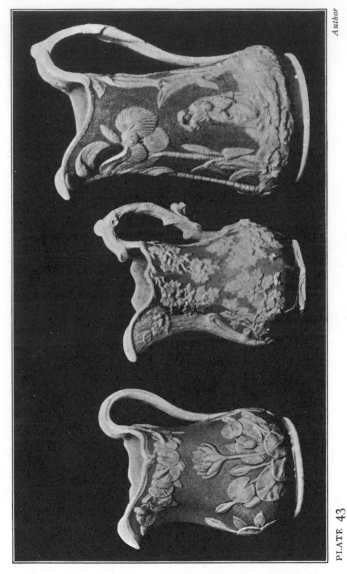

PLATE 43   Colored porcelains made at Bennington

instituting the manufacture of porcelain at Bennington.

The situation at Bennington was peculiarly favorable for such an experiment. Three generations of Nortons, including Julius, had carried on the pottery business there without interruption from 1793, and at the time there was a large pottery, making both earthenware and stoneware, one of the most successful of its kind in the country. Its permanence had brought to the pottery some of the finest potters in America. Within the town limits, easy of access, involving only a short haul, was one of the finest kaolin deposits known to exist on the American continent. Feldspar was also available locally in practically unlimited quantity. Finally, Bennington was within reasonable distance of great centers of population constituting, in the aggregate, the greatest market in the country.

John Harrison is believed to have reached Bennington late in 1843, probably at the beginning of November. He brought with him many of the latest English designs and models, according to local tradition, a fact which was destined greatly to influence the industry in America. He at once began the work of supervising the making of porcelain, and before the end of the year the first pieces successfully fired were presented to two local ladies, one of these being Mrs. Julius Norton. One end of the Norton pottery had been set aside for porcelain making. It is clear that Norton looked upon it as an experiment. He was a sound business man, enterprising but cautious, and before embarking upon the manufacture of porcelain on any large scale he desired to be quite sure of his ground.

Through 1844 the manufacture of hard-paste porcelain was carried on in a small way, some fairly good work being turned out but not on a scale large enough to influence the general character of the concern. In the meantime, Fenton had joined his brother-in-law in a joint partnership, the firm name being changed to Norton & Fenton, a name familiar to most collectors of American pottery and china. A disastrous fire in June, 1845, destroyed the pottery buildings and caused an interruption of all activities for some time. It had the effect also of postponing indefinitely the porcelain experiments, and John Harrison soon left for England. Fenton wrote on September 15, 1845, that the fire and the rebuilding of the pottery had suspended to an indefinite period all experiments in porcelain making. Except that Fenton himself may have experimented in a small way, which is most likely, Norton & Fenton did not again resume activities in that direction. It is believed that disagreement upon this subject was one of the causes which led to the dissolution of the partnership in June, 1847.

Christopher Webber Fenton then began manufacturing on his own account, and by agreement he took over all the materials and models for porcelain making. Fenton undertook to make common white, common yellow, and Rockingham, with porcelain still more or less as an experiment, or at least as a side-line. On his own resources at first, and then with Henry D. Hall as a sort of silent partner, Fenton carried on the manufacture of these wares for several months, marking his wares with a raised ornamental lozenge stamp bearing the words, "Fenton's Works, Bennington, Vermont." To this period, 1847-48, belong at least the first issues of the interesting and highly meritorious ornamental pitchers in white hard-paste porcelain which bear this mark. Care has been taken to formulate this statement of a simple fact in such a manner as to avoid misunderstanding. The stamp undoubtedly belongs to the period named, but there is evidence that it was sometimes used, whether through carelessness, accident, or deliberate intention, much later. Also, the same stamp was used in 1847-48 to mark some of the Rockingham pieces.

Fenton was not himself a great potter; in fact he can hardly be said to have been even a good one. His fame is secure enough, and he deservedly holds an honored place in the annals of the pottery industry in America. Not the least of his merits is the great impetus he gave to the industry at a critical period, particularly to the revival of porcelain making. The real potter, an artisan whose craftsmanship amounted to something akin to genius, was Decius W. Clark, who to the end of Fenton's life, through all its vicissitudes, was his trusted adviser and superintendent.

This is not the place to trace in detail all the changes of ownership and management that took place during the years when Fenton was directing the famous pottery at Bennington. Nor is it necessary to discuss in detail in this place all the types of ware that were made. These things the present writer has set forth at length, with ample detail, in "The Potters and Potteries of Bennington." It will be sufficient for our present purpose if we make

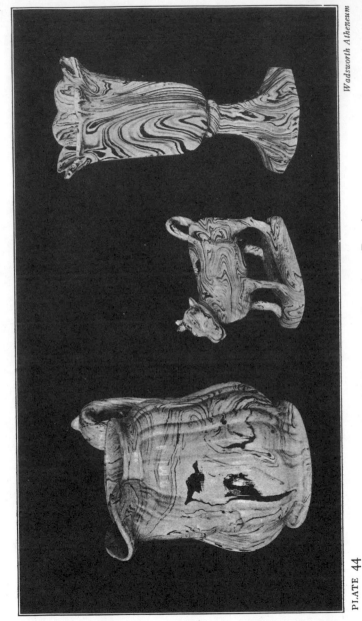

"Scroddle" or "agate" made at Bennington

PLATE 44

record of the changes of ownership, and consequently in the marking of the wares, which the collector is certain to encounter, and give a brief account of the porcelain that was made, with special reference to the much discussed, and much misunderstood, subject of Parian ware.

For some months in 1847 Fenton had no partner at all. Then for about six months he had Henry D. Hall as a partner. For legal purposes the firm-name was Fenton, Hall & Company, but it was never used on the wares, or in the ordinary business of the concern. Only when legal forms required it was that name used. From September, 1848, to November, 1849, Fenton was associated with two partners, A. P. Lyman and Calvin Park. The latter was a local dry-goods merchant, in whose business Fenton was in some way associated. Lyman was a local lawyer and politician of some note with whom Fenton was also in partnership in a local blasting-powder manufactory. The firm-name from September, 1848, to November, 1849, was Lyman, Fenton, & Park. It was used in business and local advertising but was not marked on the wares. Calvin Park withdrawing, in November, 1849, the name "Lyman, Fenton & Co." was used and stamped on the wares. Curiously, that name, while found on much of the Rockingham and other wares, is never found on the porcelain. In 1852, Lyman having left the firm, the name "United States Pottery" was applied to the works, the actual firm-name being at that time O. A. Gager & Co. While the old Lyman, Fenton & Co. mark continued to be used on Rockingham and other wares, in 1852 a raised ribbon mark came into use in connection with the porcelain. On the raised ribbon are impressed the letters "U.S.P.," the initials of the United States Pottery. In 1853, the concern having been reorganized and incorporated as the United States Pottery Company, marks bearing that name in full came into use, particularly in marking the porcelain. The company failed, and the works were shut down in May, 1858.

Such, briefly outlined, is the story of how porcelain came to be manufactured at Bennington, and of those changes in the ownership and organization of the Fenton enterprise which affect the collector because of the pottery marks that were used. An enormous quantity of wares of all sorts was made at Bennington, and collectors are often astonished to discover that in private and public collections there are numerous examples of pitchers and other articles which they have believed to be much rarer. It will help these collectors to understand this if they realize that at the height of its prosperity the United States Pottery employed more than two hundred and fifty persons, a quite extraordinary number for a pottery to employ at that time. It was probably the largest establishment of its kind in the United States.

The porcelain that was made here was nearly all of the hard-paste type. Some artificial or soft-paste porcelain was made, but the amount of it was not large. Fenton would naturally want to experiment with this type as well as all others, and the same observation applies to Decius W. Clark, one of the ablest men ever associated with the pottery industry in this country. The bone-china that was made at the United States Pottery was of fairly good quality both in body and glaze, but not particularly distinctive. With such an inexhaustible amount of kaolin of the finest quality at hand, it would have been foolish to attempt to make soft-paste porcelain as a staple manufacture.

The writer has talked with old potters who clearly remembered the keen interest with which Fenton and Clark waited to see how a batch of ware made of paste containing an unusually high percentage of bone-ash would turn out, and he possesses a small pitcher which Fenton and Clark held to be a splendid sample. So far as is known none of this bone-china was ever marked in any way, and there is no possible means of identifying it. As that is the case, it is of small interest to the average collector, and we do not need to devote any further attention to it. After all is said and done, the thing that cannot be identified, or distinguished from any one of scores of others, is for all practical purposes, from the collector's point of view, non-existent.

The hard-paste porcelain made at Bennington was very uneven in quality. Much of it, perhaps the greater part of it, was somewhat coarse and heavy. A great many pitchers, vases, and small mantel ornaments are of this coarse type. Sometimes the ware was glazed rather heavily by the direct process, and sometimes so lightly by the indirect or smear process, that it is hardly possible to be sure there has been any glazing at all. It cannot be said that either of these extremes, or any particular intermediate type of glazing, is especially characteristic of Bennington.

A great deal of the white porcelain produced was

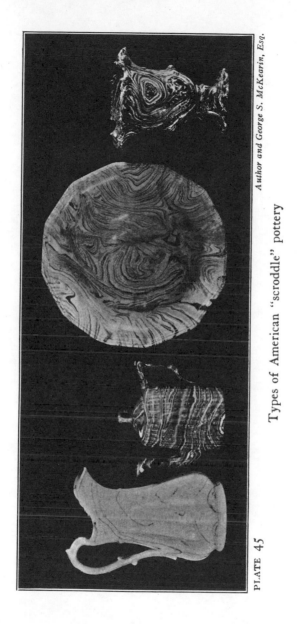

Types of American "scroddle" pottery

PLATE 45

of the biscuit type. That is to say it was ordinary white hard-paste porcelain left without glazing of any sort—at least on the outside. In the case of such articles as pitchers, mugs, and other vessels intended to hold liquids of any kind, a heavy glaze was used inside to overcome the porousness of the material. In the case of small ornaments, pin-boxes, and, in general, things not meant to hold liquids, no such reason for glazing existed, of course. In either case the outside was left entirely without glaze. Numerous pitchers, vases, and small ornaments of all kinds are found in this biscuit porcelain. The pitchers usually bear one of the pottery marks and are therefore easily identified. Only rarely, however, are any of the other objects named so marked, and except as the collector can clearly trace their origin, they belong, for the most part, to the great class of things capable of nothing better than what a friend of the writer calls "tentative attribution by shrewd guesswork."

It is noteworthy that most of this biscuit porcelain is coarse in its body texture, and quite inferior in workmanship generally. Moreover when it is marked the mark is usually the ribbon, which was used at a time when the concern was practically insolvent, and when Fenton's financial difficulties were greatest, as well as in palmier days. So, upon the basis of these facts, the writer long ago evolved the theory that this type of ware was produced at a time when Fenton was straining every nerve to lower his production cost in order to sell goods more cheaply. In other words, it was an inferior grade of ware, quality being deliberately lowered as a means of either holding or capturing a low-priced market.

At this stage it is necessary to sound a warning against a mistake which is quite commonly made by collectors, dealers, and even by the curators of our best museums. Because the Bennington pottery is so prominently identified with the early production of Parian porcelain in the United States, the fact being emphasized in every book on the subject and almost every magazine article, the classification of Bennington porcelain has been frightfully jumbled and confused. Even the most careful of our writers stumble over the simplest facts. The name "Parian" is applied to virtually every type and variety of porcelain that was ever made at Bennington. It is applied to the coarse biscuit porcelain we have been discussing. It is applied to the ware that is heavily glazed by the direct process, and to that which is only slightly glazed by smearing. It is applied to the ware with the white designs contrasting against the brilliant blue background.

All this is wrong and exceedingly stupid. It would not be a bit more stupid or erroneous to call any one of these types of ware Rockingham or luster than it is to call it Parian. Although the mistake is so common that one is inclined to say that it is constantly made by fully ninety-five per cent of those who talk or write on the subject, the matter is really simple to understand. *The collector or dealer who does not understand it cannot talk intelligently about American porcelain for ten minutes.*

Parian is the name of a quite distinct type of porcelain. When first developed in 1842 it was commonly called statuary ware. It was designed for the special purpose of making cheap miniature reproduction of famous pieces of sculpture, the portrait busts of celebrities, and the like; hence the trade-name of the time, statuary ware, or statuary porcelain. Now we know why the name Parian was applied to it. The ware was to be used for a purpose similar to that for which sculptors had for ages used marble. A close approximation in texture and appearance to the marble used for sculpture was aimed at, and the name "Parian" was applied to the ware because it met that test and approximated the appearance of Parian marble.

Obviously Parian is a silly misnomer when applied to a brilliant blue surface with white ornamentation. It would not be a bit more silly for a collector or dealer to speak of his "beautiful blue and white *basalt*" than it is for him to speak of his "blue and white Parian." It is hardly less silly to apply the name "Parian" to highly glazed white porcelain. Yet both these silly blunders are the commonplaces of recent and contemporary American writing on ceramics, and are to be found in the catalogue of almost every museum in America.

Parian is a hard-paste unglazed, or biscuit, porcelain closely resembling fine marble in its texture and appearance. The coarse white biscuit porcelain made at Bennington, which we have already discussed at some length, is not Parian, though these is some excuse for confounding the two. It is not Parian because, while it is a white biscuit porcelain, it is too coarse in its texture to imitate that of marble, which, after all, is the test of Parian. The making of Parian required a special paste, prepared

[268]

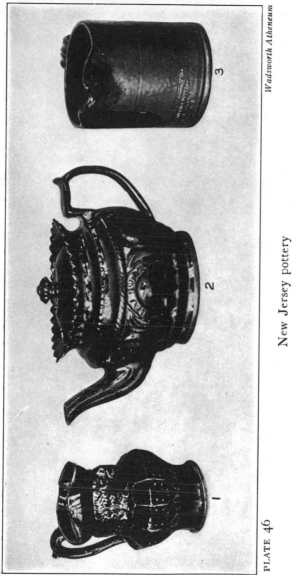

PLATE 46

New Jersey pottery

Wadsworth Atheneum

from a special formula, in a particular manner. The clay had to be ground in a special way, to a particular fineness. While it was a true hard-paste porcelain, it was mellowed somewhat by the use of bone-ash, and the kaolin was mixed with other clays. In other words, Parian is not simply a hard-paste biscuit porcelain, but a special kind of hard-paste biscuit porcelain, its special quality being its close resemblance to the smooth surface of sculptured marble.

Originally intended for the production of statuary, imitations of marble sculptures, it was admirably adapted to that purpose and not fit for making such things as pitchers and tableware. Both English and American manufacturers used it for such purposes, however, and greatly debased and discredited a really fine material. The figures made in this ware at the Bennington pottery were never marked. As a rule they are well modeled and excellently made. While they never attain the high standard of excellence reached by Copeland and Minton and other noted English firms, or even of some later American makers, they are, with few exceptions, quite admirable. Not so much can be said of the pitchers and vases. In the first place,

with very few exceptions, the designs are not suited
to the material. There is none of the illusion of
marble as there is in the case of the little figures.
Moreover, while some few of the vases are graceful in shape, they are horribly over-ornamented.
The truth is that this whole line of work at Bennington reflected the terrible debasement of taste of what
was perhaps the worst period in three centuries, from
the point of view of decorative art.

Whether a pitcher, a vase, or any other object in
porcelain known to have been made at Bennington,
either because of the pottery mark or some positive
evidence of the correctness of the attribution, is
properly to be classified as Parian or as something
else the reader must determine for himself in the
light of the foregoing discussion. In the main, it
is not a difficult matter to determine this. There
are, however, many pieces about which even the most
expert connoisseur will be somewhat in doubt. They
are the indeterminate border-line specimens, resembling the standard, but whether closely enough or
no experts will disagree. Concerning these pieces
and their classification the collector can only be
guided by common sense. The only word of advice
that can profitably be given him here is this: when

in doubt whether a piece should be classified as Parian, don't do it; classify it as biscuit porcelain and let it go at that.

The tremendous amount of blue and white porcelain, called Bennington ware or Bennington Parian, to be found in the antique-shops all over the country, is a merry jest to those who are familiar with the facts. One is reminded of the Vermont jest that more Vermont turkeys are sold and consumed in New York during a single holiday than the State of Vermont has had in it during any one year since the Civil War. There never was as much blue and white porcelain made at Bennington as the dealers are finding every year. Yet more than three score years have passed away since the United States Pottery was last in operation. The blue and white porcelain, which at its best ranks high among the products of the Bennington potters, was produced in very limited quantities. It was troublesome to make, and it was quite expensive. The pitchers in this ware almost invariably have the raised ribbon on the bottom, so that identification here is easy enough. Some of the cylindrical vases, with the so-called Paul and Virginia design in white relief, are also marked. But virtually all other articles produced in this are unmarked. Fortunately, however, there is a quality by which the collector can learn to identify this type of Bennington porcelain, despite the absence of the pottery mark. Let the collector pay no heed whatever to the fact that vases are ornamented with bunches of grapes. That was a favorite style of ornamentation on both sides of the Atlantic, and was used at a great many different potteries. Bunches of grapes clustering on the sides of vases, whether the vases be all white or decorated with blue, do not constitute a reason for believing them to have been made in Bennington, a widely prevalent belief to the contrary notwithstanding.

Most of the blue and white vases and trinketboxes which are offered as Bennington show that the blue was applied to the biscuit. That is to say, the piece was first fired in the kiln, then painted and refired to fix the color. Close examination will show that in some places the decorator got the color too far over the edges of the white, and in other places failed quite to fill the space to be colored. The evidences of hand-coloring on ware already fired are not difficult for any person to discern.

Now in the case of the Bennington porcelain the

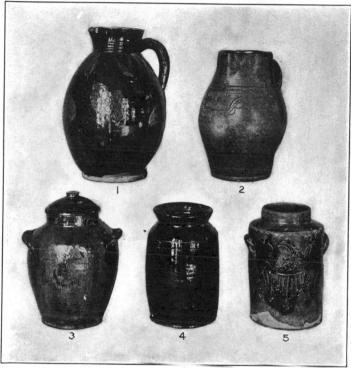

PLATE 47

Early Connecticut pottery

color was never applied to the biscuit. If a piece of genuine Bennington colored porcelain of this type is broken through the colored portions, the fractures will show, first, that the color goes through a considerable portion of the total thickness of the ware; second, that the colored part of the fracture is vitreous like the remainder. The explanation is this: All ware of this type was made by the "casting" process. That means that the materials of which the body is composed were ground very fine and mixed to the consistency of liquid paint. This "slip" was poured into plaster molds, the porousness of which insured the absorption of the water and the settling of the solid content of the slip in the mold. As the water was absorbed and evaporated more slip had to be poured into the mold. When the proper condition was reached, the mold was opened, and the article was ready for the next stage, the addition of handles, applied ornaments, and so on. Now, if it was desired to have a blue groundwork, let us say, this was done in the casting. Some of the same slip used for the body of the ware was placed in a small vessel and the necessary color added to it. Of course the only difference between the colored slip and the slip used for the body was the color. What may be termed the fictile quality was the same in both cases. With a camel's-hair brush the parts of the mold where blue was wanted were covered with the blue slip, the mold at once closed, and the uncolored slip poured in. Being of the same substance, the white slip united with the blue, and, as the color did not affect it at all, the whole fired alike. The blue on a genuine Bennington vase, therefore, not only appears to be—and in fact is—in a thicker layer than paint would be, but it has the appearance, and the quality, of the rest of the body.

The writer hopes that he has made this important matter clear enough to enable the reader to understand the process, and to apply the only test that can be relied on for the identification of the blue and white porcelain of Bennington when it is unmarked. No other pottery in America, so far as is known, used the method of applying color in slip form directly to the molds. Consequently, identification is relatively easy and certain, once the collector has grasped the significance of the process used by the Bennington potters, and the marked difference in the appearance of the ware from that which was colored by other methods.

Some Later Porcelain Makers

An interesting offshoot from the United States Pottery at Bennington was the porcelain factory that was established in 1856 at Kaolin, South Carolina, about six miles from Augusta, Georgia, and an equal distance from Aiken, South Carolina. William H. Farrar, who had sunk a large part of his capital in the Bennington works, withdrew from them and, in an effort to recoup his fortunes, went to Kaolin to start a pottery. Clay from there had been experimented with at Bennington, and it was the opinion of Decius W. Clark that good porcelain could be made at Kaolin more cheaply than at Bennington. A great market seemed to be, and in fact was, close at hand.

Farrar succeeded in interesting a number of prominent citizens of Georgia and South Carolina, and a joint-stock company was formed. It is interesting to note that Alexander H. Stephens, who later on was the vice-president of the Southern Confederacy, was an active member of the company and for a time its treasurer. Farrar took mechanics from Bennington to build his plant, and when it was ready he removed from Bennington the nucleus of his operating force, including a mixer, a modeler, and other skilled workmen. Farrar was not a practical potter and soon found himself in great difficulties. During the first year almost the entire output was unsalable. Some of it could be given away to the workmen; much of it had to be broken up. Decius W. Clark and Christopher Webber Fenton went there late in 1857 to study the problems that were involved and to advise Farrar. At one time it seemed likely that Clark and Fenton would associate themselves with the concern.

The manager of the concern was Josiah Jones, a noted designer and modeler who had been associated with Charles Cartlidge, at Greenpoint, New York. Besides being a splendid designer, Jones was a thoroughly competent potter. He had no chance at Kaolin, however. Farrar insisted that only local clay should be used, and Jones found that without the addition of some other clays to that which was found in the locality good ware could not be economically made. The principal output of the pottery was earthenware, including some rather poor Rockingham, good common white, and common yellow. Hard-paste porcelain was also produced, at times in large quantity. Some of this porcelain is fairly good in quality, and the designs, principally by Jones, are usually good. A great

PLATE 40.

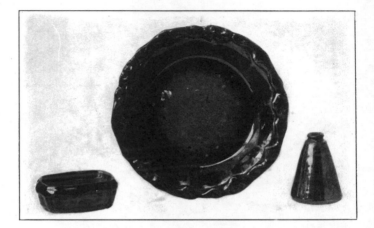

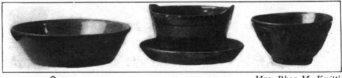

Mrs. Rhea M. Knittle

Ohio pottery

deal of the blue and white porcelain with the pitted background, so decidedly inferior to its Bennington prototype but often mistaken for it, was made at Kaolin and sent north.

Some of the porcelain made at this pottery bears the mark of the firm, an impressed shield with the initials of the company, "S.P. Company, Kaolin, S.C.," or simply "S.P.C." It appears, however, that, as in the case of the Bennington concern from which it sprang, much of the ware produced by the concern was unmarked, and positive identification is therefore extremely difficult. Throughout the Civil War the pottery was in operation, making both earthenware and porcelain. In 1865, the old company having given up the business, a new one was formed with R. B. Bullock, later govenor of Georgia, as president. After about twelve years more of fitful struggling, the works passed into the hands of McNamee & Company, a New York concern, which abandoned manufacture and devoted itself to the exploitation of the clay-beds.

The rest of the tale is soon told. Somewhat arbitrarily setting the Centennial year as the extreme limit to which the term "early American" can be extended, there is not a great deal more to be recorded. The great progress in the manufacture of porcelain which led to the present high standard of achievement came after 1876. To sketch the history of American ceramics since 1876 would be an interesting task, but it does not come within the scope of this study.

When Fenton was beginning to make porcelain for the market at Bennington he was simply one of the first, if not the first, to express in serious productive effort interest in that branch of ceramic manufacture which was widespread in this country. The interest had been greatly quickened and stimulated by the notable advances made in England in the manufacture of porcelain. The great English potters, Copeland, Minton, Ridgway, and others, were in keen rivalry not only at home but also in America. The increasing popularity of Parian, or statuary porcelain as it was then commonly called, had created a new interest in porcelain among the potters of this country, a great many of whom were British, trained in the great British potteries.

Among these men was Charles Cartlidge, of Burslem, Staffordshire, a potter belonging to one of the old potter families of Staffordshire. He was thirty-two years old when he came to the United States in 1832. He is said to have worked for some time at Jersey City under David Henderson. Later on he left the pottery industry and became the manager of an agency for the wholesale distribution of Ridgway's china and earthenware, investing all his savings in that undertaking. When financial disaster overwhelmed the Ridgway concern, causing the closing of the American agencies, Cartlidge decided to begin manufacturing porcelain. He associated himself in a partnership with Herbert Q. Ferguson, who had managed a distributing agency for Ridgway at New Orleans, the firm-name being Charles Cartlidge & Company.

They built a small kiln and shop at Greenpoint, Long Island, and in July, 1848, began to manufacture porcelain buttons to take the place of the much more expensive pearl buttons. That seems to have been the staple product on which the firm relied at the outset, but there is abundant evidence that Cartlidge had a much more ambitious program in mind. He sent to Staffordshire for his brother-in-law, Josiah Jones, who was his junior by only one year. Jones, who arrived in America before the new plant was built, was one of the most gifted designers and modelers that ever worked in an American pottery.

Soon after the pottery was started Cartlidge brought another remarkable man to this country, Elijah Tatler, a china painter and decorator whose work in that department conferred distinction upon the Greenpoint factory and has never been surpassed by anything of the same character done in this country.

At the great International Exhibition in New York in 1853, the firm exhibited a great variety of wares. These included whole tea and dinner sets, pitchers, bowls, platters, and other tableware, in bone-china; and door-knobs, drawerpulls, door-plates, escutcheons, and the like, in highly glazed earthenware. Statuettes, figurines, and portrait busts, modeled by Jones, were produced by the firm in large numbers at this time, and indeed had been almost ever since the enterprise started. It is fairly certain that a selection of these was included in the exhibit, though the available accounts are somewhat vague on the point.

These portrait busts were modeled by Jones in some cases from life, but in most instances they were either copied from engravings or from the work of other sculptors, as in the case of his general Zachary Taylor, which was copied from Gabriel's. The Taylor is one of the best of the portrait busts and one of the best known. Quite as good are those of Daniel Webster and John Marshall. A small piece made as the head of a cane is in the form of an admirably modeled likeness of Henry Clay. All these portrait busts, as well as a large variety of medallions for brooches, placques bearing bas-relief portraits, and figurines of various kinds were made in what Cartlidge himself used to describe as "bisque porcelain." He seems to have been cautious in his descriptions of these things and to have carefully avoided calling them Parian. There can be no doubt that many of them can only be classified as Parian, conforming to the English standard of that ware more successfully than even the best of the Bennington Parian does, at least in the judgment of the present writer. On the other hand, a good many of the portrait plaques and figurines are so far from having a special likeness to sculptured marble that the name "Parian" does not apply to them, and they are better described by Cartlidge's own term, "bisque porcelain." The same observation equally applies to the Bennington product.

It is one of the lesser tribulations of all collectors that a pottery which turned out such splendid wares never used a pottery mark of any kind. Fortu-

nately there are enough well authenticated specimens, notably those in the Pennsylvania Museum
and in the Metropolitan Museum, New York City,
to enable the collector who desires to go to that
trouble to visualize the contribution of Cartlidge
& Company to American ceramics, to see the really
superb decorations of Elijah Tatler and the splendid—though uneven—designing and modeling of
Josiah Jones. By the same method the collector
can obtain a general knowledge of the wares of this
important pottery that may help him to decide with
as much confidence as anybody can have in the circumstances that a particular specimen is, or is not,
a Cartlidge piece. In the meantime, if he comes
across a well modeled Parian or biscuit porcelain
bust, anywhere from six to eleven inches high, of
Daniel Webster, Zachary Taylor, John Marshall,
or Henry Clay, in the absence of any mark, or well
authenticated evidence to the contrary, he will do
well to regard it tentatively as one of the pieces
made at the Cartlidge pottery from the model of
Josiah Jones, sometime between 1848, the year when
the pottery opened, and 1856, when it closed.

In 1850 a German potter named William Boch
started a small pottery at Greenpoint, Long Island.

Some Later Porcelain Makers

He had a brother as his partner, and the firm-name was William Boch & Brother. They made a soft-paste artificial porcelain of the English type, the so-called bone-china. In 1853 they exhibited a selection of wares, ranging from elaborate table-ware to the furnishings of doors, which attracted favorable comment. Soon afterward the firm seems to have been enlarged. In 1857 Thomas C. Smith acquired an interest in the concern, and to protect his investment became manager. At the outbreak of the Civil War the concern had to wind up its affairs, and Smith became the purchaser. When he was in France, soon afterward, he conceived the idea that if the manufacture of natural or hard-paste porcelain were substituted for the other kind the business could be made profitable.

On his return to America he again started the pottery, using the old soft-paste formulas at first, presumably to use up materials on hand. In 1864 the artificial soft-paste type was given up, and from that time on natural kaolinic, or hard-paste, por-celain was produced. At first Smith was not suc-cessful. His first year was one of repeated and costly failures. It was not until well on in 1865 that he succeeded in producing ware that was sal-

[283]

able; it was a genuine hard-paste porcelain, plain white, of good body, wholly undecorated. In 1866 he undertook the decoration of the ware for the first time, as an experiment. He employed two decorators, one English, the other German, in order to study their methods.

From these men he learned that a great deal of fine ware made at Dresden was sent to England to be decorated, and then returned to Dresden and sold as Meissen ware. Acting on the information derived from his two decorators, Smith, who at the time was finding it impossible to get satisfactory results in firing his colors, submitted a piece of the Dresden-made English-decorated Meissen to the test of placing it in the same oven with his own ware. The result was that the imported piece was completely ruined. The American potter had learned the secret of the English success in decorating; namely, low temperature firing. From that time onward the decoration of its wares was one of the strong features of this pottery.

In 1874 a sculptor of some note, Karl Müller, having decided to devote himself to ceramic designing and modeling, joined the staff as chief designer and modeler. He had been led to his decision, it

[284]

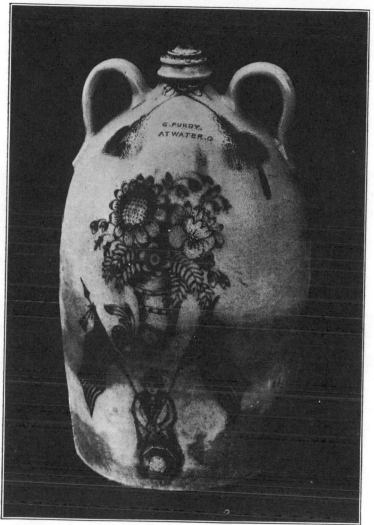

G. PURDY.
ATWATER. O

PLATE 49

Fine example of Ohio stoneware

appears, by the interest that had been evoked in the process of having some figures he had modeled produced in terra-cotta ware. Müller was responsible for some of the very best designs ever made at Greenpoint, and also for some of the very worst. Some of the things he did for the Centennial Exposition in 1876 were wholly admirable, and others were as wholly execrable. The Century vase, shown in Plate No. 53, may fairly be placed in the former class. The handles are bison-heads. The portrait medallions on both sides are fairly well done, though not notably so. The rib of gold, with the projecting heads of various animals at intervals, is rather effective, while the lower panels with their designs in white relief, depicting Indians, a Revolutionary soldier, the Boston Tea-party, and so forth, are quite admirably done. In some respects, it is a *tour de force* and is open to the criticism that it lacks artistic unity in spite of the obvious—too obvious—attempts of the artist to achieve it.

On the other hand, the Keramos vase, suggested by Longfellow's poem of that title, is about as ugly and insipid as can well be imagined. The equally famous Liberty cup and saucer which Müller designed and modeled for the Centennial Exposition exhibit both Müller's merits and his defects. The figures in low white relief on the pale lavender background are splendidly done, and the effect is entirely pleasing. But the handle, consisting of a perpendicular full-length figure of Columbia standing on an eagle, can only be described as wretched, its silliness of conception not to be atoned for by any amount of skill.

Müller was far happier in many of the little statuettes which he made, and which were turned out in Parian of good quality, in fairly large numbers. The bust of Forrest as William Tell, the statuettes illustrative of Hood's "Song of the Shirt," the statuette of the stone-mason—these and many other minor pieces show the Parian produced at the pottery at its best. Incidentally, also, it shows the art of Karl Müller at its best.

In justice to the collector as well as to a great industrial enterprise, some mention must be made of the superb applied decorations in color and gold upon some of the best pieces produced at this pottery. It is safe to say that nothing finer in this line has ever been done in America; and, bold as the assertion may seem, only rarely has anything finer been done at the great European potteries in their costliest productions. When Thomas C. Smith decided to engage the most skilled decorators to be obtained in Europe, he was derided by many as a visionary. He was told that it was hopeless to aim at equaling the standards of Sèvres, for example. To justify himself and confound his critics, he decided on a daring experiment. An elaborately ornamented Sèvres plate, which had belonged to Louis Phillippe and was purchased by an American when the king's effects were sold, was borrowed for copying. When the copy was completed both the original and the copy were set down side by side, and a number of connoisseurs and critics were asked to tell which was the original and which the copy. It is said that the people who picked the copy for the original were in the majority. The owner of the original was alarmed when he found himself uncertain which was copy and which original!

Unfortunately the early products of this pottery were never marked. So far as the writer knows there is no piece made from 1865 to 1875 that bears a pottery mark. Since 1876 when the eagle's head with the letter S in the beak was adopted to mark the pottery's wares, down to our own day and the familiar work of the Union Porcelain Company of Brooklyn, the ware made has been marked. The intelligent collector will not overlook specimens of the porcelain made at this pottery bearing the early mark.

The Parian porcelain of another pottery of the same period commands our interest and attention mainly on account of the distinctive work of a gifted artist. At the same time when Müller was designing and modeling his Centennial pieces at Greenpoint, Isaac Broome was working at Trenton, New Jersey, on a number of models of Parian pieces which the present writer believes to be superior to anything else made in that ware in this country, from the point of view both of the artistic excellence of the models and of the quality of the ware itself. The Centennial Exposition had stirred the potters of Europe as well as of America. Naturally American manufacturers and designers found in the centennial of national independence a great inspiration. Few were the American potters who did not reflect the spirit of that great occasion in their handiwork.

At Trenton John Hart Brewer, himself an artist of ability and a lineal descendent on his mother's side of that John Hart whose signature was appended to the Declaration of Independence, had

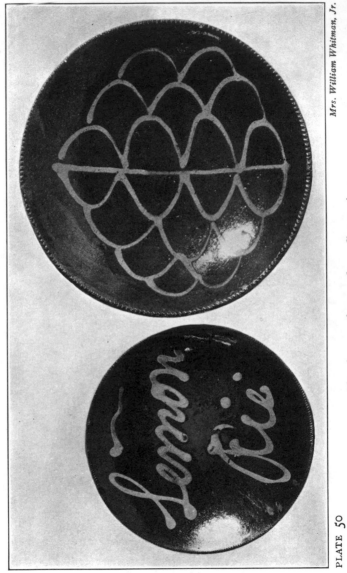

PLATE 50

Slip-decorated ware from Connecticut

Mrs. William Whitman, Jr.

become the directing head of the firm of Ott & Brewer, owners of the Etruria Pottery at Trenton. In planning the firm's exhibit for the Centennial Exposition, he decided to employ Professor Broome to make some distinctively American designs, which should be executed in Parian. In view of the fact that the firm had not previously made porcelain, this was a bold decision.

The Parian ware produced at the Etruria Pottery probably comes closer to the finest Parian of Copeland & Minton than any other made in America. Its resemblance to statuary marble is remarkable. Broome's designs are as notably distinctive as the quality of the ware. His subjects are virtually all sculptural and essentially adapted to marble or its substitute. His bust of Cleopatra and his various baseball designs rank with the best ceramic sculptures of the nineteenth century. Although the greater part of his work was done after 1876 and therefore lies beyond the limits of this volume, the writer has felt justified in seizing upon the work done for the Centennial Exposition so as to include some record of a most extraordinary achievement, and incidentally to pay his tribute to a great ceramic artist whose friendship he valued highly.

CHAPTER X

LATER NINETEENTH-CENTURY POTTERS AND POTTERIES

Soon after the Jersey Porcelain and Earthenware Company abandoned the manufacture of porcelain at Jersey City in 1829, and turned to the making of common earthenware, the works were purchased by David Henderson and his brother. At the Franklin Institute in 1830 they exhibited ware of the type generally known to the trade as stone china, a white earthenware of fine texture and density, fired to great hardness. Under the title of D. & J. Henderson the brothers carried on the business until 1833, making the white stone china, common yellow, and Rockingham, the last-named of splendid quality. So far as can be learned from the known examples that have survived, during this period the firm seems to have marked all or nearly all of its Rockingham ware, a good deal

[290]

though by no means the greater part of the common yellow, and very little of any other kind. The mark consisted of the firm name, **D. & J.** Henderson, Jersey City, arranged in a circle, and was impressed in the ware. A well known toby-jug in Rockingham upon which this mark is found is one of the best of all the jugs of this sort ever made in the United States. In 1833 the American Pottery Manufacturing Company was formed, with David Henderson at its head. Apparently the younger Henderson left the business at this time; at all events we find no further mention of him in connection with it. Two new pottery marks were now adopted, and they continued in use for about seven years, until 1840. They are both printed, under the glaze. One of these marks is in the form of a flag with the name of the firm thus: "Am. Pottery Manufg. Co., Jersey City." The other is a rather elaborate design, elliptical in form, which has the name and address of the firm effectively arranged around the edges.

It is a curious fact that in all the specimens of the wares produced at this pottery which the present writer has examined he has never seen an *impressed* mark belonging to this period. Nor has he discovered any record of such a mark by any of the numerous writers who have written of the pottery. There are many examples with the impressed mark of D. & J. Henderson, which was in general use until 1833. There are also many examples with the impressed mark of the American Pottery Company which came into use in 1840. Now we cannot suppose that Rockingham and other types of pottery which were marked from 1829 to 1833, and from 1840 to 1850, were unmarked from 1833 to 1840. With no change in the management, such a break cannot be regarded as other than extremely improbable. Some have supposed that the old Henderson mark was continued in use until 1840, but that hardly seems a more likely theory than the other. The fact which we know that, on other wares, marks were in use with the name of the company, seems to discredit this theory utterly.

The writer confesses that he does not know the explanation. It does not seem possible that no ware of the types which formerly, and afterward, bore impressed marks was made from 1833 to 1840. Of course it may be merely an accidental fact that of the Rockingham and yellow wares produced during the period in question so few pieces have survived

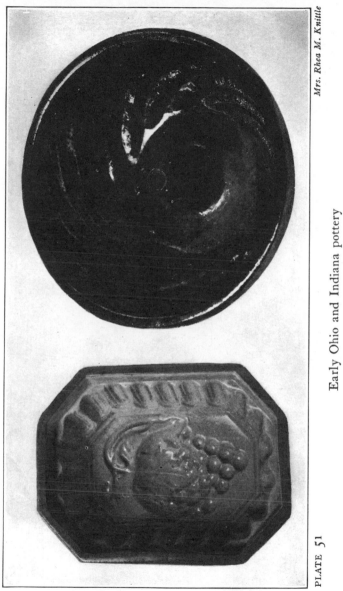

Early Ohio and Indiana pottery

PLATE 51

that the writer has never been able to find one so marked. Other collectors may be more fortunate. In any case, attention is called to the matter so that the collector who finds an impressed mark of the period may properly esteem its rarity.

It was during the period under discussion, while the pottery was operated by the American Pottery Manufacturing Company, that transfer printing in the English manner was introduced here. It is believed to have been the first use of this method of decoration in the country, and that fact alone would make the pottery of great interest to American collectors. If we knew for certain what the first transfer print was, and upon what object it was used, there can be no doubt that good marked examples would be highly regarded on account of the historical interest attached to them. The writer believes that the first use of transfer-printed designs was in the early part of 1839, and that the first subject was the Casanova pattern which was pirated from a well known dinner-service made by John Ridgway, the noted Staffordshire potter.

If this belief is correct, then the Casanova dinner-plates, marked with the elliptical pictorial design printed under the glaze, holds a peculiar historical interest. Of course the design may have been used during several years, so that, in the absence of any sort of serial mark, the owner of one of these plates cannot be sure that he has one of the early issues. The collector is entitled to know upon what grounds the writer's belief with regard to this interesting matter rests. Some twenty years ago, an old potter at Trenton, New Jersey, in the course of a long reminiscent talk about his early experiences, told the writer a story, the details of which he does not remember, but which involved a designer employed at the Jersey City pottery using one of Ridgway's patterns as his own design. There was some remonstrance by the English manufacturer; or perhaps it was Henderson who discovered it and was angry at the deception; the writer does not remember. In any case, according to the story, the designer was discharged, and his place was taken by Daniel Greatbach. The design was destroyed and a new trade-mark was decided upon, this being drawn by Henderson himself. As the story is vaguely remembered, the old potter did not profess to have been himself witness to any part of the incident, but was rather telling over a story current among the older men in his younger days.

Later Nineteenth Century

During the presidential campaign of 1840, cream-colored pitchers and mugs bearing the portrait of Harrison in black transfer print under the glaze were made and widely distributed. The writer has seen a large mug of light cream-colored earthenware of good quality, with a likeness of Harrison on one side and an inscription on the other. It was un-marked, but because the portrait was identical with one that appears on a marked pitcher, and the ware likewise seems to be identical, there is probably sufficient reason to believe that the mug was made at the Jersey City pottery. An octagonal pitcher of light cream-colored earthenware has on four of its panels a portrait of Harrison with his name under-neath, above the portrait a log cabin with the legend "The Ohio Farmer," and beneath the portrait an American eagle. The whole design is transfer-printed in black beneath the glaze, while on the bottom the flag pottery mark is printed in black underneath the glaze.

Daniel Greatbach, of all designers and modelers best known to collectors of American pottery and china, joined the staff of the Jersey City pottery in 1839, soon after his arrival from Staffordshire. Al-though he is so famous among collectors for his work here, it is a curious fact that the best of that work is little known, his fame resting upon two or three models which are not at all distinctive. One of these is the toby-mug shown on Plate No. 46; the other is the famous hound-handled pitcher, shown on Plate No. 20, which was an adaptation of a much better English model, and which Greatbach himself subsequently improved.

In 1840 the company was reorganized and its name changed by dropping the word "manufacturing." Marks used from 1840 to 1850 reflect the change of name, which is given in full, except that in some cases the word "pottery" is abbreviated to "Pott^y." At the exhibition of the Franklin Institute in 1842 the company displayed an extensive exhibit which was awarded the silver medal. The best designs exhibited at that time are supposed to have been the work of Greatbach. One of the most effective and attractive designs was used in relief on a tea-set made in a white ware closely resembling queen's-ware. Virtually the same design was later on used at Bennington, presumably introduced by Greatbach when he went there as modeler for the United States Pottery. The American Pottery Company mark is found on this tea-set and on much

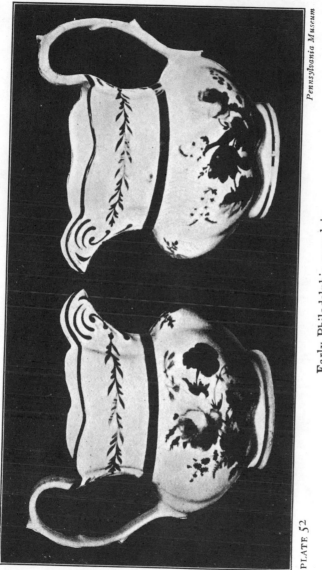

Early Philadelphia porcelain

PLATE 52

other ware of the same type, as well as on Rocking-ham and other wares.

In 1845 the business passed into new hands. The name "Jersey City Pottery Company" was adopted at this time, the members of the company being Messrs. Rhodes, Strong, and McGerron. They dropped all lines of manufacture except common white earthenware, which they continued making until 1854, when the firm sold out and dissolved, Rhodes going to Vermont. The concern was purchased by a company consisting of Messrs. Rouse, Turner, Duncan, and Henry. After a little while the last two withdrew, and the firm was reorganized once more under the title "Rouse & Turner." Although the reorganized firm made ware of a very high quality, it is of little interest to collectors, except as it derives interest from some fact other than its manufacture. The reason for this is that it was never marked, and was made for the trade, to be decorated and sold. Its only identity, therefore, was derived from its decorators, not from its makers.

In short, little or nothing that was made in the Jersey City pottery after 1845 possesses any interest for the collector. There is, however, one fact which it may be worth while to record here, since it concerns one of those curious things which arise unexpectedly to trouble the soul of the collector. On the white ware which Rouse & Turner made for decorators, they placed a mark which, whether so intended or not, would naturally be taken for the mark of a British firm. The British coat of arms with the lion and unicorn was used, and underneath it the letters "R. & T.," the initials of the firm, were placed. If the collector finds a finely decorated vase with this British mark and the letters "R. & T.," he can be sure that his British vase is really American. A good many other American potteries have used British marks in much the same fashion.

During the period which marked the decline of the industry at Jersey City from the high standards it attained under Henderson's direction, great progress was being made and an important chapter was being added to the history of American ceramics at Bennington, Vermont, under the leadership of Julius Norton and Christopher Webber Fenton. Much of the story of the association of these two men, and of their separation to pursue their individual courses, is told in the account of Bennington's contribution to the development of American porcelain, and need not here be repeated. Julius Norton, gifted grandson of Vermont's first potter, Captain John Norton, after a period of partnership with his father, Judge Luman Norton, assumed full control of the business in 1841. Like his father and grandfather, he was a good stoneware potter, a craftsman who took pride in his work. The staple produce of the pottery was the ordinary gray stoneware, salt glazed, made into crocks, churns, cider-jugs, and the like. The pottery was noted for the fine quality of the ware it made, and it catered to a market that extended over a considerable area. When Julius Norton became sole proprietor he at once began to branch out into other directions, making Rockingham ware—or dark luster as it was called—and yellow ware. An interesting example of his own workmanship is the inkstand illustrated in Plate No. 32, which is in the collection of Bennington pottery presented to the Bennington Historical Museum by the present writer, to whom it was given by Mrs. Edward Norton.

Christopher Webber Fenton was at this time in the employ of Julius Norton, whose sister he had married. While in no sense the equal of Norton as a craftsman, Fenton possessed in large measure the gift of creative imagination. No specimens of his personal craftsmanship remain; no story survives of any work of his hands commanding the admiration of his fellow-craftsmen. Yet he was destined to achieve greater fame than his more highly skilled brother-in-law. What Julius Norton would have done had he continued in business alone instead of entering into partnership with Fenton, is a subject on which old Bennington potters used to speculate in their reminiscent moods. Before the partnership he had entered upon other branches of the pottery business, and it may well be that he intended to embrace virtually the entire range of wares later produced by the concerns of which Fenton was the head. The fact that he had in his employ, along with Fenton, the man who inspired Fenton in his career, Decius W. Clark, makes that seem probable.

In the second half of 1844 the two brothers-in-law entered into partnership, the firm-name being "Norton & Fenton," which was impressed into the ware. The partnership lasted until the end of June, 1847. During that period stoneware continued to be the main product, with Rockingham, common

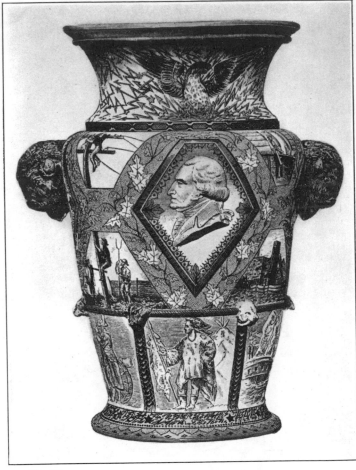

The Century Vase by Karl Müller

yellow, and common white steadily increasing in importance. Of the Rockingham ware made during this period the jug or pitcher illustrated in Plate No. 33 is a good example. It bears the mark of the firm, deeply impressed on the bottom. The modeling is good, but the Rockingham glaze is much inferior to what was later produced at Bennington. Partly because they could not agree upon the extent to which the firm should develop the manufacture of porcelain, and partly for other reasons, the two men dissolved partnership, Norton continuing the manufacture of stoneware, and Fenton starting on his own account along new lines.

From that time onward, to 1894, the Norton pottery was devoted exclusively—except for one brief period of no consequence—to the production of stoneware. Elsewhere in this volume the collector will find a chronological list of all the marks used by the Nortons from the foundation of the business in 1793 to its termination in 1894. It is not necessary to devote further attention to this phase of the pottery industry in Bennington. It is enough to say that in the opinion of the writer of these pages the stoneware produced by the several generations of descendants of Captain John Norton, within the limits of that class of ware, has never been excelled in this country.

Christopher Webber Fenton's work in the development of the several types of porcelain has been sufficiently described and discussed in a preceding chapter. Our present concern is with the work he did in the various earthenware types. He brought to Bennington the best workmen then to be found in this country. Reference has already been made to the work of Daniel Greatbach as a designer and modeler at Jersey City. He was one of the men whom Fenton brought to Bennington, and his work there was the best that he ever did, at least in this country.

Daniel Greatbach has been the subject of a great deal of silly and uncritical eulogy. He has been written about in terms which would be almost extravagant if applied to the creators of the great masterpieces of Wedgwood, Copeland, and others; to such a man as Flaxman, for example. If one were to judge from much of the writing about him, Daniel Greatbach would deserve to be ranked as one of the greatest modelers of all time. Nothing could well be more absurd. The present writer counts

himself among the enthusiastic admirers of Greatbach, but he would temper his enthusiasm with discrimination. The simple truth is that Daniel Greatbach was a good modeler, who had a knack of pleasing the fancy of simple people with no very elevated
standards or anything like cultivated taste. Facile
to a degree, but almost wholly lacking in origin-
ality, he adapted English designs—some of the best
of these by his grandfather, by the way—to American taste and American needs.

A pitcher which he designed, and which was executed in white porcelain, both directly glazed and
smear-glazed, is shown (as Fig. 1) on Plate No. 40.
The design, which is a good one, he had already
used at Jersey City on a tea-set. It is well executed,
but it can hardly be said to be original. Greatbach
also modeled the famous hound-handle pitcher, one
of the most widely known of all the pitchers made
at Bennington, and one of the best of its type. It
was made in Rockingham, and not in any other
ware so far as the writer knows, though there per-
sists in and around Bennington the legend of a white
pitcher of this type and of one vaguely described
as slate color. Persistent search over a period of
nearly fifteen years has failed to unearth either of

these, or any definite and trustworthy evidence of their existence.

On the other hand, the writer knows of one hound-handle pitcher, slate-gray in color, carefully preserved and treasured in a Bennington home, as a product of the United States Pottery, which was undoubtedly made in England and is well known to students and collectors. It is most probable that the legend referred to had its origin in the fact that English pitchers were confounded with those made in the local pottery. This raises a subject of great interest and importance to collectors, and we may as well dispose of it at this point. The lady who owns the slate-gray hound-handle pitcher in Bennington is certain that it was "brought from the pottery" by one of the workmen. She can give the most precise details. No one who knows her high character will for a moment doubt her veracity or her good faith. What, then, is the explanation? Why, simply this. In any large pottery catering to a market outside of its locality, and employing salesmen to sell its goods to dealers, samples of the wares put forth by other manufacturers in the same line were systematically acquired, for reasons easy to understand.

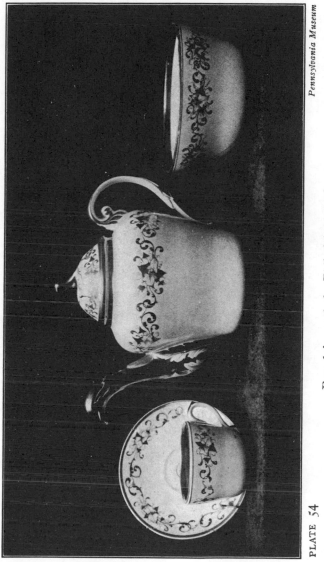

Porcelain made in Philadelphia, 1853

PLATE 54

Later Nineteenth Century

An enterprising salesman would find that pitchers of a certain type or pattern sold particularly well in Boston, let us say. Dealers would tell him that their customers preferred that type or pattern to those made by his own firm. He would secure one of the preferred kind and take it back to show his employers. That was one way, perhaps the most important way, in which wares made elsewhere would enter the pottery. At times scores of these "outsiders" would be reposing on the shelves in the office or in the modeling-room. Moreover a modeler like Greatbach would purchase or otherwise acquire specimens which he could study to "get ideas." From time to time these examples of the work of other potteries, having served their purpose and being of no further use, were taken away. Members of the firm took home such pieces as they fancied; others employees were permitted to take. Sometimes, too, such pieces were placed on counters among the seconds, and blemished and imperfect products of the pottery, offered for sale at low prices. The writer knows positively that these practices obtained at Bennington, as they did in other places, and in these various ways local families came into the possession of pieces which they knew came from the pottery, but which he is quite certain were made elsewhere.

In our desire to make clear one of the least understood phases of the game of collecting, we have digressed far from Daniel Greatbach and his work, and must retrace our steps. Greatbach modeled the several mugs and bottles of the toby type made at the United States Pottery, generally in Rockingham but also in flint enamel and in white. He modeled most of the animal pieces, including the cow creamer (an adaptation of an almost universal type), the lion with fore paw resting on a ball (a close copy of one made by Whieldon), and the deer. The deer the present writer regards as by far the best of all Greatbach's known work. It is not believed that he modeled the famous dog carrying a basket of fruit. This, it appears, was originally modeled by John Harrison, but Greatbach is said to have altered it slightly.

Among the other workmen of exceptional skill brought to Bennington by Fenton, Captain Enoch Wood deserves more than passing mention. He was a mold-maker. A descendant of a long line of potters, he personified the best traditions of the craft. One of his uncles was John Wood, long identified with the Copelands and one of the best china-painters of his day. Another uncle was Thomas Wood, of the well-known pottery firm of Wood & Challinor, of Tunstall. He belonged to the same family as the more famous Enoch Wood, so often called the "father of English pottery," the designer of the borders on the most prized of the blue transfer-printed plates with American historical scenes. Wood served in the Civil War and became a captain. After the war he superintended the Hall pottery at Perth Amboy, making a great amount of scroddle ware. Most of the surviving specimens of this ware have been attributed to Bennington, by the way.

Stephen Theiss, a Belgian, was the chief designer and modeler before Greatbach came to Bennington. He is said to have been completely master of every department of the trade. He could make molds, cast Parian ware, "throw" or "turn," or mix glazes. At a later time he was foreman of the Jefford pottery in Philadelphia. William Leake, a Staffordshire potter of great ability, was another of the remarkable group of men Fenton gathered under his employ at Bennington. Leake was a presser by trade, but there were few branches of the industry which he did not master. He could and did do excellent modeling, as examples of his work in the writer's possession prove. Some of the experiments in glazing which he later conducted at Elizabeth, New Jersey, are equal to the very best of the flint enamel ware made at Bennington, and greatly superior to most of it.

To give even a brief description of all the varieties of ware made at Bennington under Fenton's direction would far exceed the limits available in this book. We must perforce restrict our attention to the three distinctive types of pottery in which collectors are interested; namely, the Rockingham, flint enamel, and scroddle wares. They are here listed in the order of their relative importance, judged quantitatively. More Rockingham ware was made than either of the other two. Scroddle ware was produced extensively, but during a much shorter period of time than the others, and the total amount was less than either of the others. That is why good specimens of this ware are relatively scarce and hard to find.

The Rockingham ware made at Bennington ranks high in quality. Hundreds of American potteries turned out ware of this type, but only a few equalled

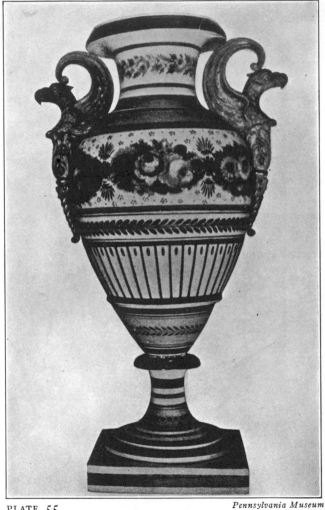

PLATE 55

Porcelain vase made at Philadelphia, 1835

the quality of that which was produced at Bennington, while none excelled it. Of course this judgment applies to the best products of the potteries concerned. To make the statement more precise and less open to possible misunderstanding, let us say that the best Rockingham that was made at Bennington in the Fenton concerns was not surpassed by the best made at any other American potteries, and was equaled only by that of a few. The criteria of judgment are fineness of body texture, good modeling, excellence of potting, brilliance of glaze, and freedom from crazing and other defects.

As in all other potteries of the period engaged in that line of production, a great deal of Rockingham of a low grade was made at Bennington. Common pie-plates, baking-dishes, soap-trays, and similar objects for use in the kitchen were made as cheaply as possible. Thousands of these objects survive in New England, and many of them are still in use. They are of no possible interest to the intelligent collector, and it is amusing to find them in the antique-shops, offered to collectors as desirable examples of Bennington pottery. Absolutely undistinguishable from the mass of objects of the same kind produced in scores of other places they derive the only value they possess from the ignorance of the purchaser. Such rubbish—for it is no less—belongs in the junk-pile, not in the collector's cabinet. To see an ugly soap-dish of this character, lacking grace or beauty of form or coloring, displayed in the best room in the house as a thing to be proud of, is to realize the gullibility of human beings and their capacity for self-delusion. Yet the present writer has seen just such a piece of this ugly nondescript stuff displayed on the mantel of a beautiful and finely furnished room. A fire-brick would be quite as decorative.

A world of difference separates the trashy stuff which we are discussing from the finer Rockingham ware. Whether the former was made at Bennington or at Mudville is of no importance and is not worth determining. It is rubbish in any case. It is quite another matter, however, when we come to the finer Rockingham. The collector who acquires a really good specimen naturally wants to be able to identify it. If no other reason existed for knowing where and when it was made, the added pleasure in the piece to be derived from such knowledge would make the matter of identification and attribution important.

Later Nineteenth Century

Roughly speaking, an examination of a large and representative collection of Bennington pottery will show that about thirty per cent of the Rockingham pieces are marked, the remaining seventy per cent being unmarked. Some articles largely made in Rockingham were never marked at all, so far as is known. Among these may be mentioned tubular candlesticks, curtain-knobs, picture-frames, tulip-vases, goblets, cow creamers, and hound-handle pitchers. Then there are a great many articles which are sometimes marked but as often not. This applies to the toby-mugs, to many pitchers, tea-pots, covered jars, and other things. If we consider only the individual articles rather than the bulk, it is probably as fair an estimate as can be made that about one-half of the articles made in Rockingham ware at Bennington were at least sometimes marked, the other half never being marked at all so far as is known.

This makes the task of the collector rather difficult. How can the wares that are unmarked be identified with any certainty? To that question no wholly satisfactory reply can be made. There are certain things which can be fairly confidently identified by pattern or design alone. For example, the

Bennington hound-handle pitcher can be readily identified, despite the fact that there are a great many variants. The same thing is true of the toby-mugs. In the case of the hound-handle pitcher with the hunting-scene on the sides, the collector can rely upon the concurrence of three things in the modeling. He will find each of these features separately on pitchers made elsewhere, *but all three together only on the Bennington pattern*. These features are: (1) the hound's head is raised well above the fore paws, so that the little finger can be inserted under the chin above the paws; (2) the dog's collar is a chain with well defined links and not a flat band; (3) the under part of the dog's body is not flattened as in some cases, nor well rounded as in most, but comes down to an angle. In the case of the toby-mugs these are sometimes marked, and the collector will do best to examine a marked specimen so as to memorize its points. A nearly flat bottom, not concaved, and a grape-vine decorating the handle, are features to remember.

So much for positive aids. There are people who say, and no doubt sincerely believe, that they can identify the Rockingham made at Bennington and distinguish it from all others. That claim is by

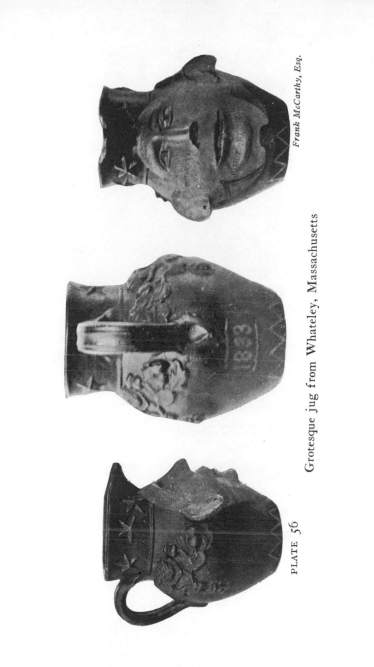

Grotesque jug from Whateley, Massachusetts

PLATE 56

itself an evidence of the little learning that is proverbially dangerous. Ask the person making the claim how he can tell, and nine times out of ten he will reply that he can tell by the fine quality of the glaze, its brilliance and fine color. In a nutshell, what he knows, and all that he knows, is the difference between the finest Rockingham glaze and the common sorts. But when you place side by side specimens of the best Rockingham ware made at Bennington, Baltimore, Zanesville, and East Liverpool, respectively, it will be found that there is no such difference. The present writer believes that he is as familiar with Bennington pottery as any man living, but he cheerfully admits that it is not at all unusual for him to have to admit that he is unable to decide whether a particular piece was made at Bennington or elsewhere. Familiarity with marked and well authenticated specimens of Bennington pottery will help the collector and perhaps endow him with expert knowledge, but it will not make him infallible in judgment.

The flint enamel ware made at Bennington was marked to about the same extent as the Rockingham. That is to say, about fifty per cent of the articles made in this ware are never marked, the remainder being marked at least sometimes. Some of the finest articles made in flint enamel never were marked at all. When the ware is marked, the mark used is the impressed elliptical stamp bearing the name "Lyman Fenton & Co., Bennington, Vt.," around the outer edge inclosing the words "Fenton's Enamel Patented 1849."

The collector should take notice of a very common misuse of this stamp. It does not follow from the fact that this mark is used on a piece of ware that it is flint enamel. It may be Rockingham, for a large percentage of pieces so marked are Rockingham, not flint enamel at all. The writer has never encountered, or evolved for himself, an explanation of this fact that seemed wholly satisfactory. It was probably due rather to a loose and slipshod method than to anything more subtle. All that is important is that the collector recognize the fact that the flint enamel patent mark is quite commonly found on Rockingham, and also that the stamp does not date the piece. As late as 1858 almost six years after Lyman ceased to be connected with the business the stamp was in use.

The use of the flint enamel stamp on Rockingham wares has tended to much confusion among collectors. As a result there has been evolved a most misleading theory concerning the two types; namely, that flint enamel is a name which Fenton devised and applied to a superior grade of Rockingham, the glaze of which was made more brilliant and rich by the use of powdered flint. The worst of a theory like that is that it makes confusion more confounded. Fenton did not invent the use of flint enamel, nor was he the first to use the name. Neither is it correct to say that flint enamel ware is simply a superior grade of Rockingham. The distinctive feature of flint enamel ware is the use of colors other than the shades of brown used in Rockingham, in a glaze which, like the Rockingham glaze, has sufficient opacity to hide the color of the body. Opacity and color are the features of flint enamel. Now if a pitcher or vase is mottled brown, after the manner of tortoise-shell, it is Rockingham, even though it may have the 1849 stamp with the words "Flint Enamel" legibly stamped upon it. On the other hand, if there are streaks of blue, green, and orange, either or all of them, it is flint enamel, even though it is not so marked.

Some of the finest flint enamel ware ever made in America was made by the Bennett brothers of

Baltimore, contemporaneously with the best period of the Bennington enterprise. Flint enamel ware of good quality was also made at Fairfax, Vermont, by S. H. Farrar. There were other potteries at which ware of this type was produced, but in none was it manufactured on such a large scale as at Bennington. Moreover while the Bennett brothers produced at their Baltimore pottery individual pieces equal to the best Bennington product, and the average level of the quality attained by them in a limited output was high, the Bennington pottery maintained its standard of excellence with the largest production reached by any pottery of the time.

The collector who will take the pains to inform himself intelligently can soon learn how to distinguish with a large measure of confidence, the Bennington flint enamel ware from other ware of the same general type. He will not be able to do this with absolute certainty in all cases, but he will not need to make many mistakes. Let him take a really good marked specimen of the Bennington ware, making sure that it is not simply Rockingham—a more or less mottled brown glaze—with the 1849 mark, but really flint enamel, with some of the other colors, blue, green, yellow, or orange. He will see

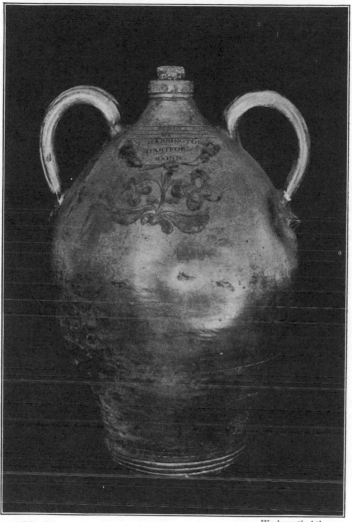

PLATE 57

Wadsworth Atheneum

Stoneware jar

on close examination that the colors are infused in the glaze, not applied underneath and then glazed over. He will be able to discern readily enough that the colors have run down, and by following the course the colors have run he will find the marks of the little stilts on which the piece rested in the kiln in which it was fired after glazing. Now these definite characteristics are the logical results of the process Fenton patented. He did not patent flint enamel, but only *a process of applying color*. That process consisted of sprinkling, from an ordinary pepper-box, powdered metallic oxides on the glaze. These oxides melted with heat and mingled with the glaze, producing the characteristics already described. No ware ever made, in the judgment of the present writer, is easier to identify in the absence of the pottery mark.

Scroddle ware, as such, is easy to classify. On the other hand, unmarked pieces in this ware are virtually unidentifiable, even by the most expert connoisseur. This creates a difficult problem for the collector, the more difficult because there exists a widespread belief that ware of this type was made only at Bennington, whereas in fact it was made at a goodly number of American potteries in the period

1845 to 1875. There are some things which can be set down for the collector's guidance, however. In the first place, then, this ware is known also as agate ware and lava ware. The three names are synonyms for the same thing. In the second place, it is frequently confused with marbled ware, though the latter is quite different and belongs to another category altogether.

"Marbling" is a method of surface decoration. It resembles the work that is done by house-painters and called by the same name, painting wood to imitate varicolored marble. Upon the surface of the ware, before glazing, generally on a thin coating of slip, such colors as amber and sienna are so worked in with sponge or rag as to create a superficial resemblance to marble. This process differs radically from "combing," which is often confounded with it by amateurs. Combing is a method of decoration similar to that used in graining varnished woodwork in houses. The ware is covered with a thin engobe of slip, either light slip on a dark body or in some cases dark slip on a light body. With steel "combs" such as grainers use in their trade, the surface slip, before firing, is combed to produce waving lines to the desired effect. It is a process related to, but different from, the form of scratching called sgraffito.

The ware which is variously, and quite properly called "scoddle," "lava," and "agate" has a laminated body. Clays of different color are first rolled out much as a cook rolls out the pastry for her pies. Then the rolled-out batches are laid layer upon layer, the different colors alternating, and the whole is then beaten into a solid mass. This is doubled up, or rolled, according to the taste or fancy of the potter. Through the mass a fine steel wire is drawn, cutting the laminated mass into slices, which can best be likened in their appearance to slices of old-fashioned marble-cake. Obviously two pieces exactly alike will almost never be found.

Some of the scroddled ware made at Bennington bears the impressed stamp of the United States Pottery Company, by which it can be identified. Much of it, however, is unmarked. American collectors have generally assumed that no other pottery in the country turned out this ware and that therefore identification was extremely easy. As a matter of fact, a number of other potteries made ware of this type in large quantities and in the same patterns that the Bennington pottery used. Plate No. 44

shows three pieces of this ware made at the United States Pottery, and it will be seen how great is the variation in appearance of authentic specimens. Plate No. 45 shows four other specimens. The tea-pot was made by Bennett Brothers of Baltimore and bears their mark. The bowl was made at Bennington and is marked. The tall pitcher was made at Bennington and is marked. The vase is unmarked. Although it has been in the author's possession for years, and was acquired as Bennington pottery, with a Bennington pedigree, he is not convinced that it was made at Bennington, or even in America. It bears a striking resemblance to the scroddle panels in the base of the monumental piece that has so long stood on the piazza of Fenton's old residence here, and the story is that the vase was made from the same batch of clay. The author does not know. Nobody does know. There is no way of identifying unmarked scroddle ware except as the history of a piece can be definitely traced.

When the United States Pottery closed in May, 1858, the finest body of craftsmen that had been gathered together in any American pottery up to that time was dispersed. They went to Peoria, Illinois, to East Liverpool, Ohio, to Kaolin, South

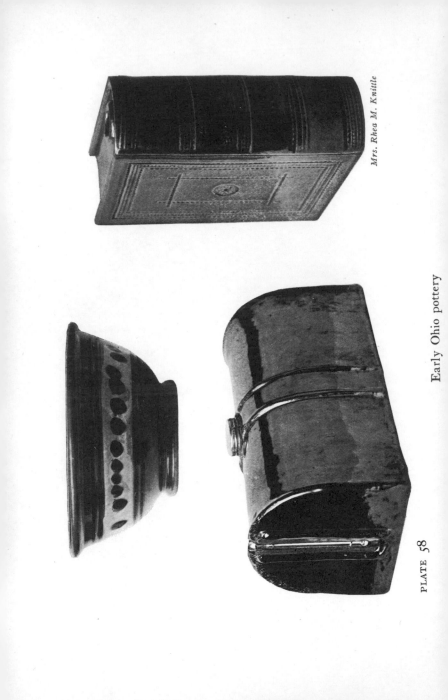

Mrs. Rhea M. Knittle

Early Ohio pottery

PLATE 58

Carolina, to Trenton, New Jersey, and to other places near and far. One interesting result of the dispersion of the craftsmen is the fact that in tracing the history of American potteries during the next thirty years or so one finds everywhere traces of men who worked at Bennington, and strongly marked influences of the work done at the United States Pottery under Fenton's leadership.

When one understands the circumstances, it is not surprising to find so many pieces which were undoubtedly made at East Liverpool marked by their great similarity to pieces made at Bennington. Any attempt to give a detailed history of the potteries that were established in East Liverpool and other Ohio centers from 1850 to 1876 would require a volume of considerable size. In the present work it is possible only to call attention to certain selected potteries as examples of the remarkable progress that was made in Ohio during the period indicated.

When James Bennett, East Liverpool's pioneer potter, with a small capital furnished by Anthony Kearns and Benjamin Harker, erected the first pottery in that section of Ohio, in 1840, he probably had not the faintest idea that he was the pioneer of one of the greatest industrial developments in our history. Situated some forty-eight miles west of Pittsburgh and one hundred miles east of Cleveland, East Liverpool was first settled by white men in 1799. At first called St. Clair, and then Fawcettstown, in honor of its first settler, the name "East Liverpool" was adopted in 1830 when the first post-office was established. It is believed that soon after 1820 a number of small potteries were established in this neighborhood, but nothing definite is known concerning them. Although barely a century has passed, they are the subject of legend rather than of historical record.

James Bennett was an experienced and skilled English potter, one of the best craftsmen in his line that this country has known. It is said that he arrived in America in 1834, finding employment at once under David Henderson at Jersey City. He remained there for about three years, going in 1837 to Troy, Indiana, to work in the pottery established there by James Clews. Forced to leave Troy on account of the malaria prevalent there, he went first to Cincinnati. Thence he walked all the way to East Liverpool in quest of employment. Finding the clay in the locality to be of good quality, he persuaded Kearns and Harker to finance a small pottery, and succeeded in getting two good men, George Thomas and George Hallingsworth, to join him. The first kiln of ware was burned in 1840 and consisted of mugs, jugs, pans, and other domestic utensils of earthenware of fairly good quality.

This ware was sold in the region at a good profit. Isaac W. Knowles bought two large crates of the ware, which he took down the river on a trading-boat, selling it at various settlements. At the same time, Bennett himself peddled ware from a wagon. The profit from the first kiln reached the respectable sum of two hundred and fifty dollars. Greatly encouraged by his initial success, Bennett decided to bring his three brothers, Daniel, Edwin, and William, from England to help him. They arrived in 1841, bringing with them John Tunnicliffe, a potter. The manufacture of common yellow was started at this time. This was maintained until 1845.

The success of the Bennett pottery did more than gratify the energetic promoter. It gave rise to the most active competition. Benjamin Harker, who had helped finance the first pottery and had been paid off, decided to build a plant on his own land, which held a considerable clay-bed. His plant was built and began operations in 1841. No sooner was it under way than a rival pottery was started by James Salt, Joseph Ogden, John Hancock, and Frederic Mear. This pottery, generally referred to as the Salt & Mear works, was started in 1842. In 1844 John Goodwin, an English potter, who had worked at the Bennett plant for about two years, set up in business for himself, making common yellow and Rockingham. Finding the competition growing keen, and having a chance to sell on favorable terms, the Bennetts withdrew and moved away, as has already been mentioned. In a long historical review of the East Liverpool potteries published in December, 1924, in the fiftieth anniversary number of the "Crockery and Glass Journal," the writer stated that "up to 1873 nothing but yellow ware had been produced in the East Liverpool potteries." The context shows, however, that in that term the author of the statement includes Rockingham ware. Certainly James Bennett always asserted that he had from the first made Rockingham ware at East Liverpool, and that he was the first in the United States to make it. That assertion should be accepted only with some re-

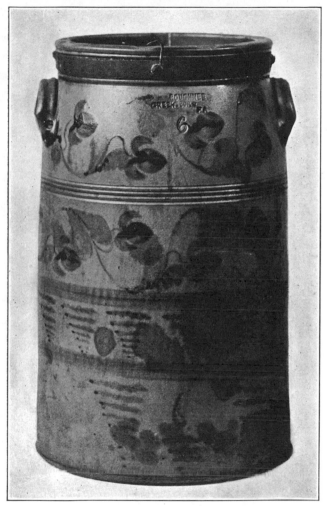

PLATE 59

Slip-decorated churn

serve, however. The present writer believes that at the Norton pottery, Bennington, Vermont, Rockingham was already being made at the time when the Bennett pottery produced its first ware. There were probably earlier makers of Rockingham than either Julius Norton or James Bennett.

In 1844, when the Bennett brothers sold out, the purchasers were four brothers, Samuel, Jesse, Thomas, and John Croxall, who were quite successful. In 1847 William Brunt started a small one-kiln plant, and in 1848 Jabez Vodrey and a man named Woodward started another small pottery under the firm-name of Woodward & Vodrey. After it had been in operation rather less than a year this pottery burned out, and Woodward and his partner, Vodrey, then took three new partners, John S. Blakely, James Blakely, and Richard Booth. The firm took a new title, Woodward, Blakely & Company, and the works were rebuilt during the summer and autumn of 1849.

It was in 1847, at about the same time when William Brunt was starting his plant, that George S. Harker, son and successor of Benjamin Harker, entered into partnership with James Taylor. This firm made one of the best of the hound-handle

pitchers, a Greatbach model, modified, it is believed, by a modeler working at East Liverpool.
Since Harker, Taylor & Company remained in business only until 1850 or 1851, all the pitchers of this
type bearing the pottery mark of the firm can be
dated 1847-51. It will be well for the collector to
compare this pitcher, illustrated on Plate No. 20
with the other hound-handle pitchers grouped on the
same plate.

In the year 1845 Isaac W. Knowles, the man
who had peddled through the river settlements part
of the first kiln of ware made by James Bennett, at
East Liverpool, joined Isaac A. Harvey in business.
They erected a small one-kiln plant and began to
make yellow ware. In 1870 Knowles, who had
bought out Harvey some time before, reorganized
the business, taking as his new partners John N.
Taylor and Homer S. Knowles. The firm name
was Knowles, Taylor & Knowles. This company
branched out after a year or two into the manufacture of white ware. Up to 1872 they made only
common yellow and Rockingham, as did all the
other firms in East Liverpool, large and small. But
in September, 1872, they began to make common
white, and in 1873 they reorganized the plant so

as to concentrate upon the white ware. That was the beginning of the manufacture of the white ware variously called ironstone china, stone china, and white granite. The firm operated three kilns at the time, but it soon began to grow, and its success was both quick and continuous.

No great gain to the collector is likely to result from continuing the narrative of the amazing growth of the pottery industry in East Liverpool. The record of the early firms has been included because it is in the products of the period from 1840 to 1875 that the collector is likely to be interested. The sketch here given, supplemented by the names and dates contained in the subjoined chronological list, will guide the collector past many pitfalls, and aid in many an attribution. To-day East Liverpool is one of the great pottery centers of the world; there is perhaps not another area of the same size which can boast of such an output.

No account of the potters and potteries of the United States in the period under discussion would be satisfactory to the collector if it omitted those of Trenton, New Jersey. For while it is true the chief contribution of the Trenton potteries has been to the development of the manufacture of porcelain, which we have sketched in another chapter, specimens of the Rockingham and other types of earthenware produced by the early potteries there are already sought after and prized by collectors. We may be sure that in the future they will be even more eagerly sought and treasured.

In dealing with the Trenton potteries we are again rather forcibly reminded of the fact that our use of the term "early American" is a special one, peculiar to our hobby. The first pottery in Trenton was established in 1852, a date within the memory of men still living! European collectors and writers on the subject can hardly comprehend our point of view.

The first pottery in Trenton was established, in 1852, by James Taylor and Henry Speeler, both previously in business at East Liverpool, Ohio. They made wares of the same types as those made by them in Ohio, namely, yellow and Rockingham. It is said that they made, among other things, a hound-handle pitcher and a cow creamer, the latter in both Rockingham and common yellow. The writer has never seen, or even heard of, any pieces bearing the mark of this pioneer pottery. He has heard old potters tell with great glee of a lottery in

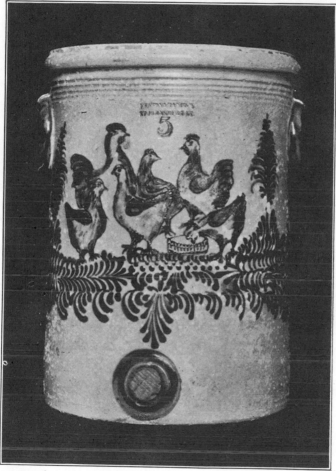

PLATE 60

Decorated stoneware water-cooler

which the prize was a Jersey cow. The winner, having first liberally treated his fellow-workmen and friends, was taken into a barn to inspect his prize and take it home. It proved to be a cow creamer, tied to a stanchion with a large rope. It is possible that a peculiar type of cow creamer which is found in that part of New Jersey, and which collectors have never been able to attribute to any pottery, may yet be found to have been made at this pioneer Trenton pottery.

In 1853 Richard Millington and John Astbury opened a small pottery on Carroll Street. They, too, began with common yellow and Rockingham, but after two or three years they began to make white ware. So far as is known, the firm used no trade-mark on its wares until 1859, so that the early pieces in Rockingham and yellow are not identifiable. In 1859 the firm was enlarged by the admission of a new partner, Mr. Poulson, said to have been a member of the famous Staffordshire family of that name, so closely associated with the history of the Mintons. The firm name became Millington, Astbury & Poulson, and an impressed stamp bearing the initials M.A.P. in an ellipse was used on the wares the firm made, or at least on some of them. One of the most notable examples of their work, made in 1861, soon after the outbreak of the Civil War, is the pitcher with the relief design showing the shooting of Colonel Ellsworth at Alexandria, Virginia.

This pitcher, which is much sought after by collectors, is generally found in white earthenware, but specimens are occasionally met with which are brilliantly colored. From time to time unmarked examples are found, and these have been attributed to a number of different potteries, including the United States Pottery at Bennington. So far as the present writer knows, there is no evidence that pitchers of this model were made by any other firm than Millington, Astbury & Poulson, and all other attributions are mere guesswork. At the same time, it is definitely established that the pitcher was modeled by Josiah Jones, of the Cartlidge works at Greenpoint, New York, and it is quite possible that some or all of the unmarked examples were made there and not at Trenton.

In 1852, the year in which Taylor & Speeler started their little pottery, Charles Hattersly built a small pottery which he operated only a few months, leasing it to William Young & Sons in

1853. They made Rockingham and common yellow at first, but soon included white ware in their output. It is said that as early as the end of 1854 or the beginning of 1855 they were making cream-colored earthenware. The writer has seen a number of well potted pitchers in this ware, of excellent design, which the owners, upon what appeared to be ample evidence, believed to have been made by Young & Sons as early as 1855. They are also believed at this time to have experimented in a small way with porcelain, a small pitcher with the design of the babes in the wood in relief having been made not later than 1855. William Young always asserted that the firm was the first to make cream-colored earthenware and the first to make porcelain in Trenton, and if the dates given are even approximately correct the assertion is hardly to be questioned. At about the same time, 1855, Taylor & Speeler, the pioneer firm, added the manufacture of white granite to its output; and in 1859 Rhodes and Yates erected the first pottery built in Trenton for the exclusive manufacture of white granite and cream-colored ware.

In the case of all these potteries it may be said that only occasional pieces are of any particular interest to the collector. As a rule, in the early stages, before the adoption of a regular mark for its wares, each pottery produced mainly common utensils in the common types of earthenware. The great period of the Trenton potteries began with 1875, the preparations for the Centennial Exposition calling forth the best talent of virtually every firm. In the main, before that development, the interest of the collector is in the occasional pieces, especially the individual pieces made by workmen on their own initiative, as gifts to their friends or for their own pleasure. It is in connection with the identification of such pieces that the collector is helped by such lists of potters as are given in these pages.

The date limits somewhat arbitrarily chosen for this work embrace only the initial period of the interesting pottery at Phœnixville, Pennsylvania. Though it was established in 1867, it was not until the latter part of 1869, or early in 1870, after W. A. H. Schreiber and J. F. Betz had taken over the plant, that its products attained any merit claiming our notice. At that time, and for some eight years, Schreiber & Betz made the numerous terra-cotta wall-pieces and other ornaments so familiar to collectors. They made also good Rocking-

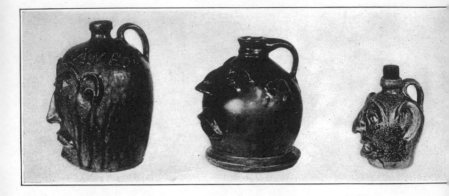

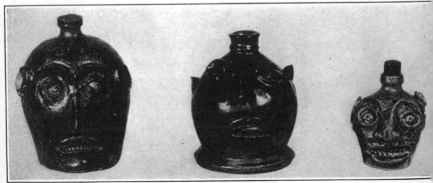

PLATE 61

Pottery grotesqueries

ham ware, including pitchers, candlesticks, picture-frames, book-flasks and dogs used for door-stops and fireplace ornaments. The stags' heads with antlers, horses' heads, eagles with spread wings, and the like which were made at this pottery before 1877 are rarely marked, but they are fairly well known to collectors. Mr. J. B. Kerfoot has a fine eagle in heavily glazed white earthenware made at this pottery. It is about sixteen inches high and is very heavy, weighing perhaps forty pounds. Whether it was made during the period when the pottery was operated by Schreiber & Betz, 1870-77, or after that time, there is no evidence to show, but the writer is of the opinion that it was made during the Schreiber-Betz régime.

From the standpoint of the collector there have been few potteries in this country of greater interest than that which Edwin Bennett established at Baltimore in 1846. Edwin Bennett was one of the brothers who had gone from East Liverpool, Ohio, to the vicinity of Pittsburgh, Pennsylvania, in 1844, as has already been mentioned. Leaving the firm of Bennett Brothers in 1846, Edwin Bennett erected a small pottery at Baltimore, Maryland, making several types of earthenware, including Rockingham of a high quality. He did not mark his wares at first, so far as the writer has discovered. In 1848 he was joined by William Bennett, one of the brothers with whom he had been associated at East Liverpool and at the Pittsburgh pottery. At this time the two brothers adopted a pottery mark consisting of the name and address of the firm, "E. & W. Bennett, Canton Avenue, Baltimore, Md." During eight years or so that mark was used on most of the wares of the firm, but after William Bennett withdrew in 1856 the initials E.B. were used as a mark. The two brothers were men of extraordinary energy and resourcefulness as well as potters of great ability. They made Rockingham of as fine quality as any that has ever been made in the United States, and, in addition, they produced splendid work in majolica, Parian, bone-china, flint enamel, and scroddle. Their chief modeler was Charles Coxon, who began his association with them early in 1850. His work is of great interest to collectors, not only by reason of its intrinsic merit, but also because of the fact that it contributes to the number and perplexity of the problems with which the collector of American pottery and china has to grapple.

He modeled the famous Rebekah at the well tea-pot, copying the design from a porcelain jug made by S. Alcock & Company, which had the figure of Rebekah in white relief on a blue ground. He modeled the wild boar pitcher, and the stag hunting pitcher with the rustic branch handle, which seems to have been made at South Amboy, New Jersey. This pitcher, shown on Plate No. 20, is believed also to have been made at Bennington, but the writer confesses that he has never been wholly satisfied with the evidence. Coxon also modeled for the Bennett brothers a pitcher with the figure of a stork standing. This was made both in Rockingham and in white ware. A pitcher with hound handle and game hanging down the sides, and another with a sort of dolphin handle and fish arranged around the sides, were also modeled by him, as was the so-called Daniel Boone pitcher.

As in the case of so many of the potteries of the period, the Bennett brothers appear to have marked only a part of their ware, and have been governed by no method that is now discernible. The writer has seen marked examples of each of the models referred to with the possible exception of the Daniel Boone pitcher. On the other hand, he has seen several times as many examples of each unmarked. Attribution is rendered more complicated by the fact that in some instances the same models are known to have been used by other concerns. So much of the Rockingham and scroddle, in particular, resembles Bennington wares of the same type that the collector will do well to be on his guard and to seek for marked specimens.

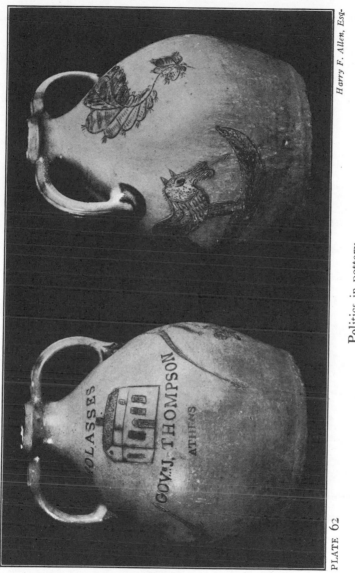

PLATE 62

Politics in pottery

Chronological List of American Potteries from 1850 to 1876

NOTE: This list is not offered as a complete one of all the potteries existing in America between 1850 and 1876. The writer believes that it is by far the most comprehensive list, and the most carefully compiled, that has ever been published. No more is claimed for it. In every case great pains have been taken to ascertain correctly such particulars as are given. In some cases, direct and positive evidence being unobtainable, the dates given have been arrived at by indirect methods, sometimes by inference from other known facts. The list can hardly fail to be of great assistance to collectors.

Date	Place	Name	Types of Ware
1851	Troy, Ind.	John Sanders & Samuel Wilson	Rockingham
1851 (*circa*)	Wilmington, Del.	Wm. Reiss	Earthenware
1851	Madison Co., Ill., (exact location not known)	George Morley & Bros.	Earthenware
1851	Akron, Ohio	Hill, Merrill & Co.	Stoneware
1852	Bergholtz, N. Y.	Charles A. Mehwialdt	Earthenware, slip-decorated, and sgraffito ware
1852	Middlebury, Ohio	Enoch Raleigh, Edwin and Herbert Baker, and Thomas Johnson	Rockingham and yellow

Date	Place	Name	Types of Ware
1852	Cincinnati, Ohio	Peter Lessel (and brother)	Rockingham and yellow ware
1852	North Fairfax, Vt.	A. S. Stearns	Stoneware
1852 (circa)	Cincinnati, Ohio	Farrar & Stearns Valentine Eichenlaub	Stoneware and common yellow
1852	Trenton, N. J.	Taylor & Speeler	Rockingham and common yellow
1852	So. Amboy, N. J.	James Carr	Yellow and Rockingham
1852	Kaolin, Mo.	E. H. Shepherd	Earthenware
1853	Trenton, N. J.	Wm. Young & Son	Rockingham, common white, common yellow
1853	Trenton, N. J.	Charles Hattersley	Earthenware
1853	East Liverpool, Ohio	Samuel & Wm. Baggott	Yellow and Rockingham
1855	Trenton, N. J.	Astbury & Millington	Sanitary ware
1853	So. Norwalk, Conn.	L. D. Wheeler	Rockingham door-knobs, etc.
1853	Philadelphia	Charles Kurbaum & John T. Schwartz	Porcelain
1853	New York City	Morrison & Carr	Majolica, stone china, white granite
1853	Burlington, Vt.	Nichols & Alford	Stoneware and Rockingham

[338]

Date	Place	Name	Types of Ware
1854	Cincinnati, Ohio	Brewer & Tempest	Rockingham and common yellow
1854	East Liverpool, Ohio	Isaac W. Knowles & Isaac A. Harvey	Yellow and Rockingham
1854	Gloucester, N. J.	American Porcelain Mfg. Co.	Soft-paste porcelain
1854	Boston, Mass.	Frederick Meagher	Rockingham and yellow
1856	Fairfax, Vt.	Lewis, Bostwick & Cady	Stoneware
1856	So. Norwalk, Conn.	Wood (Capt. Enoch) & Wheeler	Rockingham and other earthenware
1856	Cincinnati, Ohio	Skinner, Greatbach & Co.	Rockingham and yellow
1856	Cincinnati, Ohio	Tunis Brewer	Rockingham and yellow
1857	Trenton, N. J.	William Young & Sons	White ware
1857	Philadelphia	George Allen	Yellow, Rockingham, porcelain, Parian
1857	Akron, Ohio	Johnson, Whitman & Co.	Rockingham and yellow
1858	Fairfax, Vt.	Lewis & Cady	Stoneware
1858	Fairfax, Vt.	S. H. Farrar	Flint-enameled ware
1858	Worcester, Mass.	Frederick Hancock	Stoneware
1858	Philadelphia	Isaac Spiegel	Rockingham
1858	Kaolin, S. C.	Southern Porcelain Co.	Porcelain
1859	Cincinnati, Ohio	S. A. Brewer	Rockingham and yellow

Date	Place	Name	Types of Ware
1859 (circa)	Cincinnati, Ohio	Andrew Behn	Rockingham and yellow
1859	Cincinnati, Ohio	M. & N. Tempest	Rockingham, earthenware, and biscuit porcelain
1859	Trenton, N. J.	Trenton China Co.	Vitrified ware
1859	Trenton, N. J.	Rhodes & Yates	White granite and cream-colored ware
1859	Trenton, N. J.	Millington, Astbury & Poulson	White ware
1859	Peoria, Ill.	Fenton & Clark	White granite, cream ware
1859	Bennington, Vt.	Enos Adams	Rockingham
1859	Bennington, Vt.	Jacob Merz	Red ware and slip-decorated ware
1860	Akron, Ohio	Johnson & Dewey	Red ware
1860	Akron, Ohio	Johnson & Baldwin	Stoneware
1860	Akron, Ohio	H. W. Rockwell & Co.	Stoneware
1860	Cincinnati, Ohio	Wm. Bromley & Son	Rockingham, stoneware, and yellow ware
1860	Hockessin, Del.	Abner Marshall	Rockingham
1860	Cincinnati, Ohio	H. Mappes	Rockingham and yellow
1860	Trenton, N. J.	H. Speeler	White ware

[340]

Date	Place	Name	Types of Ware
1860	Peoria, Ill.	American Pottery Co.	White granite, cream ware
1860	Peoria, Ill.	Peoria Pottery Co.	Rockingham and stoneware
1861	Trenton, N. J.	James Tams and James P. Stephens	White granite
1861	Akron, Ohio	E. H. Merrill & Co.	Stoneware
1862	Akron, Ohio	Whitman, Robinson & Co.	Rockingham and yellow
1862	Cincinnati, Ohio	Tempest, Brockman & Co.	Rockingham and yellow
1863	Bath, S. Car.	Thomas J. Davis	Coarse dark brown earthenware
1863	East Liverpool, Ohio	John Goodwin	Rockingham and yellow
1863	Trenton, N. J.	Bloor, Ott & Booth	Cream ware and white granite
1863	Trenton, N. J.	Coxon & Co.	Cream ware and white granite
1863	Trenton, N. J.	John Moses	Yellow and Rockingham
1863	Troy, Ind.	Benjamin Hinchco	Yellow and Rockingham
1863	Akron, Ohio	F. J. Knapp	Stoneware
1863	Akron, Ohio	Beecher & Lantz	Stoneware
1863	Akron, Ohio	Peter Bodenbohl	Stoneware
1863	Akron, Ohio	Shenkle Bros. & Mann	Stoneware
1863	Cuyhoga Falls, Ohio	Thomas Harris	Stoneware

Date	Place	Name	Types of Ware
1864	Mogadore, Ohio	S. L. Stoll & Co.	Stoneware
1864	East Liverpool, Ohio	William Cartwright & Holland Manley	Yellow and Rockingham
1865	Cincinnati, Ohio	Fredrick Dallas	Stone china, common white
1865	Trenton, N. J.	Trenton Pottery Co.	Earthenware
1866	Spring Mills, N. J.	A. S. Moorhead & Wm. L. Wilson	Terra-cotta
1866	Chelsea, Mass.	Alexander W. Robinson	Brown ware
1867	Phœnixville, Pa.	Phœnixville Pottery Co.	Yellow, Rockingham and terra-cotta
1868	East Liverpool, Ohio	C. C. Thompson & J. T. Herbert	Yellow and Rockingham
1868	Trenton, N. J.	Greenwood Pottery Co.	White granite
1868	E. Liverpool, Ohio	E. McDevitt & Ferdinand Keffer	Yellow and Rockingham
1868	Trenton, N. J.	James Moses	Earthenware
1868	Philadelphia	J. E. Jeffords & Co.	Rockingham and yellow
1869	Phœnixville, Pa.	Schreiber & Betz	Yellow, Rockingham and terra-cotta
1869	Pittsburgh, Pa.	S. M. Kier	Earthenware
1869	Trenton, N. J.	Astbury & Maddock	White ware

Date	Place	Name	Types of Ware
1869	Trenton, N. J.	New Jersey Pottery Co.	Common white
1869	Beaver Falls, Pa.	Richard Thomas & Elijah Webster	Door-knobs
1869	Symmes Creek, Ohio	William Minner	Stoneware
1869	Akron, Ohio	Viall & Markel	Stoneware
1869	East Liverpool, Ohio	A. J. Marks	Yellow and Rockingham
1869	Akron, Ohio	Markel, Immon & Co.	Stoneware
1870	Morgantown, W. Va.	Greenland Thompson	Stoneware
1870	Akron, Ohio	Spafford & Richards	Stoneware
1870	Pittsburgh, Pa.	John Wyllie	Earthenware
1870	Akron, Ohio	Cook & Richardson	Stoneware
1870	East Liverpool, Ohio	Knowles, Taylor & Knowles	Rockingham and (1872) white ware
1870	East Liverpool, Ohio	William Burton	Yellow and Rockingham
1870	Trenton, N. J.	John Goodwin	Earthenware
1870	Trenton, N. J.	Thomas Maddock	Plumbers' sanitary ware
1871	Keene, N. H.	J. S. Taft & Co.	Red ware and stoneware
1871	E. Liverpool, Ohio	E. McDevitt & S. Moore	Yellow and Rockingham
1871	Atwater, Ohio	Purdy & Loomis	Stoneware

Date	Place	Name	Types of Ware
1871	Trenton, N. J.	Yates, Bennett & Allan	White granite
1872	East Liverpool, Ohio	John Goodwin	Yellow and Rockingham
1872	Atwater, Ohio	George Stroup	Stoneware
1872	E. Liverpool, Ohio	Manley, Cartwright & Co.	Yellow and Rockingham
1873	Mogadore, Ohio	Myers & Hall	Stoneware
1873	East Liverpool, Ohio	Richard Thomas	Brown door-knobs
1873	Fultonham, Ohio	S. A. Weller	Earthenware
1874	East Liverpool, Ohio	H. & S. Laughlin	White granite
1875	Roseville, Ohio	Baldosen & Pace	Stoneware
1875	Boston, Mass.	Thomas Gray & L. W. Clark	White Earthenware
1876	Trenton, N. J.	American Crockery Co.	White bisque, white granite
1876	Trenton, N. J.	Morris & Willmore	Belleek

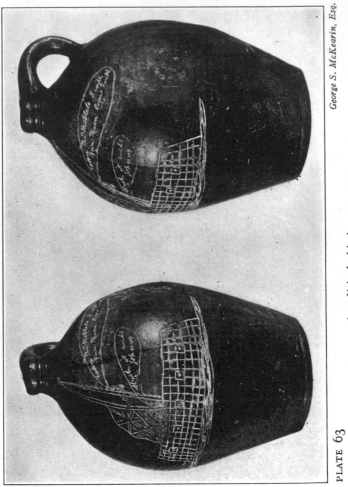

PLATE 63 A political skit in stoneware

CHAPTER XI

GROTESQUERIES, SATIRES, AND JESTS

Sooner or later almost every collector of early American pottery and china turns his or her attention to those individual pieces which were not produced for sale but to express some grotesque fancy of the potter, some satire or jest. There is no branch of ceramics which offers greater fascination to the collector who is gifted with a capacity for appreciating the whimsical. Surprisingly little has been written on the subject, in spite of the abundance of rich material. In nearly all lands and ages, potters have been fond of expressing their jests and gibes in clay.

Any reasonably comprehensive collection of old English or old German earthenware will show that a sense of humor, albeit naïve and even bucolic, characterized the men of earlier days who practised the potters' craft. The inscriptions found on some of the old Liverpool pieces and some of the old German slip-decorated pieces bear witness to this characteristic, and so do many of the early Staffordshire images and chimneypiece ornaments. What was the placing of a life-sized and lifelike frog in the bottom of a beer-jug or drinking-mug but a jest in clay?

The Vermont potter who in the old Burlington pottery of Nichols & Boynton decorated the cider-jug with the weird-looking beast may have tried to draw a horse. He may even have believed that he had successfully done so. One prefers to believe, however, that he gave merry expression to an impish mood to make a grotesque caricature; that he was of the lineage of those old Staffordshire potters whose whimsically impossible figures afford us so much delight, as indifferent to the realities of portraiture as that famous figure of Wellington by Ralph Ridgway with the strange garb of mixed naval and military uniforms and labeled "Wellington or Nelson." It did not matter a bit to Ralph Ridgway which of the famous heroes his work was regarded as representing. The possessor could claim it to be either of them, or, if he preferred, "a little of both"! So with our Vermont beast: we are free to call it either a horse or a giraffe, as we will, or, if it pleases us better, a little of both.

It is a great pity that we know practically nothing of two of the three grotesque stoneware jugs shown on Plate No. 6. The small one is believed to have been made by negro slaves on the plantation of Colonel Davies, of Bath, South Carolina, during the Civil War. It has been supposed that these roughly modeled "monkey-jugs," as they have been called, reveal some traces of "aboriginal art as practised by the ancestors of the makers" in Africa. The quotation is from a description of the jugs by Barber. Perhaps this theory rests on imagination rather than upon reality. The large jug on the same plate is not so very different, yet it was probably made in a Massachusetts pottery, though that is not certain. It seems to be related, in spirit and feeling at least, both to the Whately jug discussed in Chapter VII and to the jug made by the negro slaves in South Carolina. Who was the Joe Bamford whose name is inscribed on this old stoneware jug? Was he the maker who signed his name to his work with the pride of an artist? Or was he the butt of the potter's satire, caricatured in clay because he was no Apollo—or, perhaps, because he was good-looking enough to stir envy and malice and all uncharitableness in the breast of the maker? The other jug is fittingly placed in the middle of our illustration. It seems to come midway between the other two in feeling. One feels that it was fashioned in a kindlier spirit. The modeler's hand may have been no more skilful, but there was less malice in his heart. An artist friend of the writer, studying the photograph of the three jugs, entered upon a dissertation concerning the noses, arguing that the nose of the central one, to a greater extent than the others, indicates an attempt at portraiture. But when we are considering nasal delineation in pottery of this sort it is not well to be too critical. Shall we forget the delightful story told of Obediah Sherratt, maker of Staffordshire figures more than a century ago, that he used the same mold for Wellington's nose and for the teats of his cows?

Potters, like shoemakers and tailors, were always reputed to be keen politicians. The conditions in which they worked in the old days before the machine era may have favored conversation and discussion, and so contributed to that result. Political lampoons and satires in pottery are common enough. To this class belongs the interesting old stoneware

jug illustrated on Plate No. 62. Since its discovery in New Bedford, Massachusetts, some time
ago, this jug, which evidently was intended both as
molasses-container and political skit, has been the
theme of much speculation among collectors of early
American pottery.

Who made it we do not know. For no other
apparent reason than that there was a pottery there
during the eighteen-sixties, it has been tentatively
attributed to Athens, Ohio. To the writer of these
pages the reason seems inadequate for making a
highly improbable attribution. Some day the question may be definitely settled. In the meantime, the
jug is interesting as a sample of the way in which
potters have made political manifestoes and car-
toons, and as a sort of historical document. It seems
likely that the "Gov. J. Thompson" named was
Jacob Thompson, of Mississippi, at one time a member of Congress from that State, and a member of
President Buchanan's Cabinet as secretary of the
interior.

"When the War of Secession broke out, Jacob
Thompson became a violent upholder of the Con-
federate Cause," says Homer Eaton Keyes, whose
researches are drawn upon for this account. A man

[349]

of the wild fire-eating sort, with a positive genius for hatred, Thompson hatched a variety of schemes for bringing disaster and destruction to the Northern cause. One of his schemes was to spread plagues through the North by introducing deadly disease-germs among the population of the cities. A scheme of another character was to capture the city of Chicago and release all the prisoners confined at Fort Douglas. Many believed that he was implicated in the assassination of President Lincoln, and he fled to Europe, remaining there until it seemed safe to return.

In 1862 Thompson was a candidate for the governorship of Mississippi. He was defeated by his opponent, John J. Pettus, who had a majority of nearly twenty-seven thousand votes. So he was not governor at all in fact, though various encyclopedias have described him as governor. The crudely drawn cartoon, which is incised, seems to have been meant as a forecast, a prophecy that failed of fulfilment. There is a figure, intended to represent a man, in the doorway of the house. Presumably this indicated the artist's belief that, as governor, Jacob Thompson would enter the State Capitol.

That interpretation seems at first to be at variance

with the design itself, for how shall we view the beast which appears to represent some mythical creature, a sort of dragon with forked tail and tongue? One hardly knows how to reconcile the beast, and the wasp with the long tail, with a friendly attitude toward Thompson on the part of the potter politician. Yet a potter who felt strongly the righteousness of the cause for which Thompson stood, and remembered the Apocalypse even vaguely, might have drawn this beast. It may yet be shown that the jug was made in Ohio and that the potter's intent was not political prophecy but satire and ridicule. Until that is shown with reasonable certainty, the writer inclines to the theory of a more Southern origin at the hands of a potter who shared the sentiments of the Secessionists and hoped for Thompson's success.

One suspects that Mr. Volstead would not have been a popular personage in an old-time pottery community. As a general rule the potters were convivial souls, and that they mixed their drinking with merriment is shown by the whimsical character of the designs of their liquor bottles and flasks and the inscriptions in prose and doggerel rimes placed on many of their drinking-vessels. The jesting spirit which prevailed among old-fashioned potters is nowhere else so manifest as on articles used in connection with the worship of Bacchus.

As a motif of a design for a liquor-bottle the man astride a barrel is obvious enough. It was a commonplace long before Daniel Greatbach used it at Bennington. Jovial and well content he appears, personifying the conviviality of craftsmen in an era that knew not prohibition. It was for a local celebrity, renowned for his tippling habit, that Enoch Barber made a special bottle of this type, marking it "Bill" with raised white porcelain letters. He told the recipient that the letters were placed awry "so that they would look drunk-like and natural." We may safely conclude that the crookedness of the letters was accidental, and the "explanation" a jesting afterthought.

Sometimes joking was a collective matter. Calvin Park, a Bennington merchant and politician who had once been associated with Christopher Webber Fenton in the pottery business, was elected to the Vermont Legislature in 1864. He too was noted for his convivial habits. The stoneware potters employed in the Norton pottery made an immense two-handled jar, said to hold twenty-five gallons. On

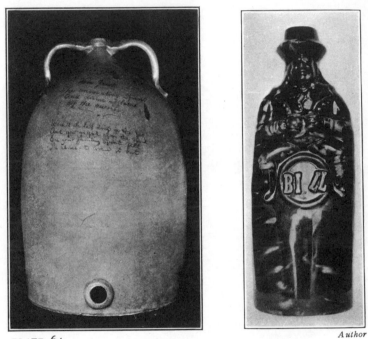

PLATE 64

Potters' little jokes

the front of this they stamped his name and then incised an elaborate inscription. At a dinner given in honor of Park's election, several potters bore the immense jar, full of ale, into the dining-hall and set it in front of the surprised legislator, who read the inscription amid laughter and cheers:

CALVIN PARK

1864

Hic Jacet

The animating spirit
and divine afflatus
of the owner

Were it the last drop in the Jug
And you gasped upon the Spout
Ere your fainting spirit fell
I'd advise—to draw it out.

Making a stoneware jar of that size must have been a task of some difficulty. No single workman could have managed it.

The stoneware jug shown on Plate No. 63 came into the writer's possession some years ago. It was found in Massachusetts. Nothing is known of its history, the only clue to which is the crudely incised drawing. A flag, obviously the British Union, is apparently being raised above a fort. Clinging to the flagstaff, half-way up, is a man who seems to be engaged either in painting it or greasing it. From the speech he is represented as making to the man hoisting the flag from below, and from the latter's reply, it would seem that he must be greasing the staff to prevent its being readily climbed. "Damn the Reblels [*sic*]. I will give them some trouble," says the man above. "Slush it well, Johnney," says the man below.

What does this drawing mean? The drawing and the inscription appear to be wholly without meaning except in connection with the War of Independence. It seems to be certain that they must refer either to the American Revolution or to the second struggle with Great Britain, the War of 1812. The point of view in either case is that of a partisan of Great Britain; the phrase "Damn the Rebels" indicates this, when taken in conjunction with the British flag. In the War of 1812 the term "Rebels" was not applied to the Americans by the British, so far as the present writer has discovered. Clearly the flag is not intended for the Stars and Bars of the Confederacy, and there is no chance that it is a product of the War of Secession.

The writer of these pages does not offer a solution

to the problem propounded by the old jug. He believes that the jug is of American origin, and not British, as a friend suggests. It is easier to believe that it was made in this country by one who sympathized with the British cause, some Loyalist during the Revolution perhaps. We know that pottery inscribed with loyalist sentiments, "Tory dishes," were much in use during the Revolution in loyalist strongholds. Here in Bennington, Vermont, older residents still tell a story relating to such a "Tory dish." On their way home after the Battle of Bennington, August 16, 1777, some of the Bennington militia under Captain Elijah Dewey stopped near the house of Benjamin Fay to refresh themselves at his well. Calling for something to drink from, a bowl was brought out from the house. Strange as it seems, this was a "Tory dish" and had "Success to British arms" on the bottom. The inscription so enraged the men that they would have broken the bowl but for Captain Dewey's firm resistance. The knowledge of that bowl so inscribed, in the home of one patriot and defended by another, makes it easy for the writer to believe that an American potter of loyalist sympathies may have made this old stoneware jug.

[355]

Early American Pottery and China

It is to be hoped that some day an enthusiastic hobbyist will give us a book devoted to those specimens of the American potter's art in which individual workmen have expressed their sense of the grotesque or the humorous, their jests, their jeers, their satires, and their sneers. What a jolly book to wait for!

APPENDIX

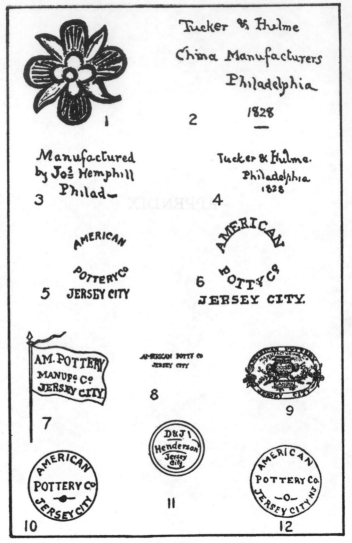

KEY TO MARKS

No.	NAME	DATE	REMARKS
1	Jacob Scholl	1830	Impressed in sgraffito ware; about size shown
2	Tucker & Hulme	1828	See text
3	Jos. Hemphill	1832	See text
4	Tucker & Hulme	1828	See text
5	American Pottery Co.	1840–45	Impressed in ware
6	American Pottery Co.	1840–45	Impressed in ware
7	American Pottery Manufacturing Co.	1840	Printed beneath glaze
8	American Pottery Co.	1842	Impressed in tableware
9	American Pottery Manufacturing Co.	1840	Printed on transfer printed ware; see text
10	American Pottery Co.	1840–45	Impressed
11	D. & J. Henderson	1829	Impressed in ware; the earliest Jersey City mark
12	American Pottery Co.	1840–45	Impressed in ware

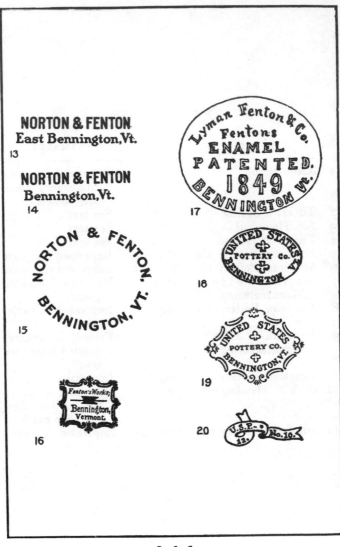

Key to Marks

No.	NAME	DATE	REMARKS
13	Norton & Fenton	1845–47	Used on Stoneware
14	Norton & Fenton		and on Rocking-
15	Norton & Fenton		ham; impressed in ware
16	C. W. Fenton	1847–48	Raised lozenge with impressed letters; used by Fenton (see text); used on Porcelain and Rockingham
17	Lyman & Fenton	1849–58	Used on flint enamel ware and Rockingham (see text); impressed in ware
18	United States Pottery Co.	1853	Impressed; used on scroddle and Rockingham wares
19	United States Pottery Co.	1853	Raised medallion impressed letters; used on porcelains
20	U.S.P. (United States Pottery)	1852	Raised ribbon with impressed initials; used on porcelain, Parian included

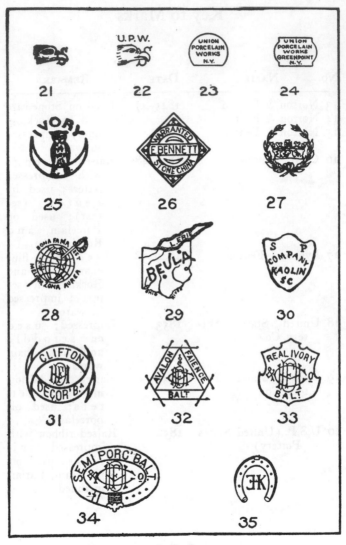

21   22   23   24

25   26   27

28   29   30

31   32   33

34   35

Key to Marks

No.	NAME	DATE	REMARKS
21	Smith & Son	1876	Impressed in ware; printed in 1877
22	Union Porcelain Works	1878	Note the "U.P.W."
23	Union Porcelain Works	1890—	
24	Union Porcelain Works	1880	
25	Edwin Bennett, Baltimore	1856—	One of the later marks; 1885
26	Edwin Bennett, Baltimore	1856—	One of the later marks; 1885
27	Edwin Bennett Pottery Co.	1890	
28	Edwin Bennett Pottery Co.		
29	Steubenville Pottery, Steubenville, Ohio	1879	Used on tableware
30	Southern Porcelain Co.	1856–64	Impressed in ware
31	Chesapeake Pottery, Baltimore, Md.	1880	Used 1882–85
32	Chesapeake Pottery, Baltimore, Md.	1880	Used 1882–84
33	Chesapeake Pottery, Baltimore, Md.	1880	Used 1882–84
34	Chesapeake Pottery, Baltimore, Md.	1880	Used 1882–84
35	D. F. Haynes (Chesapeake Pottery Co.), Baltimore, Md.	1881	Mark used for years by Haynes and his successors

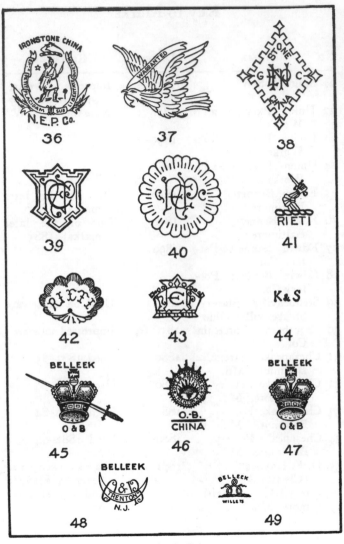

36

37

38

39

40

41

42

43

K & S

44

45

46

47

48

49

Key to Marks

No.	NAME	DATE	REMARKS
36	New England Pottery Co.	1878–83	First mark used; printed
37	New England Pottery Co.	1880 *circa*	Special mark used on private order
38	New England Pottery Co.	1883–86	Printed under glaze
39	New England Pottery Co.	1887	Used on "granite" ware—printed in black
40	New England Pottery Co.	1886	Used on cream-colored ware; mark printed in black
41	New England Pottery Co.	1886	Used on semi-porcelain, highly decorated
42	New England Pottery Co.	1888	Adopted in 1888 in place of 41 and used to 1889
43	New England Pottery Co.	1889–95	Used in place of 42 to mark "Rieti" ware
44	Kurlbaum & Schwartz	1853	See text
45	Otter & Brewer, Trenton, N. J.	1876	Used on "Belleek" ware only
46	Otter & Brewer, Trenton, N. J.	1866	Used on tableware
47	Otter & Brewer, Trenton, N. J.	1876	
48	Otter & Brewer, Trenton, N. J.	1876	
49	Willett's Manufacturing Co., Trenton, N. J.	1879	Used on "Belleek" ware only

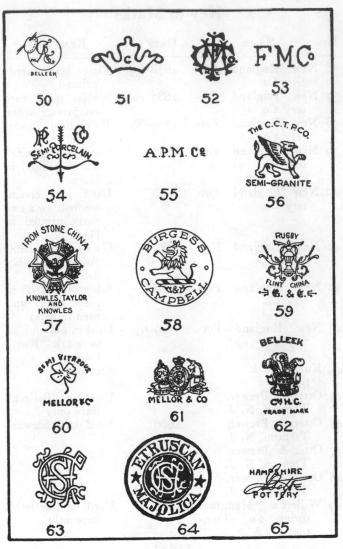

50

51

52

53 FMC°

54

55 A.P.M. C°

56

57

58

59

60

61

62

63

64

65

Key to Marks

No.	Name	Date	Remarks
50	Ceramic Art Co., Trenton, N. J.	1888	Belleek ware
51	Pauline Pottery Co., Edgerton, Wis.	1888	*Impressed* in earlier productions, *printed* in later ones
52	Faience Manufacturing Co., New York	1886	On porcelain and decorated pottery
53	Faience Manufacturing Co., New York	1886	*Incised* on majolica
54	Harker Pottery Co., East Liverpool, O.	1840–90	Mark adopted 1890
55	American Porcelain Manufacturing Co., Gloucester, N. J.	1854–57	Impressed in paste; soft porcelain
56	C. C. Thompson Potter Co., East Liverpool, Ohio	1884	Mark used on semi-granite
57	Knowles, Taylor & Knowles, East Liverpool, Ohio	1870	
58	Burgess & Campbell Trenton, N. J.	1879	Impressed in ware
59	Burgess & Campbell Trenton, N. J.	1879	Printed in brown under the glaze
60	Cook Pottery Co., Trenton, N. J.	1894	*Firm* succeeded Otto & Brewer
61	Cook Pottery Co.		
62	Cook Pottery Co.		
63	Griffen, Smith & Hill, Phœnixville, Pa.	1879	Monogram impressed in ware
64	Griffen, Smith & Hill, Phœnixville, Pa.	1879	Same with name of ware in border (also "Etruscan Ivory" etc.)
65	J. S. Taft & Co., Keene, N. H.		Printed in red over the glaze

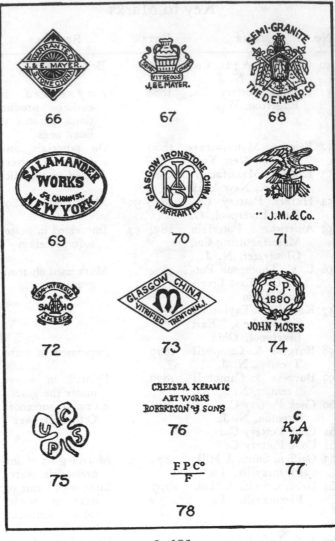

66

67

68

69

70

71   J.M. & Co.

72

73

74

CHELSEA KERAMIC
ART WORKS
ROBERTSON & SONS

76

75

77   C
K A
W

FPC°
F

78

Key to Marks

No.	Name	Date	Remarks
66	J. & E. Mayer, Beaver Falls, Pa.	1881	Mark used on white granite
67	J. & E. Mayer, Beaver Falls, Pa.	1881	Used on decorated dinner and tea services
68	D. E. McNichol Pottery Co., East Liverpool, Ohio		Mark used on white granite
69	Salamander Works	1848	Impressed in brown glazed earthenware.
70	John Moses & Co., Trenton, N. J.	1863	
71	John Moses & Co., Trenton, N. J.		These five marks were used at various times; they cover the life of the firm
72	John Moses & Co., Trenton, N. J.		
73	John Moses & Co., Trenton, N. J.		
74	John Moses & Co., Trenton, N. J.		
75	"Chelsea Pottery U. S."	1891	About 1897 became Dedham Pottery
76	Chelsea Keramic Art Works, Chelsea, Mass.	1866	Impressed up to 1880
77	Chelsea Keramic Art Works, Chelsea, Mass.	1875–89	Initials impressed
78	Franklin Porcelain Co., Franklin, Ohio.	1880	Used on granite and soft-paste porcelain

A CHRONOLOGICAL LIST OF ALL MARKS USED BY THE NORTON POTTERIES, BENNINGTON, VERMONT

NOTE: As the marks used by the Norton Potteries consisted simply of stamped plain lettering, with no ornamentation or devices of any kind, it has been thought unnecessary to list minor variations in the arrangement of the same words, as, for example, when "Bennington, Vt." is printed on two lines instead of on one. As a general rule, the name and address occupy two lines. One line and three lines are uncommon arrangements. Where the mark takes the form of an arrangement of the words in a circle, the fact is here indicated. The principal value of this list to the collector is, of course, the fact that it provides a complete and convenient check-list by means of which any piece of stoneware bearing a Norton mark may be dated with virtual certainty.

Marks Used by the Norton Potteries

L. Norton & Co., Bennington, Vt.	1823–28
L. Norton, Bennington, Vt.	1828–33
L. Norton & Son, East Bennington, Vt. ⎫ L. Norton & Son, Bennington, Vt. ⎭	1833–40
Julius Norton, East Bennington, Vt. ⎫ J. Norton, East Bennington, Vt. Julius Norton, Bennington, Vt. J. Norton, Bennington, Vt. ⎭	1841–44 (45)
Norton & Fenton, East Bennington, Vt. ⎫ Norton & Fenton, Bennington, Vt. ⎭ ¹	1844 (45)–47
Julius Norton, Bennington, Vt. ⎫ J. Norton, Bennington, Vt. ⎭	1847–50
J. & E. Norton, Bennington, Vt.	1850–59
J. Norton & Co., Bennington, Vt. ⎫ J. & E. Norton & Co., Bennington, Vt. ⎭	1859–61
E. & L. P. Norton, Bennington, Vt.	1861–81
E. Norton, Bennington, Vt.	1881–83
Edward Norton, Bennington, Vt. ⎫ Edward Norton & Co., Bennington, Vt. E. Norton & Co., Bennington, Vt. Edward Norton & Company, Bennington, Vt. ⎭	1883–94

(Sometimes the word "Company" is spelled in full)

Edward Norton Company, Bennington, Vt.	1886–94

(This last mark is uncommon.)

Bennington Factory

When the author's book, "The Potters and Potteries of Bennington," was prepared for the press, only one example of this mark had come to his at-

---

¹ Sometimes arranged in a circle.

tention. Since then, however, he has learned of several others. He is now of the opinion that this is not a pottery mark at all, but an owner's mark impressed in the ware on order. "Ralph Goldsmith, Bennington, Vermont," is another example of the same kind—made for a local tradesman.

BIBLIOGRAPHICAL NOTE

THE serious collector will desire to build up a good working library. It is at once remarkable and regrettable that there should be such a dearth of available bibliographical material that is at once reliable and illuminating. The amateur hobbyist should have upon his working book-shelf at least one good text-book covering the broad field of ceramic collecting. Taken all in all, it is doubtful whether a better book for this purpose can be had than Frederick Litchfield's "Pottery and Porcelain: A Guide to Collectors" (MacMillan Company, New York, 1925). Another treatise of a general character that is almost invaluable to the student is "The Ceramic Art: A Compendium of the History and Manufacture of Pottery and Porcelain," by Jennie J. Young (Harper & Brothers, New York, 1878). This important book is unfortunately out of print and not readily procurable. It is accessible in most of the large public libraries, however.

Bibliographical Note

The well known works of Dr. Barber, or some of them, are virtually indispensable to the student of American ceramics. While Barber was far from a careful writer, frequently jumping at conclusions, and was much given to making wide generalizations on a too scanty basis of verified fact, his more important works cannot be dispensed with. His principal book, "Pottery and Porcelain of the United States" (G. P. Putnam's Sons, New York, 1909), while it needs to be used with great caution, is one of the most important source-books that we have. His "Marks of American Potters" (Patterson & White Company, Philadelphia, 1904) is out of print and rather difficult to obtain. Far from being a satisfactory compilation, it is the most useful handbook of the kind thus far produced. From many points of view Barber's well known monograph, "Tulip Ware of the Pennsylvania-German Potters" (Pennsylvania Museum, Philadelphia, 1903), is the author's best work and the most helpful.

Practically indispensable is "The Encyclopedia of Ceramics," compiled by W. P. Jervis (New York, 1902). Lacking in discriminating scholarship though it is, this exhaustive work contains a

Bibliographical Note

vast amount of information not readily found elsewhere. Albert Hastings Pitkin's posthumously published "Early American Folk Pottery" (Hartford, Connecticut, 1918) is quite worthless, and is only mentioned here because it is so frequently regarded as authoritative by uncritical readers. Considerable information concerning early American potteries and potters can be found in the volumes of that defunct periodical, "Old China," if the reader has access to a file. The files of "The Crockery and Glass Journal," the well known trade paper of New York, contain a great deal of useful data scattered through the numerous volumes. For example, the best historical account of the East Liverpool, Ohio, potteries is that contained in the fiftieth anniversary number, December 18, 1924. The files of "Antiques," the well known monthly, provide a rich mine for the serious student. To a greater extent than any other magazine in its field, "Antiques" recognizes the responsibilities and obligations of conscientious editorship.

The best account of the potteries at Morgantown, West Virginia, is that published in the annual report of the National Museum (Smithsonian Institution, Washington, D. C.), for 1899. This is a valuable

Bibliographical Note

monograph by Walter Hough, assistant curator of the Division of Ethnology, Smithsonian National Museum. The Quarterly Bulletin of the New York Historical Society, July, 1926, contains an altogether admirable study by Dr. John E. Stillwell, entitled "Crolius Ware and Its Makers." This is a study which no student of American ceramics can afford to ignore. "The Potters and Potteries of Bennington," by the author of the present work, will interest those collectors who specialize in collecting Bennington porcelain and pottery.

INDEX

Index

Index

Index

Index

East Greenwich, R. I., colonial pottery, 92

East Liverpool, Ohio, amazing growth of pottery industry, 326–327; Benjamin Harker's pottery, 324; first kiln fired, 50; first kiln of ware burned, 323; first pottery erected, 321; Goodwin pottery started, 324; Harker & Taylor partnership, 324–325; its first settlement by white men, 322; James Bennett, its pioneer potter, 321–323; manufacture of common yellow started, 323; pottery, 222–223, 225, 338–339, 341–344; Rockingham ware made, 324; Salt & Mear works started, 324; success of Bennett pottery engenders competition, 323; Woodward & Vodrey pottery, 324; 198–199; 320, 333–334

Eichenlaub, Valentine, potter, 338

Elers, English potter, 55

Elizabeth, N. J., pottery, 124–125, 155, 217, 308

Ellsworth, Colonel, shooting, 330

Ensminger, A., potter, 219

Etruria Pottery, Trenton, N. J., 289

Euwatse, John, potter, 54

Fairfax, Vt., pottery, 175, 220, 330–339

Fairlee, Vt., 176

Farrar, Caleb, Vermont potter, 174, 216

Farrar, E. L., potter, 175, 220

Farrar, S. H., 316, 339

Farrar, William H., 275–276

Farrar & Stearns, potter, 338

Fay, Benjamin, 355

Fennemore, Jason, 242–243

Fenton, Christopher Webber, associated with A. P. Lyman and Calvin Park, 261; Bennington potter, 41; begins at Bennington, 171–172; craftsmen brought to Bennington, 302, 306–307; engaged in powder manufacture, 261; experiments with porcelain making, 259; financial difficulties, 266; goes to Kaolin, S. C., 276; has Henry D. Hall as partner, 259; association with Clark, 260; flint-enamel process, 315, 317; limitations as potter, 261; Lyman leaves firm, 262; operates pottery at Dorset, Vt., 173; Park withdraws from firm, 261; partnership with Julius Norton, 258; partnership with Julius Norton dissolved, 259; revives porcelain industry, 256; starts manufacture on his own account, 259; wares made by, 259; 298, 352

Fenton, Jacob, 213

Fenton, Jonathan, born at Windham, Conn., 173; establishes pottery at Dorset, Vt., 172; ink-well, 173; wares made 173; 213

Fenton, Leander W., 174

Fenton, Richard L., potter, 173

Fenton, Richard Webber, 173, 214

Fenton & Clark, potters, 340

Fenton, Hall & Co., 261

Index

Index

Index

[384]

Index

Index

Index

Index

Index

Index

Index

Index

Index

T